ESA Women International

HOLIDAYS
a la Carte

RECIPES FOR HOLIDAYS YEAR-ROUND

© Favorite Recipes® Press/Nashville EMS MCMLXXVIII
Post Office Box 77, Nashville, Tennessee 37202

Library of Congress Cataloging in Publication Data
Main entry under title:

Favorite Recipes of ESA Women Internation

At head of title: ESA holidays 'a la carte.
Includes index.
1. Cookery. I. Title: ESA holidays 'a la ca.
TX652.S39   641.5   78-14729
ISBN 0-87197-122-4

Dear Homemaker

ESA Women International probably *exchange* more good deeds, good will and good fellowship than any other organization of women in the world. We are a very select group of women, because of our real determination to dedicate part of our lives to change helplessness and human misery into radiant hope and happiness! In July of this year, we began our 50th Anniversary Celebration.

Now ESA Women are *exchanging* one of the most delightful commodities that women possess the world over . . . *"Our Favorite Recipes!"* This is our way of inviting you to know ESA Women and acquaint you with our leadership and service. We thank you for your contributions to our goals, through the ESA Cookbooks. We know you will receive many hours of pleasurable eating and entertaining with these excellent recipes from ESA Women around the world.

Our Sorority has exchanged our ingenuity and hours of work and personal sacrifice for *dollars* in amounts of over THREE MILLION, donated to the St. Jude Children's Hospital For Leukemia Treatment And Research. We have exchanged our prayers, kindness and help as well as dollars to further "Project Hope." More noticeable to you, may be the exchange of our philanthropic dollars through programs right in your own community! All of our endeavors are genuine *exchanges* of our love for our own neighbor . . . You! We ask for your continued support of our Cookbooks as we invite you to join ESA Women International in loving and sharing with thy neighbor.

Sincerely,

Gennie Haralson

Gennie Haralson, President
International Council
ESA Women International

5

Contents

Epsilon Sigma Alpha International

ESA women are among the best hostesses in the world and at holiday time they really shine. These recipes are the very finest that ESA members have to offer. We urge you to sample the delights described in each recipe and enjoy the results.

Epsilon Sigma Alpha International members are women from every walk of life. They have come together to share their collective talents, to experience personal growth, to aid those less fortunate, and to be part of an organization that is making a very positive impact on our world. The chapter is the basic unit of ESA and normally is made up of 10 to 15 members. Membership in Epsilon Sigma Alpha International is by invitation only and any women eighteen years old and above are eligible for membership.

The organization was founded in 1929 and is celebrating fifty years of caring. During ESA's fifty years the members have established an impressive record of achievements. Their philanthropic work is indicative of ESA's stated purpose of giving "aid to those less fortunate." Annually, ESA women raise and donate in excess of three million dollars for worthy causes and national charities. Of particular note is ESA's untiring efforts on behalf of St. Jude Children's Research Hospital in Memphis, Tennessee. Two Million Dollars has been raised through the ESA Million Dollar Bike Ride for the defeat of catastrophic illnesses in children.

The threefold purposes of ESA are Education, Service and Association. Currently, 25,000 women in the United States and several foreign countries make up the membership of ESA. Anyone desiring further information about ESA should contact the local Epsilon Sigma Alpha International Chapter or ESA International Headquarters, Drake Office Center, 333 West Drake Road, Fort Collins, Colorado 80521.

Any Day Is A Holiday

When a holiday begins, the work-a-day world comes to an end for a while, and everyone prepares for a whirlwind of fun, friendship, and festive foods that special occasions always bring. It seems that feasts and festivals are as common to human nature as happiness and laughter. People of every land have been celebrating their most memorable events and important persons since the start of civilization. The Japanese are famous for their appreciation of nature and the four seasons by celebrating in many ways, while Germans are known for their harvest-time beer-fests, and then Chinese are noted for their colorful observance of New Year's.

Christian countries observe a great number of religious occasions, many of which tie in with seasonal or everyday events. Martinmas, which honors St. Martin, the patron saint of France, falls on November 11, at the end of the harvest. So, in France and other European countries it is celebrated with autumn feasts and new wine; in Belgium children are given nuts, apples and traditional autumn foods; in Britain, they roasted a goose as Martinmas marked a yearly quarter when rents and bills came due, and in the past, a goose very often was included as part of the landlord's or creditor's payment.

The United States, probably because it has become the home of so many diverse cultures, has an overflowing calendar of festivals and holidays. In fact, from New Year's in January to Christmas in December every month has one and often more, commemorative days that are happily observed by

thousands of people. Some of these days are recognized by no more than just a mention on a desk calendar, while others have at least a customary greeting, characteristic decorations, or typical costumes. The favorite holidays are usually the most meaningful ones and the festivities are extended to include not only the immediate family, but neighbors, relatives, friends, and sometimes entire communities. These festivities often feature parades, fireworks, singing and there is plenty of traditional foods to accompany these celebrations.

IT ALL STARTS AT THE BEGINNING . . .

January has marked the beginning of The New Year since the ancient days of Rome. They set aside a day to honor *Janus,* their god of gates, doors, starts and finishes. Today, we celebrate the arrival of The New Year with gala parties featuring upheld glasses of champagne to toast the stroke of midnight, ushered in with hugs and kisses amidst the din of noisemakers, fireworks, whoops, and cheers. In the 19th Century, January 1st was the occasion for very formal house-to-house visiting. Today, people follow this same custom in a far more relaxed way, enjoying one another's talk of New Year's resolutions, as well as televised parades and football bowl games, which have become such an integral part of New Year's Day.

THEN IT STEALS YOUR HEART AWAY.

February, which falls in the cold of winter, is the perfect month for celebrating the warmth of Valentine's Day. This celebration for sweethearts and loved ones is linked to an Old English belief that birds begin choosing their mates on February 14th. Stories about St. Valentine are varied, although it seems certain that he was beheaded about 270 AD, then canonized some 200 years later. According to two stories, Valentine was jailed either for marrying young couples against the will of Claudius II (who preferred that the young men stay single and become soldiers), or for refusing to worship the Roman gods. Greatly loved by the children of Rome, they would pass notes of love through the iron bars of the cell's window. The traditional customs surrounding Valentine's Day, therefore, include sending sentimental greeting cards to loved ones, and giving candy and flowers to sweethearts.

Two great Americans were born in February: George Washington on February 22nd and Abraham Lincoln on February 12th. Many homes fly an American flag outside on these days, while school children review the many unique contributions these two presidents made to the history of the United States. Cherry recipes and pioneer foods are favorites on these holidays.

BUT SPRING FINALLY COMES . . .

St. Patrick's Day on March 17th is the only popularly-celebrated holiday that falls in the month of March — only a few days before Spring officially begins. It is actually a celebration of the Irish, as St. Patrick is their patron saint and was responsible for bringing Christianity to Ireland. The traditional "wearin' o' the green" symbolizes the green of the three-leaf shamrock that St. Patrick was said to have used in explaining The Holy Trinity to his converts. Today, the Irish and many other Christians, as well, commemorate St. Patrick's Day with parades, Irish ballads, leprechaun legends and feasts of hearty Irish food.

Together, March and April are the harbingers of Spring, and of the most important of Christian celebrations, Easter time. It is a time for gaily decorated eggs, symbolizing the happy, new life that Spring brings, as well as the belief in the new life that the Resurrected Christ can give. Little girls demurely show off new pastel dresses, while little boys tug, pull, and adjust their crisp spring suits. Lamb, a symbol of Christ, is traditional Easter food, as are Hot Cross Buns, and cookies and cakes shaped and decorated to resemble rabbits, eggs, lambs and crosses.

The first day of May has long been celebrated with outdoor festivals to honor this beautiful flower-filled month. Dancers erect a blossom-trimmed Maypole, then holding onto ribbons streaming from the top dance happily around it until the pole is colorfully covered. This is also the day that Swedes and Finlanders celebrate the return of the sun after a long, dark winter. The second Sunday in May is a tradition all families have come to look forward to since 1915, because it was proclaimed Mother's Day, set aside specifically to honor the nation's mothers. Memorial Day has been observed on May 30th since 1868 as a legal holiday commemorating those who have given their lives in the military service of the United States. Patriotic programs and special services are held at Arlington National Cemetery and local cemeteries throughout the nation. This day, long marked by military parades, American flags, and political speeches, has also come to mark the start of the summer recreation months. Children are through with school in most areas, so families head for the mountains, lakes and parks for water sports, fishing, sunbathing and picnics.

AND SUDDENLY, IT'S SUMMER!

June is the month for school graduations, weddings, Flag Day, and a very important date — Father's Day. The Romans, who named the month of June after Juno, their goddess of marriage, believed this month was the best in which to marry — a custom that is followed by young couples to this very day. Flag Day on June 14 marks the day on which the 1777 Continental Congress chose the Stars and Stripes (13 of each, then) as the official flag of the new United States. Father's Day, although not a holiday officially proclaimed by Congress, is as enthusiastically noted as Mother's Day. Dad sits back and puts his feet up, while mom and the kids prepare his favorite meal and do his chores. Summer officially begins with the longest day of the year on June 21 or 22, and by this time, people have begun a round of summer activities that will continue through the month of August. Families take vacation trips to lakes, beaches and camping areas, to national parks and historic areas, and kids look forward to days of relaxation and royal treatment at grandma's house in the country.

July 4th is usually the peak of all this summer fun, with everyone's attention focused upon celebrating the anniversary of the nation's independence. In the founding days of the United States, John Adams predicted that this day would, forevermore, be an occasion for great parades and shows, for games and athletic events, and for patriotic music, bonfires and ringing bells — and it seems that he was exactly right. With undying enthusiasm this is just how Americans do celebrate The Fourth of July, and undoubtedly how they always will.

AUTUMN, THE GYPSY, TAKES OVER FROM HERE . . .

Labor Day, always observed on the first Monday in September as a nation-wide holiday for working people, is the final chance to get away from it all in the summer outdoors. Some families pack up and head for popular recreation areas, while still others use the day to rest and relax at home with a traditional cookout or baseball game, or to attend the company or church barbecue. September also heralds the annual visit of traveling circuses and fairs, and the coming of the autumn harvest. Children settle into a school day routine, birds begin to head south for the winter, and the trees begin to don their bright autumn colors of gold, orange and yellow.

It is on October 12th at this time of year that Americans set aside a day in honor of Christopher Columbus, who first arrived on the shores of the New World on October 12, 1492. Then, the month of October ends on a spooky note with imaginative Halloween happenings. Goblins, witches, black cats and ghosts (in costume, of course!) wait around every corner with demands of "Trick or Treat!" Halloween parties feature couples bobbing for apples that float in a washtub, as well as eerie stories, scary sounds, fortune-telling and unearthly decorations.

Nature becomes very quiet in November, with the glory of autumn well on its way and only a nip in the air to warn of the approaching winter. People are happy and content because the harvest is in, and the end of another year beckons in the distance. For this reason, families gather to celebrate Thanksgiving, just as the Pilgrims did after their first successful harvest in the New World. Thanksgiving dinners are traditionally bountiful feasts, and today, the

day is not quite complete without televised parades and spirited football games between rival colleges.

UNTIL WINTER WINDS BEGIN TO BLOW.

December brings us Christmas, the most beloved holiday of the year because it celebrates the birthday of Jesus Christ. At no other time of the year are people busier or happier than they are during the Christmas season because it is a holiday with so many joyous traditions. In most areas, the festivities get into full swing when the family brings their Christmas tree home to decorate and crown with a star like the one that led the shepherds and the Wise Men to Bethlehem. Boxes of adored and sparkling decorations are brought from storage, and soon the entire house is festooned with gay Yule decor.

But, even before this, family members have been secretly buying special gifts for loved ones and wrapping them in colorful papers and shining ribbons. Best of all, the delightfully myriad aromas of candymaking and home baking pervade every corner of the house until divinity, fudge, and marzipan fill brightly colored tins, and the cookie jars overflow. Fruitcake and nut breads crowd the refrigerator and the anticipation of Christmas dinner whets everyone's appetite for days in advance. This is the season of the year that gives children and adults alike the warmest of memories to carry with them for a lifetime.

YOU ARE INVITED . . .

Birthdays, anniversaries, wedding teas, baby showers and a host of other meaningful occasions appear all through the year, and are celebrated with as much exuberance as any full-fledged holiday. Even election nights, athletic events, promotions, retirements, graduations, and bon voyages make people think festively. And, for every friendly reason, nothing reflects the happiness and good wishes of these events like a lively party. Certainly, too, nothing brings out the sparkling creativity of a hostess than an upcoming special event. Ideas for decorations, table settings, color schemes, guest lists, the menu, and the entertainment will determine if the party will be formal or casual, and certainly whether or not it will be a memorable one.

The type of party depends, of course, on the event or the honoree. Time and place depend on the size of the hostess' home, her budget, the number of guests to be invited and their life-styles. For example, if most of the guests work throughout the week, weekend parties are usually the best. The guest list can include old friends, new acquaintances, or a convivial mixture of both. Decorations are in order if the party has an important theme — such as a child's birthday, a 25th Wedding Anniversary, or a Halloween or Famous Names costume party. But, even a small, casual gathering of close friends can be brightened with arrangements of flowers, autumn leaves, seashells, candles or whatever seems appropriate.

There is no doubt that almost everyone loves holidays and the excitement they bring. This is probably because they provide a good excuse for friends and family to gather and enjoy jovial company, delicious food, and a delightful atmosphere. Yet, even with all the holidays that a year's calendar provides, we still look for reasons to entertain — just for the sake of having fun. The following is a list of the unique, and probably lesser-known reasons to invite friends, relatives or acquaintances over for a hospitable time. This list also includes suggestions for themes or menu ideas.

Appetizers

One of the most popular holiday parties of all is a lively and informal gathering where the guests just talk, laugh and relax. Because the activities are unstructured and no formal dinner is served, the hostess provides a bounteous and attractive selection of appetizers and finger foods for her guests to choose from and enjoy. This kind of party is perfect any time of the year, indoors or outside, in the afternoon or at night — just as long as there is plenty of room, lots of people, a few chairs and good food.

Appropriate holiday appetizers are virtually unlimited, including selections of meats, seafood, poultry, cheese and vegetables, and even fruit and dessert tasty bites. Most importantly, appetizers should be bite-sized and colorful, as well as varied in texture and temperature, so each guest will feel free to taste each food, and will be sure to find any number of individual favorites.

A great conversation topic is to include dishes that let the guests participate in the preparation of their own appetizers. Miniature shish kabobs cooked hibachi-style are as much fun as they are palate-pleasing. If a hibachi is not available, a number of clay flower pots filled with glowing coals will serve the same purpose, and will lend a decorative note to the table, as well. If a family-sized barbecue grill is used, be sure that the cooking grate is not too large for the foods. Wire mesh can be used to make sure that the food does not fall through to the coals. Fondue is another holiday guest pleaser, as are various spreads with breads cut in assorted shapes for tiny, fix-it-yourself sandwiches.

The best Holiday in the year to plan an Appetizer Party is New Year's Eve. As hostess, you can relax and enjoy the evening with your guests without too much fuss and bother in getting ready. Foods left over from Christmas adapt perfectly into appetizers — from the celery, cranberries, and turkey to the fruitcake, fudge, and roasted pecans and chestnuts. On the other hand, if you know everyone is tired of turkey and fruitcake leftovers, you can be sure your guests will welcome the change of pace that seafood bits, fresh vegetables, tiny pizzas, and oriental flavors have to offer. This same party theme is just as appropriate on New Year's Day, as people enjoy informal gatherings for watching parades and football games on television.

Probably the most enjoyable part of any Holiday party is creating the decorations — especially at New Year's. It could be planned as "Chinese New Year's," with candles, paper lanterns, bamboo mats, low tables and lacquered trays — even chop sticks and barefoot guests. Or, more traditionally, the decorations can include festive hats, paper horns, streamers, a television to watch the midnight countdown, and as many chiming and ringing clocks as can be found — all set to go off at midnight! Best of all, the appetizers can be prepared and garnished to be as colorful as the event itself.

Appetizers are just as palate-pleasing when they are not the focal point of the menu, but the introduction to a more formal meal, instead. Here, the selection of foods should be small and fancy. Impressive formal appetizers might include crisp crackers spread with cream cheese and artfully topped with a touch of colorful pepper jelly, fruit preserves, caviar, olives or anchovies; chicken livers or eels wrapped and broiled in bacon strips; or a compote of fresh fruits accompanied by powdered sugar, bourbon balls and bits of various fancy cheeses. The elegant effect is heightened when the foods are served on glimmering silver trays, with small cloth napkins, silver appetizer forks and cheese knives and small china plates. Appetizers like these should be followed by a dinner fit for royalty for an evening of entertainment and dining your guests will long remember.

Fun or formal, but always fabulous — that is the ESA definition for appetizers. And, as anyone who frequently entertains already knows, appetizers can only be compared to a kaleidoscope, always revealing a new pattern of color, flavor, taste and enjoyment. The following selection of recipes for appetizers will soon have you convinced — not another holiday or special occasion should go by without a party featuring your favorite finger foods!

CHRISTMAS SALMON-CHEESE BALL

1 can salmon, drained and flaked
1   8-oz. package cream cheese,
   softened
1 roll sharp Cheddar cheese
1 tsp. finely chopped onion
1 tbsp. lemon juice
1 tsp. horseradish
1/4 tsp. liquid smoke (opt.)
1/2 c. chopped pecans or 1/4 c.
   chopped parsley

Remove skin and bones from salmon. Combine all ingredients except pecans; mix well. Chill until firm enough to handle. Form in 1 large ball or 2 small balls. Roll in pecans. Refrigerate for several hours. Serve with crackers.

Helen McSpadden
State Coun. Jr. Past Pres.
Epsilon Epsilon No. 1896
Littleton, Colorado

FESTIVE HOLIDAY CHEESE BALL

2   8-oz. packages cream cheese,
   softened
1   8-oz. package Cheddar cheese,
   grated
1 tbsp. chopped pimento
1 tbsp. chopped green pepper
1 tsp. chopped onion
1 tsp. lemon juice
2 tsp. Worcestershire sauce
Dash of cayenne pepper
Dash of salt
Finely chopped pecans

Combine cream cheese and Cheddar cheese; mix well. Add remaining ingredients except pecans; mix well. Shape with hands into 1 large ball or 2 small balls. Roll in chopped pecans. Wrap in waxed paper; refrigerate until firm. Let come to room temperature before serving. This freezes well.

Beth Evans, Pres.
Beta Upsilon No. 2416
Harrison, Arkansas

HOLIDAY CHEESE LOGS

1/2 lb. Swiss cheese,
   finely grated
24 slices pimento cheese, finely
   chopped
24 slices American cheese,
   finely chopped
2   8-oz. packages cream cheese,
   softened
1 lb. sharp cheese, finely
   grated
2 garlic cloves, crushed
1 lg. onion, grated
2 tsp. lemon juice
Mayonnaise
Paprika (opt.)
Crushed pecans

Combine all cheeses, garlic, onion and lemon juice; mix well, adding just enough mayonnaise to hold mixture together. Shape into logs or rolls. Roll logs in paprika and crushed pecans. Refrigerate for at least 1 hour before using. May store in freezer, if desired.

Lorine Caldwell, Publ. Chm.
Beta Zeta No. 3889
Fishersville, Virginia

CHRISTMAS PARTY CHEESE BALL

2   8-oz. packages cream cheese
1/2 lb. sharp Cheddar cheese,
   shredded
2 tsp. grated onion
2 tsp. Worcestershire sauce
1 tsp. lemon juice
1 tsp. dry mustard
1/2 tsp. seasoned salt
1/4 tsp. salt
1/2 tsp. paprika
1   2 1/4-oz. can deviled ham
2 tbsp. chopped parsley
2 tbsp. chopped pimento

Soften cream cheese; beat in all remaining ingredients. Shape into ball. Refrigerate for several hours. This freezes well. May roll in chopped nuts, if desired.

Delilah Miller
Alpha Eta No. 3320
Rupert, Idaho

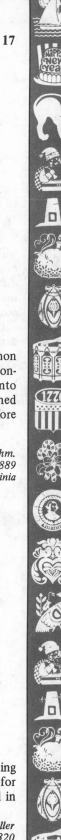

BLUE VEIN CHEESE CRISPS

3/4 c. all-purpose flour
1/2 tsp. salt
1/4 c. butter or margarine
Lemon juice
1/4 c. grated blue vein cheese
1 egg, beaten
Paprika
Sesame seed

Sift flour and salt into bowl; work in butter with fingertips. Add enough lemon juice to make a firm dough. Roll out thin between 2 sheets waxed paper. Spread cheese over half the pastry; fold other half over cheese. Roll out again until cheese shows through. Cut with hors d'oeuvre cutters. Brush lightly with egg; sprinkle with paprika and sesame seed. Place on greased baking sheet. Bake at 375 degrees for 8 to 10 minutes or until lightly browned. Loosen slightly; cool and remove from baking sheet. Store in airtight container.

Marjorie Ridley, Pres.
Beta Theta No. 4607
Brisbane, Queensland, Australia

CHEESE PUFFS

2 c. grated sharp American cheese
1/2 c. butter or margarine, softened
1 c. flour, sifted
1/2 tsp. salt
1 tsp. paprika
48 stuffed olives

Blend cheese with butter; stir in flour, salt and paprika, mixing well. Wrap 1 teaspoon cheese mixture around each olive, covering completely. Arrange on greased baking sheet. Bake in preheated 400-degree oven for about 15 minutes.

Helen J. Gard, V.P.
Alpha Upsilon No. 157
San Antonio, Texas

CHEESE AND WINE MOLD

2 1/2 c. finely shredded sharp
    Cheddar cheese
1/8 tsp. nutmeg

1/8 tsp. white pepper
1/4 c. dry white wine
1/4 c. softened butter

Combine cheese, nutmeg and pepper in small mixer bowl. Heat wine just to boiling point; pour immediately over cheese. Beat with mixer for about 10 minutes or until smooth. Beat in butter. Spoon into well-oiled 2-cup mold. Cover; chill overnight. Unmold onto serving plate. Cover; let stand at room temperature for 1 to 2 hours. Serve with fresh fruit wedges and crackers.

Ellaine Coscarella, Rec. Sec.
Alpha Omicron No. 770
Salida, Colorado

NIPPY CHEESE SNACKS

1/2 lb. Cheddar cheese
1 c. butter or margarine
2 c. flour
1/2 tsp. cayenne pepper
2 c. Rice Krispies

Grate cheese into large bowl; add butter. Let stand until soft. Mix with hands until well combined. Mix in remaining ingredients. Shape into small balls; flatten slightly with fork on ungreased cookie sheet. Bake at 350 degrees for 15 minutes.

Margaret Alexander, Pres.
Alpha Omega No. 715
Edmonds, Washington

OLIVE-CHEESE AND HAM SWIRLS

1 3-oz. package cream cheese,
    softened
1 tbsp. mayonnaise or salad dressing
1/2 tsp. mustard
1/3 c. chopped stuffed olives
1/4 tsp. paprika
1/4 tsp. onion powder
4 thin slices boiled ham

Combine cream cheese, mayonnaise and mustard; stir in olives, paprika and onion powder. Spread evenly onto ham slices; roll up. Chill for several hours or until firm. Slice ham rolls into 1/4-inch pieces. Place on picks. May stick picks in ham rolls first, then slice between picks.

Carol Rodgers, Treas.
Alpha Theta No. 4623
Griffin, Indiana

PIMENTO CHEESE SPREAD

1   8-oz. package cream cheese,
      softened
3 hard-boiled eggs, chopped
1 jar chopped pimento
3 sm. green peppers, chopped
1 c. chopped celery
1 c. chopped green onions
1 to 1 1/2 c. mayonnaise
Salt to taste
Paprika
Cayenne pepper to taste

Beat cream cheese until creamy. Add eggs, pimento, green peppers, celery and onions; mix well. Stir in mayonnaise, salt, paprika and cayenne pepper. Chill. Serve as a sandwich spread or for stuffing celery.

Suzanne Linville, Treas.
Zeta Eta No. 4009
Del City, Oklahoma

OLIVE-CHEESE BALL GIFT

2   8-oz. packages cream cheese,
      softened

1 c. shredded sharp Cheddar cheese
1 tbsp. milk
1 tsp. Worcestershire sauce
2/3 c. chopped stuffed Spanish green
      olives
3/4 c. coarsely chopped pecans

Blend cream cheese, Cheddar cheese, milk and Worcestershire sauce together; mix in olives and 1/2 cup pecans. Shape into ball; chill thoroughly. Place ball on a tile; press remaining pecans over ball. Garnish with sliced stuffed olives.

Photograph for this recipe on this page.

SNAPPY CHEESE WEDGES

12 slices white bread
1/2 c. process Cheddar
      cheese spread
1/4 tsp. Tabasco sauce
1/4 tsp. prepared mustard

Remove crusts from bread. Slice diagonally to make 4 wedges from each slice. Combine cheese spread, Tabasco sauce and mustard until well blended. Spread on bread wedges. Bake in 400-degree oven for 5 minutes or until cheese is bubbly. Place rolled anchovies on wedges, if desired. Serve immediately. Yield: 48 wedges.

Photograph for this recipe on page 16.

TOASTED PARMESAN SQUARES

White bread, crusts removed
Mayonnaise
Finely chopped onion
Grated Parmesan cheese

Cut each slice bread into 4 squares. Spread small amount of mayonnaise on each piece; sprinkle with onion, then Parmesan cheese. Place under broiler until lightly browned.

Jane McCoy, V.P.
Alpha Nu No. 4710
Waynesboro, Virginia

CHEESY DEVILED DIP

1   5-oz. jar pimento cheese spread
1   2 1/4-oz. can deviled ham
1/2 c. mayonnaise or salad dressing
2 tbsp. minced parsley
1 tbsp. minced onion
4 drops of Tabasco sauce
Salt and pepper to taste

Combine cheese spread, deviled ham, mayonnaise, parsley, onion and seasonings; beat
with electric mixer. Chill until ready to use.
Serve with assorted crackers and potato
chips. Yield: About 1 1/2 cups.

Jeanne Williams, Pres.
Alpha Mu No. 346
Muncie, Indiana

CURRIED VEGETABLE DIP

1 c. mayonnaise
2 tsp. grated onion
2 tsp. tarragon
1/2 tsp. curry powder
1/8 tsp. thyme
2 tbsp. catsup
Salt and pepper to taste

Combine all ingredients; mix well. Chill for
at least 2 hours but preferably 24 hours before serving.

Judy Rowlan, Parliamentarian
Beta Omicron No. 3701
Rogers, Arkansas

GREEN CHILI PEPPER DIP

1 can cream of mushroom soup
1 can Ortega green chili peppers, mashed
2 c. grated Cheddar cheese

Combine all ingredients in top of double
boiler; cook until cheese is melted, stirring
frequently. Serve hot as dip or topping for a
chicken casserole, potato casserole or cauliflower topping.

Mrs. Rosa D. Roberts, Dir.
Theta Rho No. 1560
Farwell, Texas

GUACAMOLE DIP

1 ripe avocado
1/2 tsp. diced onion
1/4 c. sour cream
4 drops of lemon juice
Pinch of salt

Chop avocado fine; place avocado and onion
in blender container. Blend until fine. Stir in
sour cream, lemon juice and salt. Serve with
corn chips.

Rose Cedillo
Zeta Lambda No. 2395
Salina, Kansas

TABASCO AVOCADO DUNK

2 ripe avocados
1/2 c. mayonnaise
3 tbsp. lemon juice
1 tsp. chili powder
1 sm. clove of garlic, pressed (opt.)
1/4 tsp. Tabasco sauce
1/4 tsp. salt

Mash avocados with fork or place in blender
and blend until smooth. Stir in remaining
ingredients. Refrigerate for about 1 hour before serving to let flavors blend. Serve with
fresh vegetable dunkers such as cauliflower
buds, green pepper slices, carrot and cucumber sticks. Yield: 1 1/2 cups.

Photograph for this recipe on page 16.

HAWAIIAN PECAN DIP

2 lg. packages cream cheese, softened
1/4 c. milk
2 tbsp. dried onion flakes
2 tbsp. chopped green pepper
1 tsp. garlic salt
1 c. sour cream
1/2 tsp. pepper
1   6-oz. jar dried beef, finely chopped
1/4 c. butter
1 c. finely chopped pecans

Blend cream cheese and milk together; add
onion flakes, green pepper, garlic salt, sour
cream, pepper and beef. Mix well. Pour into
shallow baking dish. Heat butter; add pe-

cans. Pour over top. Bake at 375 degrees for 20 minutes.

Sydney Feraco, Philanthropic Chm.
Delta Omega No. 4369
Loveland, Colorado

SPICY BEEF DIP

1 lb. ground beef
1/2 c. chopped onion
1 clove of garlic, minced
1 8-oz. can tomato sauce
1/4 c. catsup
1 tsp. sugar
3/4 tsp. dried oregano leaves, crushed
1 8-oz. package cream cheese, softened
1/3 c. grated Parmesan cheese

Cook ground beef, onion and garlic in skillet until beef is lightly browned and onion is tender. Stir in tomato sauce, catsup, sugar and oregano. Cover; simmer for 10 minutes. Spoon off excess fat. Remove from heat. Add cream cheese and Parmesan cheese. Heat and stir until well blended and cream cheese is melted. Keep warm in fondue dish and serve with crackers or tortillas. Yield: 3 cups.

Dolores Holmgren, Soc. Chm.
Zeta Lambda No. 2395
Salina, Kansas

FESTIVE SHRIMP DIP

1 8-oz. package cream cheese,
*   softened*
3/4 c. mayonnaise
2 tsp. lemon juice
3 or 4 dashes of Tabasco sauce
2 tbsp. chopped parsley
2 green onions, chopped
Salt and pepper to taste
2 cans shrimp, drained

Whip cream cheese until light with electric mixer. Add mayonnaise by hand. Blend well. Add lemon juice, Tabasco sauce, parsley, onions, salt and pepper; mix well. Blend in shrimp. Serve with fresh vegetables such as celery, cauliflower and carrots.

Carolyn Jones, Sec.
Epsilon Epsilon No. 3475
Portland, Oregon

ALL-HOLIDAY CRAB DIP

1 8-oz. package cream cheese, softened
Milk
6 oz. frozen crab meat, thawed and
*   drained*
1/2 sm. onion, minced
2 dashes of Worcestershire sauce
1/2 bottle chili sauce
3 tbsp. horseradish

Blend cream cheese with a small amount milk. Add crab meat; mix well. Blend in onion and Worcestershire sauce. Chill well. Combine chili sauce and horseradish. Pour over crab mixture. Serve with crackers as dip or spread.

Janet Cullen
Beta Beta No. 4142
Longwood, Florida

REAL VISTA BALLS

6 hard-boiled eggs, chopped
2 slices crisp bacon, crumbled
1 tsp. minced onion
1/2 tsp. salt
1/4 tsp. prepared mustard
1/4 c. mayonnaise
Dash of pepper
2/3 c. grated cheese
Paprika

Combine all ingredients except cheese and paprika. Shape into balls. Roll in cheese; sprinkle with paprika. Chill for 12 hours before serving for improved flavor. Yield: About 3 1/2 dozen.

Shirley A. Hayward
Gamma Epsilon No. 25700
Veradale, Washington

DO-AHEAD FINGER SANDWICHES

When making finger sandwiches, spread bread with light coat of soft butter or margarine before adding spread and the bread will not get soggy. Make these several hours ahead; cover with a damp paper towel, then cover with aluminum foil. Keep refrigerated until ready to use.

Pat Bolin, Parliamentarian
Alpha Omicron No. 577
Enid, Oklahoma

SMOKEY EGG SPREAD

6 hard-cooked eggs, sieved
1/3 c. mayonnaise
1 tbsp. soft butter or margarine
1/2 tsp. salt
2 tsp. prepared mustard
1 1/2 tsp. lemon juice
1 1/2 tsp. Worcestershire sauce
1/8 tsp. liquid smoke
2 drops of hot pepper sauce
Dash of pepper
4 slices cooked bacon, crumbled (opt.)

Combine all ingredients except bacon; beat by hand until smooth. Chill until serving time. Fold in bacon; garnish with paprika. Serve with cocktail crackers.

Shirley Dean, Pres.
Alpha Athena No. 001
Albuquerque, New Mexico

NEW YEAR'S EVE COCKTAIL MEATBALLS

1 lb. ground beef
1/2 c. dry bread crumbs
1/3 c. minced onions
1/4 c. milk
1 egg
1 tbsp. snipped parsley
1 tsp. salt
1/8 tsp. pepper
1/2 tsp. Worcestershire sauce
1/4 c. shortening
1 12-oz. bottle chili sauce
1 10-oz. jar grape jelly

Combine all ingredients except shortening, chili sauce and jelly; mix well. Shape into 1-inch balls. Melt shortening in large skillet; brown meatballs. Remove meatballs from skillet; pour off all fat. Add chili sauce and jelly to pan; heat, stirring constantly, until jelly is melted. Add meatballs; stir until thoroughly coated. Simmer, uncovered, for 30 minutes.

Susan Greer, Treas.
Epsilon Upsilon No. 1626
North Manchester, Indiana

PARTY HAM CUBES

2 tbsp. prepared horseradish
2 tbsp. mayonnaise
1 tsp. Worcestershire sauce
1/2 tsp. seasoned salt
1/8 tsp. pepper
1   8-oz. package cream cheese
6 thin slices boiled ham

Beat horseradish, mayonnaise, Worcestershire sauce, seasoned salt, pepper and cream cheese together until creamy and of spreading consistency. Place 1 ham slice on piece of waxed paper. Spread part of the creamed mixture over slice. Place another slice of ham on top of creamed mixture; spread with more cheese mixture. Repeat, ending with ham slice on top. Wrap securely in waxed paper; place in freezer for 2 hours or longer. Remove from freezer about 1 hour before serving time; cut lengthwise and crosswise into small cubes. Insert an hor d'oeuvre pick in each cube.

Mrs. Roberta G. Evans, W. and M. Chm.
Beta Omicron No. 2997
Madison, Wisconsin

PIZZA SNACKS

1 lb. bulk sausage
1 lb. hamburger
1 tsp. garlic salt
1 tsp. oregano
Salt and pepper to taste
1 lb. Velveeta cheese, melted
Party rye bread

Brown sausage and hamburger in skillet; drain off excess fat. Add seasonings and mix. Pour melted cheese over mixture and stir. Spread on rye bread slices. Make ahead and heat just before serving. Yield: About 5 dozen.

Marsha King, Pres.
Beta Rho No. 681
Independence, Kansas

PARTY SNACKS

1 lb. ground beef
1/2 lb. bulk pork sausage
Salt and pepper to taste

3/4 lb. Velveeta cheese, cubed
Pepperidge Farm party rye bread
Grated Parmesan cheese
Strips of mozzarella cheese

Combine beef and sausage; season with salt and pepper. Brown in skillet; pour off excess fat. Add Velveeta cheese; stir until melted, mixing well. Spread on bread slices; top with Parmesan cheese and several strips of mozzarella cheese. Garnish each with stuffed olive slice. Broil for about 5 minutes or until cheese is melted just before serving.

Judy Schlink, Pres.
Alpha Rho No. 2035
New Berlin, Wisconsin

CHRISTMAS BRAUNSCHWEIGER LOAF

2 lb. braunschweiger
Cream cheese, softened
Mayonnaise
2 tbsp. (heaping) horseradish
2 dashes of Worcestershire sauce
Milk
Stuffed olives

Let braunschweiger stand at room temperature until softened. Combine braunschweiger and one 8-ounce package cream cheese. Add enough mayonnaise to make of spreading consistency. Add horseradish and Worcestershire sauce; mix well. Form into loaf. Blend two 3-ounce packages cream cheese until smooth, adding enough milk to make of spreading consistency. Spread over loaf. Decorate top with sliced stuffed olives.

Betty Lou Caplinger, Past State Pres.
Gamma Nu No. 2261
Indianapolis, Indiana

BRAUNSCHWEIGER SPREAD

10 oz. braunschweiger
4 hard-boiled eggs, mashed
1 sm. onion, finely chopped
2 sweet pickles, finely chopped
3/4 c. mayonnaise

Bring braunschweiger to room temperature. Mash with potato masher or pastry blender to cream well. Do not grind. Add eggs, onion and pickles. Blend in mayonnaise until of desired consistency. Chill for several hours. Remove from refrigerator 2 hours before serving. Serve with crackers or potato chips as a spread or dip.

Edith M. Reida, Awards Chm.
Gamma Omega No. 4408
Rago, Kansas

SPECIAL OCCASION BRAUNSCHWEIGER

1 lb. braunschweiger
1/4 c. mayonnaise
1/4 tsp. garlic powder
2 tbsp. catsup
1 tbsp. Worcestershire sauce
1 tbsp. minced onion flakes
1 8-oz. package cream cheese, softened
Milk

Combine all ingredients except cream cheese and milk; mix thoroughly. Shape into ball. Chill thoroughly. Combine cream cheese with just enough milk to make of spreadable consistency. Spread over ball; garnish with parsley flakes. Serve with snack crackers.

Bobby Johnson, Parliamentarian
Sigma Rho No. 4730
Indianapolis, Indiana

CHEESY SAUSAGE APPETIZER

3 lb. Italian tube sausage
1 can Cheddar cheese soup
3 tbsp. diced jalapeno peppers
1/2 c. milk

Cut sausage into about 1 1/2-inch lengths. Brown well; drain. Combine soup, peppers and milk in fondue pot or saucepan; cook over low heat, stirring until well blended. Add drained sausages to cheese sauce; simmer for 30 to 45 minutes to blend flavors. Allow guests to spear sausages with toothpicks or serve on plates.

Jane Long, Sec.
Kappa Nu Chap.
Englewood, Colorado

DELICIOUS SAUSAGE BALLS

2 c. Bisquick
1 lb. bulk hot sausage
2 tsp. salt
1 10-oz. package sharp Cheddar
   cheese, grated

Combine all ingredients; mix well. Shape into small balls. Place on ungreased cookie sheet. Bake in 400-degree oven for 15 minutes. Drain on paper towels.

Mary Lou Bates, Pres.
Epsilon Mu No. 1986
Odessa, Texas

TURKEY-CHEESE BALL

1 8-oz. package cream cheese
1 c. finely chopped cooked turkey
3/4 c. finely chopped toasted almonds
1/3 c. Hellman's mayonnaise
2 tbsp. chopped chutney
1 tbsp. curry powder
1/4 tsp. salt
Chopped parsley

Combine all ingredients except parsley; mix well. Chill for several hours. Shape into ball; roll in parsley. Serve with crackers.

Edith M. Reida, Awards Chm.
Gamma Omega No. 4408
Rago, Kansas

CHICKEN WINGS PACIFICA

3 lb. chicken wings
1 c. soy sauce
1 c. (packed) brown sugar
1/2 c. butter or margarine
1 tsp. dry mustard

Disjoint chicken wings, discarding tips. Arrange remaining wing pieces in shallow baking dish or pan. Combine soy sauce, brown sugar, butter, mustard and 3/4 cup water; heat until sugar and butter are dissolved. Cool; pour over wings. Marinate for 2 hours, turning occasionally. Bake in 350-degree oven for 45 minutes, turning once and spooning sauce over chicken occasionally.

Drain on paper towels; serve hot or cold. Yield: 20 servings.

Eloise Whitehair, Parliamentarian
Gamma Upsilon No. 3429
New Smyrna Beach, Florida

CLAM PUFFS

1 7 1/2 or 8-oz. can minced clams
1/2 c. butter
1/2 tsp. poultry seasoning
1/4 tsp. salt
1 c. flour
4 eggs

Drain clams; reserve liquor. Add enough water to clam liquor to make 1 cup liquid. Combine clam liquid, butter, poultry seasoning and salt in saucepan; heat to boiling point. Add flour; cook, stirring, until mixture forms a ball. Remove from heat; add eggs, one at a time, beating well after each addition. Stir in clams. Drop by teaspoonfuls onto greased cookie sheet. Bake in preheated 450-degree oven for 10 minutes. Reduce oven temperature to 350 degrees; bake for 10 minutes longer. Serve warm or cold. Yield: About 60 puffs.

Helene Duffy, Ed. Dir.
Alpha Delta No. 1711
Milford, Utah

ELEGANT CRAB BALLS

2 7-oz. cans crab meat
1 c. fresh bread crumbs
3 tbsp. cooking Sherry
1 tbsp. lemon juice
1 tbsp. grated onion
1 tsp. dry mustard
1/2 tsp. salt
Pepper to taste
Bacon slices

Drain and flake crab meat; combine with remaining ingredients except bacon. Mix well. Shape into walnut-sized balls. Wrap with bacon; secure with toothpicks. Broil under medium heat for about 10 minutes or until bacon is crisp, turning to brown evenly.

Garnish with parsley and lemon. Yield: About 2 dozen.

Hazel Kaiser, Corr. Sec.
Alpha Phi No. 1438
Winner, South Dakota

CRAB AMERICAINE

    1   6-oz. package frozen crab meat,
        thawed, drained and flaked
    1   8-oz. package cream cheese,
        softened
    1 sm. onion, finely chopped
    1 tbsp. milk
    1 tsp. lemon juice
    1/2 tsp. prepared horseradish
    1/4 tsp. salt
    Dash of pepper
    1/4 c. slivered toasted almonds

Combine crab meat, cheese, onion, milk, lemon juice, horseradish, salt and pepper in bowl; beat until well mixed. Spread mixture in ungreased 1 1/2 to 2-cup baking dish; sprinkle top with almonds. Bake at 350 degrees for 20 minutes. Garnish with parsley. Serve with unsalted crackers or Melba toast.

Photograph for this recipe on page 27.

CAVIAR MOLD

    3 env. unflavored gelatin
    2 c. chicken broth

    1   2-oz. jar Romanoff red caviar
    2 hard-cooked eggs, sieved
    1   2-oz. jar Romanoff black caviar

Soften gelatin in chicken broth in 1-quart saucepan. Stir over medium heat until gelatin is dissolved. Chill until slightly thickened. Divide into 3 portions, 2/3 cup each. Fold red caviar into one portion, eggs in another and black caviar in the third portion. Pour red caviar portion into 3-cup greased mold. Chill until set. Add egg portion; chill until set. Add black caviar portion; chill until firm. Unmold onto serving plate.

Photograph for this recipe on this page.

RED CAVIAR MOUSSE

    1 tbsp. unflavored gelatin
    1 tbsp. Worcestershire sauce
    1 tbsp. lemon juice
    2 tbsp. mayonnaise
    1 c. sour cream
    4 oz. whipped cream cheese
    2   4-oz. jars red caviar

Soften gelatin in 2 tablespoons cold water; add 1/2 cup boiling water. Stir until gelatin is dissolved. Add Worcestershire sauce and lemon juice. Combine mayonnaise, sour cream and cream cheese; stir in gelatin mixture. Fold in caviar. Pour into 4-cup mold. Chill until set. Unmold; serve with Melba toast. Yield: 24 servings.

Peggy Shepard
Alpha Nu No. 1596
Wilmington, North Carolina

SHRIMP AND CHEESE SPREAD

    1 jar Kraft pimento cheese spread
    1 jar Kraft jalapeno pepper cheese
        spread
    1 can cocktail shrimp, rinsed and drained
    1 tbsp. Worcestershire sauce
    1 tbsp. lemon juice

Combine all ingredients; mix well. Refrigerate for several hours before serving.

Jane Habel, Jonquil Girl
Zeta Chi No. 3878
Fort Collins, Colorado

PICKLED SHRIMP

1/3 c. wine vinegar
1/3 c. oil
2/3 c. Burgundy
1 med. onion, chopped
1 clove of garlic, cut in half
1 tsp. pickling spices
1 tsp. salt
1/2 tsp. Tabasco sauce
1 lb. cooked shrimp, shelled and
    deveined

Combine 2/3 cup water with all ingredients except shrimp; bring to a boil. Simmer for 15 minutes. Add shrimp; return to a boil. Remove from heat; cool. Store in covered glass container in refrigerator. Drain well before serving.

Juanita Gleason, Ed. Dir.
Beta Nu No. 510
Pueblo, Colorado

TUNA SPREAD

1 7-oz. can tuna, drained
2 hard-boiled eggs, chopped
1/4 c. pickle relish
1/3 to 1/2 c. sour cream
Paprika

Combine first 4 ingredients; mix well. Turn into serving bowl. Sprinkle with paprika. Chill thoroughly. Serve with crackers.

Virginia Bernbaum, Rec. Sec.
Epsilon Zeta No. 1928
Los Angeles, California

HAM-STUFFED TOMATOES

1 pt. cherry tomatoes
2 2 1/4-oz. cans deviled ham
2 tbsp. sour cream
2 tbsp. horseradish

Cut thin slices from tops of tomatoes. Remove pulp; drain shells upside down. Combine deviled ham, sour cream and horseradish. Fill drained shells. Refrigerate. Garnish with parsley before serving.

Leona Murdock, Coun. Pres.
Alpha Upsilon No. 3295
Renton, Washington

TOMATO TEASERS

1 pt. cherry tomatoes
1/2 lb. bacon, fried and crumbled
1/4 tsp. Tabasco sauce

Cut small hole in top of each cherry tomato. Combine crumbled bacon with Tabasco sauce. Fill tomatoes with bacon mixture. Serve with food picks. Yield: About 24 tomatoes.

Photograph for this recipe on page 16.

MUSHROOMS AVERY

1/2 lb. medium mushrooms
1/4 c. oil
2 tbsp. minced onion
1/2 c. bread crumbs
1/4 tsp. Tabasco sauce
1/4 tsp. dried leaf thyme
1/4 c. Sherry or water

Remove stems from mushrooms. Chop only enough stems to measure 2 tablespoons chopped stems. Heat 2 tablespoons oil in skillet. Add onion and mushroom stems; saute lightly. Add bread crumbs, Tabasco sauce and thyme; mix well. Fill mushroom caps with stuffing. Clean skillet. Add remaining oil to skillet and heat. Add stuffed mushrooms; saute for about 3 minutes. Add Sherry; cover. Simmer for about 10 minutes or until tender. Serve immediately. Yield: About 12 stuffed mushrooms.

Photograph for this recipe on page 16.

MUSHROOMS IN WINE

16 med.-sized mushrooms
1/2 lb. bulk sausage
1/2 clove of garlic, minced
1 c. tomato sauce
1 c. white wine
1/8 tsp. oregano

Wash mushrooms; remove and chop stems. Add stems to sausage; mix well. Stuff into caps, rounding sausage mixture into high crown. Place in shallow baking pan. Bake in 350-degree oven for 30 minutes. Mash garlic into paste. Heat tomato sauce, wine, garlic and oregano in chafing dish. Add mushrooms;

cover. Heat until sauce bubbles. Spear mushrooms with toothpicks to serve.

Barbara E. Slodyskso, Sec.
Beta Beta No. 4142
Altamonte Springs, Florida

CHEESE-STUFFED MUSHROOMS

2 pt. fresh mushrooms
1 tbsp. finely chopped onion
1 tsp. cooking oil
1/4 c. finely chopped Genoa salami
1/4 c. sharp cheese spread
1 tbsp. catsup
Fine soft bread crumbs

Hollow out mushroom crowns; chop enough stems to measure 1/3 cup. Cook mushroom pieces with onion in oil. Stir in salami, cheese spread and catsup until well blended. Stuff mixture into mushroom crowns; sprinkle with crumbs. Place on cookie sheet. Bake at 425 degrees for 6 minutes. Serve immediately.

Shirley Mooney
Alpha Sigma No. 3514
Raleigh, North Carolina

BICENTENNIAL STUFFED MUSHROOMS

3/4 lb. small or med. fresh mushrooms
6 tbsp. butter or margarine
1/4 c. chopped pecans
3 tbsp. finely chopped onion
1/2 tsp. salt
Dash of pepper
Dash of garlic powder
3/4 c. fresh bread crumbs
2 tbsp. chopped parsley

Rinse mushrooms; dry with paper towels. Remove stems from mushrooms; set caps aside. Chop stems finely; set aside. Melt 3 tablespoons butter in large skillet; saute mushroom caps for 1 to 2 minutes or until lightly browned. Arrange mushroom caps, rounded side down, in shallow baking dish. Melt remaining 3 tablespoons butter in skillet; add chopped stems, pecans, onion, salt, pepper and garlic powder. Saute for 5 minutes. Stir in bread crumbs and parsley. Spoon pecan stuffing into mushroom caps.

Bake, uncovered, in 350-degree oven for 15 minutes. Serve warm.

Photograph for this recipe above.

SAUERKRAUT-SAUSAGE BALLS

1 onion, finely chopped
Margarine
1 lb. bulk sausage
1/2 clove of garlic, finely chopped
1/4 c. flour
1/2 c. broth
3 c. sauerkraut, drained and
*   finely chopped*
1 tbsp. chopped parsley
1 egg, beaten
1 c. milk
Fine bread crumbs

Brown onion in small amount of margarine; add sausage and garlic. Brown lightly. Stir in flour; cook thoroughly. Add broth, sauerkraut and parsley; cook for several minutes or until mixture is thick. Chill. Roll into bite-sized balls. Chill again. Roll balls in additional flour; dip in combined egg and milk mixture. Roll in bread crumbs. Fry in deep hot fat; remove with slotted spoon. Keep warm until ready to serve. May prepare ahead and freeze. Reheat in 300-degree oven. Serve in chafing dish.

Dolores Martensen
Beta Phi No. 2199
Pasco, Washington

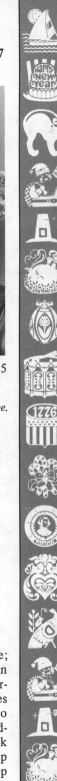

Soups and Salads

Whether it's for Mother's Day, Father's Day or a Family Birthday, when families gather to celebrate, there will always be plenty of enjoyable talk, laughter and smiles, and a memorable meal. But, because the hostess doesn't want to be distracted with cooking, serving and cleaning up, she knows to fix something simple that everyone is sure to enjoy. The answer? Soups and salads, of course! Served as a pair, or separately with sandwiches, crackers, or crepes, both soups and salads make the perfect entree for a midday menu — casual or formal — because neither is too filling, and both are satisfying and refreshing.

The basic appeal of soups and salads is their adaptability — to almost any occasion, season, budget or taste. Whatever follows will be a delicious product of the cook's creativity. A fruit-filled salad, cool and sweet, pairs perfectly with cheese spreads and crackers or a light, savory crepe. A hot poultry salad, served with nuts and fresh, juicy peach slices makes a memorable menu, as does a fresh garden salad served with warm homemade bread, or a meal-in-itself chef's salad. Soups, too, are equally varied in personality. A clear, savory bouillon, served Oriental-style with slivers of crisp vegetables, complements to perfection a hearty sandwich made with dark bread and a robust cream cheese filling. Or, a soup can be hearty and satisfying in itself, accompanied only by a beverage and light dessert for a complete meal. For a doubly delicious menu, soups and salads can be served together, with their flavors and textures planned to complement one another.

For your next holiday party, it would be taste-tempting fun to treat your guests to a soup and salad bar resembling a Scandinavian smorgasbord. Set out a steaming variety of clear, meaty, creamy and vegetable soups accompanied by a choice of croutons, crackers and cheeses to sprinkle over the soup. For the salad selection, choose a variety of lettuce, cheeses, congealed and fresh fruits, pickles, onions, fresh vegetable garnishes, and a choice of piquant dressings. Also include various breads, crispy crackers and spreads for imaginative sandwich-making.

Decorations and food on any chosen theme can be built into a buffet menu as flexible as a smorgasbord. For example, if you want your focus to be on the autumn harvest, lay your tableware and serving dishes on a bed of glorious autumn leaves. For a centerpiece, create a cornucopia overflowing with harvest products, including golden stalks of grain, dusky nuts and acorns, colorful squashes and gourds, deep purple eggplant, and sun-bright chrysanthemums. The food selection could include prepared versions of the same foods, as well as cabbage, onion, pickled beets, marinated carrots, sausages, apples, as well as potato, French onion, and split pea soups. For Mother's Day, use baskets of flowers and follow a picnic theme — sunny yellow napkins with a sky blue tablecloth. Use paper plates, etc. for easy cleanup. Your salad selection could include Mom's favorite recipe for Hot Potato Salad, or Hot Chicken Salad, as well as baked beans, egg salad, corn relish, dill pickles, a choice of Vichyssoise or Gazpacho for the soup, and an icebox pie for dessert. For Father's Day, choose a savory spinach salad or chef salad packed with meat and cheese, then serve Brunswick Stew accompanied by crackers, dark bread and pimento cheese. Build the decor around Dad's favorite sport or hobby. If possible, tune in to a baseball game on TV or another sports show and eat on TV trays.

Soups and salads are excellent family foods. Each is highly nutritious, and easy on the household budget. For a family always on the go — as so many of today's families are — soups and salads are the best choice of all the "fast foods" available. A cool crisp salad of fresh fruits or vegetables provides a balance for savory entrees, hot breads and rich side dishes. Soups are an excellent addition to a lunchbox meal and can be real money-savers when made from leftover pasta, meat, gravy, poultry, seafood, or vegetables. Soups never have to go to waste, either, because they can be frozen and used when needed.

ESA members recommend soups and salads because they offer a free reign to homemakers creative imagination. They can be dollar-saving family food or elegant party fare, and casual or fancy, but a cook can always count on soups and salads to be unquestionable palate pleasers. Don't let many days, especially Holidays, go by without putting soups and salads on your menu.

CANADIAN CHEESE SOUP

1/4 c. butter
1/4 c. finely diced onion
1/4 c. finely diced carrots
1/4 c. finely diced celery
1/4 c. flour
1 1/2 tbsp. cornstarch
4 c. chicken stock
4 c. milk
1/8 tsp. soda
1 lb. Old English process Cheddar
   cheese, grated
Salt and pepper to taste

Melt butter; saute vegetables until soft. Add flour and cornstarch; cook until bubbly. Add stock and milk; simmer, stirring until smooth. Add soda and cheese. Heat until cheese is melted. Season with salt and pepper.

Coni Osborn, Treas.
Iota Zeta No. 4424
Plano, Texas

CREAM OF ONION SOUP

2 or 3 onions, sliced
1/4 c. butter or margarine
1 beef bouillon cube
1 c. evaporated milk
1 tsp. salt
1/8 tsp. thyme
Pepper to taste

Cook onion slices in 3 cups water until tender; add butter and bouillon cube. Stir in remaining ingredients; heat through.

Nora Marshall, Historian
Epsilon Beta No. 1653
Stockton, Kansas

CREAMY FRENCH ONION SOUP

1/4 c. butter
7 c. sliced onions
2 tbsp. all-purpose flour

1 tsp. salt
3 tbsp. beef stock base or 12 beef
   bouillon cubes
4 c. milk

Melt butter in 4-quart saucepan; saute onions for about 15 minutes or until tender. Stir in flour and salt. Add 4 cups water and beef stock base. Bring to a boil; reduce heat. Cover; simmer for 30 to 40 minutes. Stir in milk. Heat to serving temperature but do not boil. Yield: About 9 cups.

Croutes

1/2 c. butter
1 sm. clove of garlic, crushed
8 slices French bread, cut 1 in.
   thick
2 c. shredded Swiss cheese

Melt butter in saucepan; stir in garlic. Dip both sides of bread in butter. Place on a jelly roll pan. Bake in preheated 325-degree oven for 10 minutes; turn and toast 5 minutes longer or until lightly browned. Place about 1 cup soup in ovenproof soup bowls. Top each bowl with 1 croute and 1/4 cup Swiss cheese. Place in oven for 10 minutes or until cheese melts.

Photograph for this recipe above.

CABBAGE SOUP

1 clove of garlic, minced
1 lg. onion, diced
1 c. diced celery
2 tbsp. bacon drippings
3 c. chicken stock
1 No. 303 can tomatoes
1 sm. head cabbage, chopped
1 sm. ham hock

Saute garlic, onion and celery in bacon drippings until almost tender. Add chicken stock and tomatoes; simmer for 30 minutes. Add cabbage and ham hock; simmer until cabbage and ham are tender.

Joanne Reynolds, Treas.
Epsilon Sigma No. 3628
Orlando, Florida

CAULIFLOWER-CHEESE SOUP

1 sm. head cauliflower, broken into
  flowerets
1 carrot, grated
1/4 c. chopped celery
2 chicken bouillon cubes
3 tbsp. butter or margarine
3 tbsp. flour
3/4 tsp. salt
1/8 tsp. pepper
2 c. milk
1 c. grated Cheddar cheese

Combine cauliflowerets, carrot, celery, bouillon cubes and 3 cups water in large saucepan. Bring to a boil. Reduce heat; cover. Simmer for 20 minutes or until vegetables are tender. Melt butter in small saucepan; blend in flour, salt and pepper. Add milk; cook, stirring, until mixture comes to a boil. Add cheese; cook and stir just until cheese is melted. Stir cheese sauce into cauliflower mixture. Yield: About 1 1/2 quarts.

Teresa Davis, V.P.
Kappa Chi No. 4457
Brush, Colorado

DELUXE POTATO SOUP

3 c. diced potatoes
1/2 c. diced onion

1 c. diced celery
2 chicken bouillon cubes
2 c. milk
1 carton sour cream with chives
1 tbsp. flour

Combine potatoes, onion and celery in large saucepan. Dissolve bouillon cubes in about 1/2 cup hot water. Add bouillon and 1 cup water to potato mixture. Cook until vegetables are tender. Mash slightly with potato masher. Stir in 1 cup milk. Blend sour cream and flour together; stir into potato mixture. Add remaining 1 cup milk. Heat thoroughly. Garnish bowls of soup with shredded cheese, if desired.

Roberta McDowell
Beta Phi No. 485
Cherokee, Oklahoma

WEST STEAK SOUP

1 1/2 lb. beef chuck steak, cubed
3/4 c. butter
1 1/4 c. flour
1 16-oz. can tomatoes, cut up
3 tbsp. beef base
1 tsp. salt
1 tsp. pepper
1 10-oz. package frozen mixed
  vegetables
1 c. diced celery
1 c. chopped onions
1 c. chopped carrots

Brown beef in 1/4 cup butter. Combine 1/2 cup soft butter and flour; blend in 2 cups water gradually. Add to beef mixture. Add 6 cups water, tomatoes, beef base, salt and pepper. Bring to a boil; cover. Reduce heat; simmer for 30 minutes. Add mixed vegetables, celery, onions and carrots. Cook, stirring frequently, until vegetables are tender and mixture is thickened.

Dot Walker, W. and M. Com.
Delta Xi No. 3038
Clearwater, Florida

Recipe on page 160.

ANY-OCCASION CRAB BISQUE

1 1/2 c. milk
1 tsp. Worcestershire sauce
4 to 5 drops of Tabasco sauce
1 can cream of mushroom soup
1 can tomato soup
Dash of cayenne pepper
5 oz. (or more) crab meat
1 tbsp. Sherry

Combine all ingredients except crab and Sherry; bring to a very slow boil, stirring frequently. Add crab meat; simmer for 1 minute. Add Sherry; serve hot. Yield: 5 servings.

Paula McFarland
Eta Beta No. 2286
Denver, Colorado

CRAB-ASPARAGUS BISQUE

1 can cream of mushroom soup
1 can cream of asparagus soup
1 1/2 soup cans milk
1 c. cream
1 7 1/2-oz. can crab meat
1/4 c. dry white wine

Blend soups together; stir in milk and cream. Heat just to boiling point. Add crab; heat through. Stir in wine just before serving.

Rose Graham, Pres.
Zeta Omicron No. 4409
Plano, Texas

TABASCO OYSTER STEW

1 tsp. celery salt
1/2 tsp. paprika
1 tbsp. Worcestershire sauce
2 doz. oysters with liquid
1 qt. milk
1/2 tsp. Tabasco sauce

Add celery salt, paprika and Worcestershire sauce to oysters and liquid in a deep kettle. Heat until edges of oysters curl slightly. Add

Recipes on pages 105 and 111.

milk; bring to a boil. Remove from heat; stir in Tabasco sauce. Serve with a lump of butter in each bowl. Yield: 4 servings.

Photograph for this recipe on page 30.

CURRIED RICE SALAD

1/4 c. French dressing
2 c. cooked rice
1 10-oz. package frozen peas,
   cooked
1 c. diced celery
1/2 c. chopped onions
3/4 c. mayonnaise
1/2 tsp. (scant) curry powder
1/4 tsp. salt

Drizzle French dressing over rice; let stand for 1 hour. Combine rice, peas, celery and onions; mix well. Combine mayonnaise, curry powder and salt; stir into rice mixture. Garnish with olives and green pepper slices.

Frances Brown, Ed. Dir.
Epsilon Gamma No. 1563
Manhattan, Kansas

HOT CHICKEN SALAD

4 cooked chicken breasts, chopped
2 cans cream of chicken soup
1 c. diced celery
1/3 c. chopped onion
1 c. slivered almonds (opt.)
1 1/2 c. Hellman's mayonnaise
2 c. crushed corn flakes
Melted margarine

Combine first 6 ingredients with 1 cup crushed corn flakes; mix well. Place in baking dish. Combine remaining 1 cup corn flakes with small amount margarine; sprinkle over top. Bake at 300 degrees for 45 minutes.

Jean Nickols, Pres.
Alpha Gamma No. 779
Hot Springs, Arkansas

TOSSED CHICKEN IN A SALAD

        1   1-lb. can bean sprouts, rinsed
              and drained
        4 c. coarsely chopped cooked chicken
        1 1/2 tsp. monosodium glutamate
        1 c. thinly sliced radishes
        1 c. diced unpared cucumber
        1 c. thinly sliced celery
        1 c. snipped watercress
        2 scallions, chopped
        1/4 c. finely chopped green pepper
        2 tsp. garlic salt
        2 c. sour cream
        2 tsp. salt
        1/4 tsp. pepper
        2 to 3 c. cooked rice, chilled
        Fresh salad greens

Layer first 9 ingredients in order listed in large bowl, ending with green pepper. Cover and refrigerate until well chilled. Combine garlic salt with sour cream; cover and refrigerate. Sprinkle chicken mixture with salt and pepper; toss lightly with rice and sour cream mixture. Turn into large salad bowl or platter lined with salad greens; garnish with parsley. Yield: 8-10 servings.

Sally Richison, Pres.
Gamma Beta No. 4513
San Diego, California

CHRISTMAS NOEL SALAD

        2 oranges
        2 apples
        1 qt. cranberries
        1/2 c. chopped celery
        3 c. sugar
        2 3-oz. packages red gelatin
        Chopped nuts to taste

Grind unpeeled oranges, apples and cranberries; add celery and sugar. Let stand until sugar dissolves. Dissolve gelatin in 2 cups boiling water; add fruit mixture and nuts. Chill until firm.

Myrtle Mae Atkinson
Alpha Omicron No. 577
Waukomis, Oklahoma

CHRISTMAS SALAD SUPREME

        1 pkg. lime gelatin
        1 pkg. lemon gelatin
        1 3-oz. package cream cheese,
              softened
        1/2 lb. miniature marshmallows
        1 No. 2 can crushed pineapple, drained
        1/2 c. whipped cream
        1/2 c. Miracle Whip salad dressing
        1 pkg. strawberry or cherry gelatin

Dissolve lime gelatin according to package directions. Pour into oblong or square dish; chill until firm. Combine lemon gelatin, cream cheese, marshmallows and 2 cups boiling water; cool. Add pineapple, whipped cream and salad dressing. Pour over firm lime gelatin; refrigerate until firm. Dissolve strawberry gelatin according to package directions; cool. Pour over firm gelatin mixture; chill until firm. Cut into squares to serve.

Iris DeWilde, Pres.
Delta Rho No. 2397
Savoy, Illinois

HOLIDAY CRANBERRY SALAD

        1 pkg. cranberries
        1 orange
        1 c. chopped nuts
        1 6-oz. package black cherry gelatin
        2 c. sugar
        1 9-oz. can crushed pineapple

Put cranberries, orange and nuts through food chopper, using medium blade; drain and reserve juices. Dissolve gelatin in 2 2/3 cups hot water. Add sugar; stir until dissolved. Add reserved juices. Chill until partially congealed. Stir in pineapple, cranberries, orange and nuts; chill until firm.

Helen Scofield, I.C. Assn. of Arts Chm.
Omicron No. 374
Tacoma, Washington

LAYERED CRANBERRY-APPLE SALAD

        1 3-oz. package raspberry gelatin
        1 16-oz. can whole cranberry sauce

2 apples, diced
1/2 c. diced celery
1 3-oz. package lemon gelatin
1/4 c. lemon juice
1 8-oz. package cream cheese, diced
1/2 c. cashews, chopped
1 3-oz. package lime gelatin
1 8-oz. can grapefruit sections

Dissolve raspberry gelatin in 1 cup boiling water; chill until partially set. Add cranberry sauce, 1 apple and celery. Place in 8-cup mold. Chill until set. Dissolve lemon gelatin in 1 1/4 cups boiling water; add lemon juice. Chill until partially set. Add cream cheese, remaining apple and cashews. Pour over raspberry mixture. Chill until set. Dissolve lime gelatin in 1 cup boiling water; chill until partially set. Add grapefruit; pour lime mixture over lemon mixture. Chill until set.

Sharon R. Welch, V.P.
Theta Rho No. 4635
Walsenburg, Colorado

DREAMY ORANGE SALAD SUPREME

1 No. 2 can crushed pineapple
1 6-oz. box orange gelatin
1 c. chopped nuts
1 box Dream Whip
1 8-oz. package cream cheese,
   softened
1 tbsp. lemon juice
3/4 c. sugar
2 tbsp. all-purpose flour
2 eggs, beaten

Drain pineapple; reserve juice. Dissolve gelatin according to package directions; pour into 8 x 12-inch dish. Chill until partially set. Stir in pineapple. Sprinkle half the nuts over top; chill until firm. Prepare Dream Whip according to package directions; blend in cream cheese. Spread over gelatin mixture, covering completely. Return to refrigerator. Combine reserved pineapple juice, lemon juice, sugar, flour and eggs in saucepan. Cook, stirring constantly, over low heat until thick. Chill thoroughly. Spread over Dream Whip mixture. Sprinkle remaining nuts over top. Refrigerate until ready to serve.

Marybelle Comparato, Pres.
Gamma Phi No. 2561
Haines City, Florida

PADDIE'S AVOCADO MOLD

1 6-oz. package lime gelatin
1 tbsp. instant minced onion
1 tsp. curry powder
1 tsp. garlic salt
2 tbsp. vinegar
2 California avocados
1/2 c. mayonnaise
1/2 c. chopped green pepper
1/3 c. sliced stuffed olives

Combine gelatin, onion and seasonings. Add 1 1/2 cups boiling water; stir until gelatin is dissolved. Stir in 1 cup cold water and vinegar. Chill until mixture mounds on spoon. Cut avocados lengthwise into halves; remove seeds and skin. Sieve avocado; blend with mayonnaise, green pepper and olives. Blend into gelatin mixture. Pour into 5-cup mold. Chill until set. Unmold; garnish with avocado slices, if desired. Yield: 6-8 servings.

Photograph for this recipe below.

EASTER LEMON CHEESE SALAD

1 can pineapple tidbits
1 pkg. lemon gelatin
2 bananas, sliced
2 eggs, beaten
1/2 c. sugar
2 tbsp. flour
15 marshmallows, cut up
1 c. whipping cream, whipped
Grated longhorn cheese

Drain pineapple; reserve juice. Dissolve gelatin according to package directions; chill until partially set. Add pineapple and bananas. Chill until set. Add enough water to reserved pineapple juice to measure 1 cup liquid. Add eggs, sugar and flour. Cook until thick, stirring constantly. Stir in marshmallows; cool. Fold in whipped cream. Pour over gelatin; chill until firm. Sprinkle with cheese.

Pauline Drips, Contact Chm.
Delta Lambda No. 2469
Overland Park, Kansas

FOURTH OF JULY SALAD MOLD

1 29-oz. can peach halves
1 1-lb. 4-oz. can crushed pineapple
1 1/4 c. canned blueberries
6 candied or maraschino cherries
1 3-oz. package red raspberry
   gelatin
2 3-oz. packages lemon gelatin
1 8-oz. package cream cheese,
   softened
1 c. sour cream
1 pkg. black raspberry gelatin

Drain peaches, pineapple and blueberries; reserve each juice. Drain peaches on paper towels. Place 1 cherry in center of each of 6 peach halves; arrange, cut side down, in oiled 10-inch tube pan or 12-cup mold. Dissolve red raspberry gelatin in 3/4 cup boiling water; add 3/4 cup reserved peach liquid. Chill until slightly thickened. Pour over peaches in mold. Chill until firm. Dissolve lemon gelatin in 1 1/2 cups boiling water; add 1 1/2 cups reserved pineapple liquid. Chill until slightly thickened. Beat cream

cheese with sour cream until smooth; stir into lemon gelatin mixture. Fold in pineapple. Pour over firm raspberry layer in mold; chill until firm. Dissolve black raspberry gelatin in 3/4 cup boiling water; add 1 cup reserved blueberry juice. Chill until slightly thickened. Fold in blueberries; pour over firm pineapple layer. Chill for several hours or until firm. Loosen gelatin around top edge with a small sharp knife; dip mold in hot water and unmold. Garnish with cherries, if desired.

Pauline Gard
Alpha Omicron No. 440
Knightstown, Indiana

CUPID'S RIPE OLIVE MOUSSE

2 env. unflavored gelatin
2 8-oz. cans tomato sauce with
   tomato bits
2 tbsp. lemon juice
2 tsp. white wine vinegar
1/2 tsp. Worcestershire sauce
1/4 c. mayonnaise
1 tbsp. chopped green onion
1 2/3 c. quartered pitted California
   ripe olives
1 c. whipping cream, whipped

Sprinkle gelatin on 1/2 cup cold water to soften. Place over low heat; heat, stirring until gelatin dissolves. Remove from heat;

blend in tomato sauce, lemon juice, vinegar and Worcestershire sauce. Cool until slightly thickened. Blend in mayonnaise, onion and olives. Fold in stiffly whipped cream. Turn into 6-cup heart-shaped mold; chill until firm. Unmold; garnish with ripe olives.

Photograph for this recipe on page 38.

PLUM PUDDING SALAD

1 pkg. lemon gelatin
Dash of salt
3/4 c. raisins, cooked
3/4 c. cooked prunes, chopped
1/4 c. chopped black walnuts
1/2 tsp. cinnamon
1/4 tsp. ground cloves
1/4 c. diced red maraschino cherries
1/4 c. diced green maraschino cherries

Dissolve gelatin in 2 cups boiling water; add salt. Chill until partially set. Add remaining ingredients; pour into mold. Chill until firm.

Leona Luecking
Alpha Omicron No. 1827
West Burlington, Iowa

CHRISTMAS FROZEN FRUITCAKE SALAD

1 c. sour cream
1/2   4 1/2-oz. carton frozen whipped
    dessert topping, thawed
1/2 c. sugar
2 tbsp. lemon juice
1 tsp. vanilla extract
1   13-oz. can crushed pineapple,
    drained
2 med. bananas, diced
1/2 c. sliced green candied cherries
1/2 c. sliced red candied cherries
1/2 c. chopped walnuts

Blend sour cream, dessert topping, sugar, lemon juice and vanilla together. Fold in fruits and walnuts. Turn into 4 1/2-cup ring mold. Freeze for several hours or overnight. Unmold onto lettuce-lined plate. Garnish with additional candied cherries, if desired.

Let stand for 10 minutes before serving. Yield: 8 servings.

Ruth E. Hunt
Alpha Omicron No. 1827
Burlington, Iowa

FROZEN HOLIDAY SALAD

1   8-oz. package cream cheese,
    softened
1/2 c. powdered sugar
1/4 c. lemon juice
1 c. sour cream
2 c. miniature marshmallows
1 c. pecan halves or lg. pieces
1 c. glazed red cherries or maraschino
    cherries
2/3 c. drained chunk or tidbit
    pineapple
1 can mandarin oranges

Beat cream cheese, sugar and lemon juice together until smooth. Stir in sour cream. Fold in reamining ingredients. Turn into aluminum foil-lined 9 x 13-inch pan. Freeze until firm.

Vi Hamann
Beta Xi No. 4398
Longmont, Colorado

FRUIT SALAD ICE

1 c. (scant) sugar
3   10-oz. packages frozen strawberries
1 sm. can frozen orange juice
    concentrate
1   17-oz. can apricots, drained and
    chopped
1 No. 2 can crushed pineapple, drained
3 bananas, quartered and sliced

Heat 1 cup water and sugar together until sugar dissolves. Add strawberries, orange juice concentrate, apricots, pineapple and bananas; mix well. Place cupcake liners in muffin pans; fill with fruit mixture about 2/3 full. Freeze until firm. Remove from pans; store in plastic bags. Remove from freezer 5 to 10 minutes before serving.

Marjory Rubel, Treas.
Alpha Mu No. 1895
Denver, Colorado

CREAMY FROZEN SALAD

2 c. sour cream
2 tbsp. lemon juice
3/4 c. sugar
1/8 tsp. salt
1 9-oz. can crushed pineapple, drained
1/4 c. sliced cherries
1/4 c. chopped pecans
1 banana, sliced

Blend first 4 ingredients together until well mixed. Add remaining ingredients; mix well. Turn into 1-quart mold. Freeze until firm. Unmold; wrap in freezer paper. Refreeze. Slice and serve on salad greens.

Linda R. Hodge, Pres.
Alpha Tau Chap.
West Columbia, South Carolina

RED-WHITE AND BLUEBERRY DELIGHT

1 can sweetened condensed milk
1/3 c. ReaLemon lemon juice
2 tsp. grated lemon peel
2 c. plain yogurt
2 c. miniature marshmallows
1/2 c. chopped pecans
1 pt. fresh strawberries, sliced and
    well drained
1 c. fresh or frozen blueberries,
    well drained

Combine milk, lemon juice and lemon peel in large bowl; mix well. Stir in yogurt, marshmallows and pecans. Spread half the milk mixture in 13 x 9-inch baking dish; arrange half the strawberries and blueberries on top. Cover with remaining milk mixture. Top with remaining fruits. Cover with foil; freeze until firm. Remove from freezer 10 minutes before cutting. Yield: 15 servings.

Norma Jean McCord, Rec. Sec.
Beta Kappa No. 697
Seymour, Indiana

FROSTY PINK SALAD

2 10-oz. packages frozen red
    raspberries, thawed
1 3 1/2-oz. package dessert topping mix
Milk

1 12-oz. package frozen peach
    slices, thawed and drained
1 8-oz. can crushed pineapple, drained
1/4 c. chopped walnuts
2 tbsp. mayonnaise
1/2 c. whipping cream

Drain raspberries, reserving juice. Sieve raspberries, if desired. Prepare topping mix according to package directions, using milk required on package and substituting reserved raspberry juice for water. Stir in raspberries, peaches, pineapple, walnuts and mayonnaise. Whip cream; fold into fruit mixture. Turn into 9 x 9 x 2-inch pan. Freeze until firm. Remove from freezer 15 minutes before serving. Cut into squares; place on lettuce-lined plates. Top each serving with mayonnaise and chopped walnuts, if desired. Yield: 8-10 servings.

Donna Sanford, Rec. Sec.
Gamma Nu No. 4508
Winter Park, Florida

MANDARIN WALDORF SALAD

1 11-oz. can mandarin oranges
1/2 c. crushed pineapple
1/2 c. raisins
1 med. red apple, chopped
1/2 c. chopped celery
1/4 c. chopped walnuts or pecans
1/3 c. mayonnaise
4 lettuce leaves

Drain oranges and pineapple; reserve juices. Boil raisins in reserved juices for 1 minute. Drain and cool. Combine all ingredients except mayonnaise and lettuce in bowl; toss well. Chill. Add mayonnaise just before serving. Arrange salad on lettuce leaves. Yield: 4 servings.

Lois Kochenower
Theta Tau No. 4563
Kingfisher, Oklahoma

MEXICAN TACO SALAD

1 lb. ground beef
1 can kidney beans
1 sm. onion, chopped
1 head lettuce, chopped
1 lg. tomato, chopped

8 oz. Cheddar cheese, shredded
1 bottle Catalina French dressing
Tabasco sauce to taste
1 family-sized bag Doritos

Combine ground beef, beans and onion in skillet; cook until browned. Drain and cool completely. Add to lettuce and tomato; mix well. Top with cheese. Add dressing, Tabasco sauce and crushed Doritos just before serving. Mix well.

Mrs. Joyce Lucas
Beta Lambda No. 3199
Gainesville, Florida

GEORGE WASHINGTON'S CHERRY SALAD

1 can fruit cocktail
1 c. drained pineapple chunks
1/2 c. diced maraschino cherries
1 3-oz. package strawberry gelatin
1/4 c. pineapple juice
1 tbsp. cherry juice
1 3-oz. package cream cheese, softened
1 tbsp. lemon juice
1/2 c. whipping cream, whipped
1 c. miniature marshmallows

Drain fruit cocktail; reserve 1/4 cup juice. Chill all fruits. Dissolve gelatin in 1 cup hot water. Add pineapple juice, cherry juice and reserved fruit cocktail juice. Chill until partially set. Blend cream cheese with lemon juice; fold in whipped cream. Beat chilled gelatin until light and fluffy; fold in cream cheese mixture, fruits and marshmallows. Pour into mold. Freeze until firm. Remove from freezer 30 minutes before serving.

Carol Serres, Pres.
Delta Tau No. 3684
Creve Coeur, Missouri

FAVORITE LUNCHEON SALAD

1 can tomato soup
1 lg. package cream cheese, cubed
2 env. unflavored gelatin
1 c. salad dressing
1 c. diced celery
1 c. chopped onions
1 c. chopped pickles
1 c. relish olives
1 12 1/2-oz. can tuna, drained

Heat soup in top of double boiler; add cream cheese. Stir until smooth. Remove from heat; pour into large mixing bowl. Soften gelatin in 1/2 cup cold water; stir into soup mixture. Cool. Add remaining ingredients; mix well. Pour into mold; chill until firm. Yield: 8-10 servings.

Woody Huselton, Sec.
Sigma Nu No. 4713
Pine Bluff, Arkansas

PEGGY'S SHRIMP SALAD

2 c. cooked elbow macaroni, chilled
2 tbsp. finely chopped onion
1 tsp. salt
1/8 tsp. pepper
1 tsp. prepared mustard
2 tbsp. salad oil
1 tbsp. cider vinegar
1 lb. cooked shrimp, diced
3/4 c. chopped celery
1/3 c. chopped green pepper
1/3 c. diced sweet red pepper
1/3 c. mayonnaise

Combine first 4 ingredients. Blend mustard with oil and vinegar; pour over macaroni mixture. Toss lightly. Cover; marinate for 2 to 3 hours in refrigerator. Add remaining ingredients; mix well. Chill. Serve on bed of lettuce. Garnish with green pepper rings.

Betty Newcomb, Rec. Sec.
Alpha Tau No. 2046
Richmond, Virginia

SHRIMP ASPIC SALAD

1 3-oz. package lemon gelatin
2 c. tomato juice
Dash of salt
1 tbsp. vinegar
1 c. finely chopped celery
1 green pepper, finely chopped
1 tbsp. chopped onion
1 can shrimp, drained and halved

Dissolve gelatin in 1 cup hot tomato juice; stir in remaining tomato juice. Add salt and vinegar. Add remaining ingredients; mix well. Pour into mold. Chill until firm. Serve with salad dressing.

Libby Steffens, Sec.
Beta Sigma No. 415
Grand Junction, Colorado

LAND AND SEA SALAD

4 c. torn mixed salad greens
1 1/2 lb. frozen king crab legs
1 lb. cooked shrimp, peeled and
  deveined
1 c. cherry tomatoes, halved
2 tbsp. sliced green onion
1 lg. avocado
Curry Dressing

Place salad greens in salad bowl; top with crab meat, shrimp, cherry tomatoes and green onion. Chill. Peel and slice avocado; add to salad just before serving. Toss with chilled Curry Dressing. Yield: 6 servings.

Curry Dressing

1 c. mayonnaise
1/4 c. milk
1 clove of garlic, minced
2 tsp. curry powder
1/4 tsp. Worcestershire sauce
6 to 8 drops of bottled hot pepper
  sauce

Combine all ingredients; mix well. Chill thoroughly before using.

Peggy Kay, Sec.
Sigma Kappa No. 4684
Claflin, Kansas

SHRIMP LOUIS

1 c. mayonnaise
1/2 c. chili sauce
3/4 tsp. Worcestershire sauce
1 tbsp. grated onion
1 tbsp. chopped parsley
3/4 tsp. prepared horseradish
6 crisp lettuce cups
2 lb. cooked shrimp, shelled and
  deveined

Combine mayonnaise, chili sauce, Worcestershire sauce, onion, parsley and horseradish in bowl. Beat with rotary beater until smooth and well combined. Refrigerate, covered, for several hours or until well chilled. Arrange lettuce cups on individual luncheon plates. Chop shrimp coarsely; divide evenly

in lettuce cups. Spoon dressing over shrimp. Yield: 6 servings.

Sandy Winger, Pres.
Epsilon Upsilon No. 1626
North Manchester, Indiana

SHRIMP-POTATO SALAD

3 lg. cooked potatoes, diced
8 hard-boiled eggs
2 cans shrimp, drained and rinsed
3 tbsp. sweet pickle relish
10 stuffed olives, sliced
10 tbsp. mayonnaise
1/2 tsp. finely chopped onion
1/2 tsp. lemon juice
Salt and pepper to taste

Combine potatoes, 7 chopped eggs, 1 can shrimp, pickle relish, olives, mayonnaise, onion and lemon juice; season with salt and pepper. Mix well. Garnish top with remaining egg and shrimp. Refrigerate for 5 hours.

Margaret Webb
Alpha Chi No. 292
Canon City, Colorado

PARTY ASPARAGUS SALAD

2 14 1/2-oz. cans chopped asparagus
2 c. sugar
1 c. white vinegar
1 tsp. salt
4 env. unflavored gelatin
2 c. chopped celery
1 c. chopped pecans
1 4-oz. jar chopped pimentos
2 sm. onions, grated
Juice of 1 lemon

Drain asparagus, reserving juice. Add enough water to asparagus juice to measure 2 cups liquid. Combine liquid with sugar, vinegar and salt. Bring to a boil. Soften gelatin in 1 cup cold water; add to hot mixture, stirring until dissolved. Chill until consitency of unbeaten egg whites. Add remaining ingredients; mix well. Pour into 8-cup mold. Chill until firm.

Sarah Jones, State Coun. Pres.
Alpha Omega No. 3443
Smyrna, Georgia

FOURTH OF JULY MEXICAN BEAN SALAD

1 16-oz. bottle Catalina dressing
1 lg. tomato, chopped
1 green pepper, diced
1 lg. red onion, thinly sliced
1 can ranch-style beans
1 lg. head lettuce
1 lb. longhorn cheese, grated
1 med.-sized pkg. Fritos

Combine Catalina dressing with tomato, green pepper, onion and beans. Marinate overnight in sealed container. Add lettuce, cheese and crushed Fritos just before serving. Toss to combine.

Sunya Decker, Pres.
Gamma Zeta No. 2179
McCook, Nebraska

COLESLAW SOUFFLE

1 3-oz. package lemon gelatin
2 c. (scant) mayonnaise
1 sm. onion, chopped
1 green pepper, chopped
1 head cabbage, chopped
Salt and pepper to taste
Celery seed to taste
1/4 c. sugar
1/2 c. vinegar

Dissolve gelatin in 1 cup hot water; chill until partially congealed. Add mayonnaise; whip until fluffy. Add remaining ingredients; pour into mold. Chill until firm.

Nora Chase, Pres.
Epsilon Upsilon No. 2154
Liberal, Kansas

FREEZER SLAW

1 med cabbage, grated
1 lg. carrot, grated
1 green pepper, minced
1 med. onion, minced
1 tbsp. salt
1 c. vinegar
1 tsp. celery seed
1/2 tsp. mustard seed
2 c. sugar

Combine cabbage, carrot, green pepper and onion; add salt. Mix well. Combine vinegar, 1/4 cup water, celery seed, mustard seed and sugar in small pan; boil for 1 minute. Cool. Pour over slaw. Mix until well combined. Spoon into plastic freezer containers; freeze. May add mayonnaise to thawed slaw before serving, if desired.

Phyllis Rahill, Awards Chm.
Epsilon Omega No. 1981
Marion, Indiana

SAVE AND SERVE SLAW

1/2 cabbage, grated
1 green pepper, grated
1 onion, grated
1/2 c. vinegar
1/2 c. sugar
1 tsp. celery seed
1/2 c. cooking oil
Salt to taste

Combine cabbage, green pepper and onion. Combine remaining ingredients for marinade; pour over cabbage mixture. Store in covered dish in refrigerator. This keeps well for several days.

Mary Waller, Past Pres.
Epsilon Gamma No. 2959
Deland, Florida

PICNIC CORN SALAD

2 cans white corn, drained
3/4 c. diced cucumber
2 sm. tomatoes, diced
1/4 c. diced onion
1/4 c. sour cream
2 tbsp. mayonnaise
1 tbsp. vinegar
1 tbsp. sugar
1/4 tsp. dry mustard
1 tsp. celery seed

Combine first 4 ingredients in bowl. Combine remaining ingredients; mix until well blended. Pour over corn mixture. Mix well.

Winifred Gilbert, Treas.
Gamma Omega No. 4408
Kingman, Kansas

CAULIFLOWER SALAD BOWL

4 c. thinly sliced cauliflower
1 c. chopped pitted ripe olives
2/3 c. chopped green peppers
1/2 c. chopped pimento
1/2 c. chopped onion
1/2 c. salad oil or olive oil
3 tbsp. lemon juice
3 tbsp. wine vinegar
2 tsp. salt
1/2 tsp. sugar
1/4 tsp. pepper

Combine cauliflower, olives, green peppers, pimento and onion in bowl. Combine remaining ingredients; beat with rotary beater until well blended. Pour over cauliflower mixture. Refrigerate, covered, until well chilled. Toss before serving. Yield: 8-10 servings.

Donna Jones
Alpha Rho No. 373
Danville, Indiana

SPECIAL CARROT SALAD

2 lb. carrots, sliced
1 sm. green onion, chopped
1 green pepper, thinly sliced
1 can tomato soup
1/2 c. salad oil
1 c. sugar
3/4 c. vinegar
1 tsp. prepared mustard
1 tsp. Worcestershire sauce
Salt and pepper to taste

Cook carrots in small amount water until just tender. Drain and cool. Add onion and green pepper. Combine remaining ingredients; pour over carrot mixture. Mix well. Cover. Refrigerate overnight. This keeps well for several days.

Virginia Fisher, Publ. Chm.
Gamma Omega No. 4408
Kingman, Kansas

CUCUMBER SALAD

1 med. cucumber, peeled and sliced
Salt

3/4 tsp. sugar
1/8 tsp. dry mustard
2 tbsp. vinegar
2 tbsp. oil
1 med. onion, thinly sliced

Sprinkle cucumber generously with salt; let stand for at least 1 hour. Drain off water. Combine sugar, 1/4 teaspoon salt, mustard and 1 tablespoon water; stir until dry ingredients are dissolved. Add vinegar and oil. Pour over sliced cucumber and onion; mix well. Refrigerate for several hours or overnight.

Mrs. Nancy Meyer, Treas.
Gamma Phi No. 2561
Winter Haven, Florida

DIETER'S TOMATO ASPIC

2 1/4 c. tomato juice or V-8 juice
1 env. lemon D-Zerta
2 tbsp. vinegar
1/4 c. chopped celery
1/4 c. chopped onion
2 tbsp. minced green olives
2 tbsp. minced fresh parsley

Bring tomato juice to a boil; add D-Zerta. Stir until dissolved. Add vinegar; chill until thick. Add celery, onion, olives and parsley. Pour into individual molds or 1 1/2-quart mold. Chill until firm. Unmold onto crisp salad greens. Yield: 6 servings.

Pauline Burman, Past Pres.
Alpha Chi No. 292
Canon City, Colorado

GARDEN SALAD

Torn lettuce
1 lg. carrot, grated
1 sm. package frozen green peas,
*   partially cooked*
1 onion, cut into rings
1/4 c. sugar
6 tbsp. salad dressing

Arrange layer of lettuce in large glass bowl. Add carrot, peas and onion rings in layers over lettuce. Sprinkle with sugar. Spread salad dressing over top. Cover. Refrigerate for 8 to 10 hours. Toss together just before serving.

Joan Davis, Sec.
Beta Theta No. 4270
Waynesboro, Virginia

MARINATED VEGETABLE PICNIC SALAD

1 jar marinated artichoke hearts, drained
1 can lima beans, drained
2 stalks celery, chopped
3 green onions with tops, chopped
1 sm. bottle Italian dressing

Combine all ingredients in bowl; cover. Refrigerate overnight. Drain; serve on a lettuce leaf.

Carolyn Best, Rec. Sec.
Delta Tau No. 3684
Ellisville, Missouri

NEAPOLITAN VEGETABLE MEDLEY

2 3-oz. packages lemon gelatin
1 tsp. salt
3 tbsp. vinegar
1/2 c. shredded carrots
1/2 c. mayonnaise
1 c. chopped cabbage
1 1/2 c. chopped spinach
1 tsp. grated onion

Dissolve gelatin and salt in 2 cups boiling water; add 1 1/2 cups cold water and vinegar. Measure 1 1/3 cups gelatin into bowl; place bowl in larger bowl of ice and water. Stir until slightly thickened. Stir in carrots. Pour into 8 1/2 x 4 1/2-inch loaf pan; chill until partially congealed. Measure 1 cup remaining gelatin into bowl; beat in mayonnaise. Chill over ice until thickened. Stir in cabbage; spoon into pan over first layer. Chill. Chill remaining gelatin over ice until

slightly thickened. Stir in spinach and onion; spoon over second layer. Chill for about 4 hours or until firm. Unmold and garnish as desired. Yield: 10 servings.

Merna Haggin, Ed. Dir.
Beta Pi No. 1939
Waterloo, Iowa

PICKLED VEGETABLE SALAD

1 10-oz. package frozen mixed vegetables
1 17-oz. can kidney beans, drained
1 c. diced celery
1/2 c. diced onion
1/2 c. chopped green pepper
3/4 c. sugar
1 tbsp. flour
1 tbsp. prepared mustard
1/2 c. vinegar

Cook frozen vegetables according to package directions; drain and cool. Add kidney beans, celery, onion and green pepper. Combine remaining ingredients in saucepan; cook over low heat until thickened, stirring constantly. Pour over vegetables. Chill for at least 6 to 8 hours.

Mary E. Carter
Delta Upsilon No. 2842
Fort Lauderdale, Florida

SAUERKRAUT SALAD

1 2 1/2-lb. can sauerkraut
1 can bean sprouts
1 med. onion, chopped
1 med. green pepper, chopped
1 c. vinegar
1 1/2 c. sugar

Drain sauerkraut and bean sprouts; rinse well with cold water. Drain well. Place in 2-quart casserole. Add onion and green pepper; mix well. Combine vinegar and sugar in saucepan; bring to a boil. Pour over sauerkraut mixture; cover. Chill overnight.

Fran Ashley, V.P.
Alpha Lambda No. 3592
Arlington, Virginia

Vegetables and Side Dishes

The seasons of the year each have wonderfully distinct personalities, but it seems that no other season is as glorious as autumn. Along with the colorful leaves and clear blue skies in contrast with the mottled browns of the earth, there is an unseen force in the air that seems to energize almost everyone. Most exciting of all is the abundant treasure of harvest food that fills pantries, food stores and roadside markets at this time of year. What a colorful sight! Succulent green beans, bold red tomatoes and bright summer squash have been packed into glistening jars for wholesome winter eating; aromatic scarlet and golden apples begin burgeoning the trees, ready to be picked and shipped to market.

What a fantastic time for a party — a Halloween Harvest Party! And, its just the right time of year to let vegetables take the spotlight on the holiday menu. Colorful contrasts can be the overall theme of a Halloween Harvest Party, whether it's for children, teen-agers or adults. Decorations of black witches and cats with grey ghosts and skeletons can stand in contrast to a crazy quilt array of the vegetable entrees on the menu. Take your choice of carrots, cauliflower, broccoli, beets, green beans, limas, corn, sweet potatoes, eggplant and green peppers. Some of these such as the broccoli, cauliflower and carrots, can be served uncooked with a creamy and flavorful dip, others cooked just until tender with a touch of herbs or glazed. Many of these vegetables can also be made into delicious rolls, puddings, salads, soups and cakes. Side dishes can include macaroni and other pastas, as well as accompaniments of baked fruit dishes, pickles, chowchows, jellies and jams. You'll have plenty to choose from so take advantage of the autumn abundance of vegetables in planning your party menu.

A Halloween Harvest Party can be a very convivial gathering, not only because it suggests gala costumes, but because it is an ideal party to feature games for all ages. For one, have plenty of large pieces of paper handy. Then let each guest (child or adult) lie on one sheet while someone else traces their outline on the paper. The resulting full-size paper doll can then be cut out and decorated and painted as desired. This gives children something fun to take home and older people a good chance for laughter and enjoyment. You can also have your guests bob for apples, play "pin-the-hand-on-the-skeleton," and have a pumpkin-carving contest. Don't forget to award prizes! What an escape from the real world a Halloween Harvest Party can be, with its eerie decor, far-out costumes, and all round enjoyment of friends.

Luckily though, the vegetables you feature on your menu are a part of the real world that you can serve everyday. Many are at their freshest in the middle of summer, when they should be picked from the garden and eaten as soon as possible, or canned or frozen so that the family can enjoy their fresh flavor, vitamins and minerals all through the year. Most cooks count on vegetables alone to add personality to a meal, and they are right. There is just no other group of food that can add as many flavors, textures, and colors to family eating. They can be mixed and matched, and brightened with sauces, spices, nuts, onions, mushrooms and herbs. Be sure to make full use of the many kinds of vegetables there are available so that your family will never grow tired of them.

Someone once said that vegetables have an image problem, and most homemakers would probably agree. Sometimes children have to be forced to eat them, probably because they are overcooked, lifeless, colorless, and flavorless. The only real rule for proper vegetable preparation is to cook them in the least amount of water for the shortest possible time. This preserves not only their color, crispness and flavor, but their extraordinary nutrition content, as well. Properly prepared vegetables usually delight children and open older people's eyes to a world of eating they may have never before known. Because they are so colorful, vegetables are also perfectly suited to taste-tempting serving ideas. Placed attractively on a serving platter and garnished with a sprinkling of herbs, fresh parsley, pimentos, or cheese, there is nothing more appetizing than vegetables.

ESA members think it's time to rediscover vegetables, all the year through — everyday and on holidays. In addition to their color, flavor, texture and nutritive value, vegetables are also low in cost and calories. Perfect family foods! Be bold with your use of vegetables. Try picking one that you have never tried, or learning new ways for preparing the ones you know your family loves. Any day can be a holiday with taste-tempting vegetables!

LEMON-CHEESE SAUCE AND ASPARAGUS

2 tbsp. butter
2 tbsp. all-purpose flour
1/4 tsp. dry mustard
Dash of salt
1 c. milk
1 c. shredded Cheddar cheese
1/4 c. grated Parmesan cheese
1 tbsp. grated lemon peel
1 tsp. lemon juice
2 10-oz. packages frozen asparagus
  spears or 1 1/2 pounds fresh
  asparagus, cooked and drained

Melt butter over medium heat; stir in flour, mustard and salt. Cook until bubbly, stirring constantly. Remove from heat; stir in milk gradually. Bring to a boil over medium heat, stirring constantly. Boil and stir for 1 minute. Remove from heat. Stir in Cheddar cheese until melted. Stir in Parmesan cheese, lemon peel and juice. Serve over hot asparagus. Garnish with lemon slices and chopped pimento, if desired.

Photograph for this recipe on page 49.

FIREWORKS ASPARAGUS CASSEROLE

2 cans asparagus, drained
1 sm. can mushrooms, drained
1 sm. jar sliced pimentos, drained
1 can French-fried onion rings
1 can cream of mushroom soup
1 c. grated sharp cheese
Butter

Arrange half the asparagus, mushrooms, pimentos, onion rings and mushroom soup in layers in buttered casserole. Repeat layers. Top with cheese; dot with butter. Bake in 350-degree oven for about 30 minutes.

Karen Bond, V.P.
Beta Gamma No. 4267
Hampton, Virginia

JIFFY BAKED BEANS

Bacon
1 sm. onion, chopped
1 32-oz. can pork and beans
2 tbsp. mustard
1/3 c. (packed) brown sugar

Fry 5 strips bacon until crisp; reserve drippings. Fry onion in bacon drippings until lightly browned; drain. Place pork and beans in casserole; add onion, crumbled fried bacon, mustard and brown sugar. Mix well. Top with bacon slices. Bake at 350 degrees for 1 hour or until beans begin to thicken.

Cheryl Peters
Kappa Tau No. 4527
Burlington, Colorado

CAMPFIRE BEANS

1/2 lb. bacon, diced
1 med onion, chopped
1 lg. can pork and beans

Brown bacon and onion in skillet; add pork and beans. Simmer for 30 to 45 minutes, stirring occasionally.
This is a great dish to take on a camping trip. Prepare beans before leaving home and at campground all that is necessary is a warm fire.

Peggy Hensley
Epsilon Theta No. 598
North Manchester, Indiana

FOURTH OF JULY BAKED BEANS

2 1-lb. cans pork and beans
1/4 c. catsup
2 1/2 tbsp. brown sugar
2 tbsp. molasses
1/4 tsp. liquid smoke
1/4 tsp. Tabasco sauce

Combine all ingredients in a casserole; mix well. Bake at 350 degrees for 45 minutes. May add chopped green pepper, chopped onion and sliced wieners, if desired.

Linda Nelson
Sigma Kappa No. 4684
Claflin, Kansas

MIXED BEAN POT

2 cloves of garlic, minced
3 med. onions, thinly sliced
1/4 c. bacon drippings
1 can pork and beans
1 can red kidney beans
1 can sm. green lima beans, drained
1/2 c. (packed) brown sugar
1/4 c. vinegar
1/2 c. catsup
1 tsp. mustard
1/2 tsp. pepper
1 tsp. salt

Fry garlic and onions in bacon drippings until tender but not brown. Combine all ingredients; mix well. Pour into a 2-quart bean pot or baking dish. Bake at 350 degrees for 1 hour to 1 hour and 15 minutes. Yield: 6-8 servings.

Margie McCollum, Corr. Sec.
Gamma Sigma No. 4729
Madison, North Carolina

CREAMY GREEN BEAN CASSEROLE

Melted butter
2 tbsp. flour
1/4 tsp. pepper
1 tsp. sugar
1/2 tsp. grated onion
1 c. sour cream
2 c. drained green beans
Grated cheese
1/2 c. corn flake crumbs

Combine 3 tablespoons melted butter and flour; cook, stirring, until well blended. Remove from heat; stir in pepper, sugar, onion and sour cream. Fold into beans. Place in shallow casserole. Cover with cheese. Mix crumbs with 1 teaspoon melted butter; sprinkle over top. Bake at 350 degrees for 30 minutes.

Pat Warsop, Treas.
Beta Rho No. 3969
Green River, Wyoming

ITALIAN GREEN BEANS WITH HERBS

2 pkg. frozen Italian beans
1/4 c. butter
3/4 c. minced onion
1 clove of garlic, minced
1/4 c. minced celery
2 tbsp. sesame seed
1/4 tsp. rosemary
1/4 tsp. sweet basil
3/4 tsp. salt
1/4 c. parsley flakes

Cook beans according to package directions; drain. Melt butter in saucepan; add onion, garlic, celery and sesame seed. Saute for 5 minutes, stirring frequently. Add rosemary, basil, salt and parsley; cover. Simmer for 10 minutes. Spoon over hot beans; toss well to coat.

Vic Hamele
Beta Zeta No. 2556
Windsor, Wisconsin

SPECIAL MARINATED GREEN BEANS

2 1-lb. cans green beans, drained
1 tbsp. vinegar
1 tbsp. salad oil
1 sm. onion, thinly sliced
Salt and pepper to taste
1 c. sour cream
1/2 c. mayonnaise
1 tsp. lemon juice
1/4 tsp. dry mustard
1 tsp. horseradish
2 tsp. chopped chives

Mix green beans with vinegar and oil in bowl; place onion over top. Season with salt and pepper. Cover. Marinate for several hours in refrigerator, stirring occasionally. Drain. Combine sour cream with remaining ingredients; blend into bean mixture. Let stand for 1 hour before serving.

Sandy Stormzand, Historian
Beta Theta No. 3478
Springfield, Missouri

coat. Stir horseradish into sour cream; spoon over beets just before serving. Garnish with sprinkle of chopped parsley, if desired. Yield: 3-4 servings.

Elcie Harrison
Beta Lambda No. 3199
Gainesville, Florida

GOLDEN GLORY BEETS

    1   13 1/2-oz. can pineapple chunks
    1/3 c. vinegar
    3 tbsp. brown sugar
    2 1/2 tbsp. flour
    1/2 tsp. seasoned salt
    2   1-lb. cans party-sliced beets,
        well drained

Drain pineapple; reserve syrup. Combine reserved syrup, 1/2 cup water and vinegar. Stir in brown sugar blended with flour and salt. Cook, stirring, for about 10 minutes or until mixture boils and thickens. Add beets. Heat for several minutes longer. Add pineapple chunks. Serve hot. Yield: 6-8 servings.

Photograph for this recipe above.

DAIRY FARM BEETS

    2 c. whole small beets
    1/4 tsp. dry mustard
    1/4 tsp. salt
    1 1/2 tbsp. butter
    1 tbsp. prepared horseradish
    1/2 c. sour cream

Heat beets, mustard and salt in small amount beet liquid; drain. Add butter; toss gently to

EASTER BROCCOLI CASSEROLE

    1/2 c. chopped celery
    1 c. chopped onion
    1/3 c. butter
    1 can cream of mushroom soup
    1 sm. jar Cheez Whiz
    1 pkg. frozen chopped broccoli, thawed
    2 c. cooked Minute rice

Saute celery and onion in butter until transparent. Add remaining ingredients; mix well. Place in buttered casserole. Bake at 350 degrees for 45 minutes.

Jean Early, Pres.
Zeta Pi No. 2513
Dodge City, Kansas

FAVORITE BROCCOLI CASSEROLE

    6 tbsp. margarine
    1 med. onion, chopped
    1   10-oz. package frozen chopped broccoli
    1 can cream of chicken soup
    1/2 c. chopped pasteurized cheese
    1/2 c. milk
    1 c. Minute rice
    Grated cheese

Melt margarine in saucepan. Add onion; saute until transparent. Cook broccoli according to package directions. Combine all ingredients except grated cheese; place in 2-quart baking dish. Sprinkle grated cheese over top; cover. Bake in 350-degree oven for 30 minutes.

LaNese Grim
Beta Pi No. 2225
Benton, Arkansas

BROCCOLI WREATH WITH CURRIED ONIONS

2 pkg. frozen chopped broccoli
Butter
1 tbsp. chopped onion
1 c. bread crumbs
1/2 tsp. sugar
1/2 tsp. salt
1/8 tsp. pepper
1 c. grated longhorn cheese
1 can cream of mushroom soup
3 eggs, well beaten
2 cans boiled onions
3 tbsp. flour
1 tbsp. curry powder

Cook broccoli according to package directions; drain. Melt 1/2 cup butter; add chopped onion, crumbs, sugar, salt, pepper, cheese and soup. Mix thoroughly; fold in eggs and broccoli. Pour into greased 2-quart ring mold. Place mold in pan of water. Bake in preheated 350-degree oven for 45 minutes. Unmold onto serving platter. Drain onions; reserve juice. Melt 3 tablespoons butter in pan; stir in flour and curry powder. Stir in reserved onion juice gradually. Cook until thickened, stirring constantly. Season with additional salt and pepper; add onions. Heat through. Pour in center of broccoli wreath. Garnish with shamrocks cut from green sweet peppers for St. Patrick's Day or with bells made from red pimento for Christmas.

Genie Gilliland, Parliamentarian
Kappa Theta No. 4343
Gainesville, Texas

CABBAGE AND CELERY CASSEROLE

1 sm. head cabbage, sliced
1 med. bunch celery, diced
1 can cream of celery soup
1/2 c. milk
Salt to taste
1/2 c. blanched almonds
1 c. buttered seasoned bread crumbs

Steam cabbage and celery for 10 minutes; drain. Combine soup, milk and salt in sauce-pan; cook over low heat, stirring until smooth. Arrange 1/2 of the cabbage and celery in buttered 9 x 12-inch casserole; add 1/2 of the almonds. Cover with 1/2 of the soup mixture. Repeat layers; top with bread crumbs. Bake at 350 degrees for 30 minutes.

Virginia Hunter
Theta Chi No. 4536
Greensburg, Kansas

YANKEE CABBAGE ROLLS

4 lg. cabbage leaves
1   15 1/2-oz. can corned beef hash
1   10 1/2-oz. can Franco-American
    chicken gravy
1/2 c. sliced cooked carrots
1/2 tsp. caraway seed

Cook cabbage in salted water for several minutes to soften; drain. Divide hash among cabbage leaves; fold in sides and roll up. Secure with toothpicks, if necessary. Place, seam side down, in 10 x 6 x 2-inch baking dish. Pour gravy over cabbage rolls; stir in carrots and caraway seed. Bake at 350 degrees for 30 minutes or until heated through. Yield: 4 servings.

Photograph for this recipe below.

CABBAGE-CHEESE CASSEROLE

1 med. head cabbage, chopped
Velveeta cheese slices
Milk
50 Ritz crackers, crushed
1 tsp. celery seed
1 tsp. minced onion
Salt and pepper to taste
1/2 c. melted butter

Cook cabbage in small amount of water until just tender; drain. Arrange alternate layers of cabbage and cheese slices in buttered casserole; fill with milk. Combine remaining ingredients; mix well. Pat crumb mixture over top, sealing well. Bake at 350 degrees for 30 minutes or until hot and bubbly.

Helen Goodlive, Treas.
Alpha Chi No. 463
Franklin, Indiana

CAMOUFLAGED CARROTS

2 c. grated carrots
1 c. soda cracker crumbs
1 sm. onion, grated
1 c. milk
1/4 c. melted butter
Salt and pepper to taste

Combine all ingredients; mix well. Place in baking dish; cover. Bake at 325 degrees for 50 minutes. Uncover; bake for 10 minutes longer.

Janet Massagli, Treas.
Lambda Delta No. 4224
Redway, California

FOURTH OF JULY COPPER PENNIES

1 can tomato soup
1/2 c. salad oil
1/2 c. vinegar
1 tsp. Worcestershire sauce
1/2 c. sugar
Dash of salt
2 lb. cooked sliced carrots
2 med. onions, sliced in rings
1 lg. green pepper, sliced in rings

Combine first 6 ingredients; mix well. Arrange carrots, onions and green pepper in layers in bowl. Pour dressing over top; cover. Refrigerate overnight. Serve cold. Yield: 8 servings.

Marie Puckett, Treas.
Alpha Xi No. 1610
Chesapeake, Virginia

EASTER BAKED CARROTS

3 c. thinly sliced carrots
3/4 c. bread crumbs
2 tsp. minced onion
2 tbsp. melted butter
1/4 tsp. pepper
1/2 c. grated cheese

Boil carrots in salted water until tender; drain, reserving 1/2 cup liquid. Stir bread crumbs, onion, butter and pepper into carrots. Turn into greased baking dish. Cover with reserved liquid. Dot with additional butter; sprinkle with cheese. Bake at 350 degrees for 15 minutes or Microwave on Cook for 6 minutes. Serve with ham or roast pork.

Carolyn Houser, Rec. Sec.
Alpha Omicron No. 3217
Eustis, Nebraska

HELEN'S CARROT CASSEROLE

1 pkg. carrots, cooked and mashed
2 eggs, beaten
1 sm. onion, chopped fine
1 c. cracker crumbs
1 tbsp. butter
1 c. milk
Salt and pepper to taste
1/2 c. grated sharp Cheddar cheese

Combine all ingredients except cheese; mix well. Place in greased baking dish; cover. Bake at 350 degrees for 45 minutes. Remove from oven; sprinkle grated cheese on top. Return to oven; bake until cheese is melted.

Helen Addington, Pres.
Iota Zeta No. 4424
Plano, Texas

SHAMROCK CAULIFLOWER

1 lg. head cauliflower
1/3 c. oil
2 1/2 tbsp. wine vinegar
1 3/4 tsp. salt
Pepper to taste
1 1/2 c. sieved avocado
1 1/2 tbsp. grated onion
1 tbsp. lemon juice
Dash of Tabasco sauce

Cook whole cauliflower in boiling salted water until just tender. Lift from cooking water; drain. Blend oil, vinegar, 1/4 teaspoon salt and pepper together; pour over hot cauliflower. Cool thoroughly. Chill. Combine avocado, onion, remaining salt, lemon juice and Tabasco sauce. Frost cold cauliflower with avocado mixture. Garnish with radish roses and shamrocks cut from avocado. Yield: 6 servings.

Photograph for this recipe above.

CAULIFLOWER A LA CHEESE

1 cauliflower
1/2 lb. fresh mushrooms, sliced
1/4 c. diced green pepper
1/3 c. butter
1/4 c. flour
1 c. milk
1 tsp. salt
1/4 lb. Kraft pimento cheese, grated
Paprika

Wash cauliflower; break into small pieces. Cook just until tender. Saute mushrooms and green pepper in butter. Stir in flour until smooth; add milk and salt. Cook, stirring, until thickened. Add cheese; cook until melted. Pour cheese sauce over cauliflower. Sprinkle with paprika.

Jean Evans
Rho No. 7198
Nashville, Tennessee

THOUSANDS-LIKE-IT CORN

1 17-oz. can cream-style corn
2 eggs, beaten

1/2 c. milk
2 tbsp. flour
5 tbsp. sugar
2 tbsp. melted butter
1 tsp. salt
1 tsp. pepper
Fine cracker crumbs

Combine all ingredients except crumbs in large mixing bowl. Pour into medium-sized baking dish. Bake at 375 degrees for about 30 minutes. Top with crumbs. Bake for 30 minutes longer or until set.

Janice E. Foreman
Alpha Phi No. 1261
Macy, Indiana

THANKSGIVING CELERY CASEROLE

4 c. diagonally sliced celery
1 can water chestnuts, thinly sliced
1/4 c. chopped pimento
1 can cream of chicken soup
Salt and pepper to taste
1/2 c. buttered bread or cracker crumbs
1/2 c. toasted sliced almonds

Cook celery in boiling water for 8 minutes; drain. Mix with water chestnuts, pimento and soup; season with salt and pepper. Pour into greased 2-quart casserole. Top with crumbs and almonds. Bake at 350 degrees for 35 minutes. Yield: 6-8 servings.

Judy Patterson, V.P.
Beta Iota No. 2748
Madison, Wisconsin

EGGPLANT-SAUSAGE CASSEROLE

2 med. eggplant
Salt
Flour
Cooking oil
1 1/2 lb. Italian sausage
3 ripe tomatoes, sliced
1/2 c. grated Romano cheese

Slice eggplant 1/2 inch thick; sprinkle lightly with salt. Let stand for 30 minutes. Rinse and drain. Dredge with flour; brown in oil. Drain on paper towels. Brown sausage separately; drain well. Arrange eggplant, toma-toes, sausage and cheese in single layers in casserole until all ingredients are used. Bake in preheated 350-degree oven for 45 minutes.

Dorothy Tekavec, Pres.
Alpha Delta No. 178
Pueblo, Colorado

HOLIDAY VEGETABLE CASSEROLE

1 10-oz. package frozen cauliflower, thawed
1 15-oz. can green beans, drained
1/2 c. chopped celery
1/2 c. chopped onion
1/2 tsp. salt
2 cans cream of mushroom soup
1 c. seasoned stuffing mix
1/4 c. butter
1/2 c. (or more) grated Cheddar cheese

Mix cauliflower, green beans, celery, onion and salt with soup and stuffing mix. Turn into greased 2-quart casserole. Dot with butter. Bake at 350 degrees for 30 minutes. Remove from oven; sprinkle with cheese. Return to oven; bake for 8 to 10 minutes longer.

Toni Livelsburger, Philanthropic Chm.
Gamma Kappa No. 2250
Gary, Indiana

GOURMET MUSHROOMS

2 lb. fresh mushrooms
3/4 c. butter
2 tsp. minced onion
1 clove of garlic, minced
1/2 tsp. dried rosemary
1 tsp. Worcestershire sauce
1/2 tsp. salt
1/4 tsp. pepper

Wash mushrooms; remove stems. Melt butter in saucepan. Add remaining ingredients; mix well. Place mushrooms in 2-quart casserole; pour butter mixture over mushrooms. Bake, covered, in 325-degree oven for 30 minutes or until heated through. Yield: 8 servings.

Bea Casad
Zeta Mu No. 2412
Stockton, Kansas

MARINATED ORIENTAL VEGETABLES

1 can French-cut green beans, drained
1 can white Shoe Peg corn, drained
1 can bean sprouts, drained
1 sm. can water chestnuts, sliced
1 4-oz. can sliced mushrooms,
     drained
1 c. thinly sliced celery
1 med. onion, chopped
1 green pepper, chopped
2 pimentos, chopped
1 lg. head cauliflower, broken in
     flowerets
2 lg. carrots, grated
1 c. salad oil
2 c. sugar
2 1/2 c. cider vinegar
1 tsp. salt
Coarsely ground pepper to taste

Combine all vegetables in large bowl. Combine remaining ingredients for marinade; pour over vegetables. Refrigerate overnight or for 48 hours. Keeps for 2 weeks in refrigerator.

Judy Pierson, V.P.
Beta Omega No. 743
Lamar, Colorado

PIMENTO-PEAS AND CORN

1 10-oz. package baby peas frozen
     in butter sauce
1 10-oz. package Shoe Peg corn
     frozen in butter sauce
1/3 c. diced onion
1/3 c. chopped celery
1 tbsp. chopped parsley
1 2-oz. jar sliced pimento, drained
1/2 tsp. basil
1/2 tsp. salt
Dash of pepper
1 tsp. lemon juice
1/2 c. sour cream

Cook peas and corn according to package directions. Open pouches partially; drain

butter sauce into medium saucepan. Saute onion, celery and parsley in butter sauce until tender. Add peas, corn, pimento, basil, salt and pepper. Stir in lemon juice and sour cream; heat through. Yield: 6-8 servings.

Photograph for this recipe on opposite page.

BAKED STUFFED ONIONS

6 lg. onions, peeled
1/2 lb. bulk pork sausage
3/4 c. soft bread crumbs
Beef broth or melted butter (opt.)
Buttered bread crumbs

Cook onions for 10 minutes in enough boiling salted water to cover; drain and cool. Remove center of onions, leaving about a 1/4-inch shell. Invert shells to drain; chop onion centers. Cook sausage in skillet over medium heat for about 10 minutes or until done, stirring with a fork to crumble; drain. Combine sausage, soft bread crumbs and chopped onion; stir in enough broth to moisten. Stuff into onion shells; sprinkle with buttered bread crumbs. Place onions in shallow baking dish; pour 1/2 cup hot water in dish. Bake at 350 degrees for 25 to 30 minutes or until stuffing is hot and onions are tender.

Mrs. Marcelle Heathcock, Pres.
Alpha Alpha No. 1116
Nashville, Tennessee

BAKED POTATOES IN A HURRY

Soak potatoes in hot water for 10 minutes before baking. Rub potatoes with butter to make skins crisp and tasty.

Cynthia G. Webster, Pres.
Eta Omicron No. 4095
Great Bend, Kansas

GRILLED ONIONS IN SHERRY

6 med onions, quartered
6 pats of butter
6 tbsp. Sherry or sweet vermouth

Place each quartered onion in piece of heavy-duty foil. Place pat of butter and 1

tablespoon Sherry on each onion. Seal tightly. Cook on slow grill for 45 minutes. May be baked in 350-degree oven, if desired.

Nancy Reece, Pres.
Alpha Xi No. 1610
Norfolk, Virginia

AUNT ROSE MARY'S AU GRATIN POTATOES

2 qt. grated potatoes
1 tbsp. flour
Garlic salt to taste
1 lb. charp Cheddar cheese, coarsely grated
1/2 lb. Kraft American cheese, grated
Butter
Salt and pepper to taste
2 c. half and half

Soak grated potatoes in cold water for 1 hour; rinse in hot water and drain. Place layer of potatoes in buttered 9 x 13-inch pan; sprinkle with flour and garlic salt. Add layer of cheeses. Dot with butter; season with salt and pepper. Add another layer of potatoes, then remaining cheeses. Pour half and half over all. Bake at 375 degrees for 1 hour and 45 minutes.

Carolyn M. Hayes
Beta Omicron No. 2997
Waunakee, Wisconsin

CHEESE ROSTI

6 lg. Idaho potatoes
6 tbsp. butter or margarine
8 oz. Swiss cheese, grated
Salt and pepper to taste

Boil potatoes in jackets until tender but firm. Cool, peel and grate potatoes. Melt butter in large nonstick skillet; add layer of potatoes and layer of cheese. Sprinkle with salt and pepper. Repeat layers. Sprinkle 2 tablespoons hot water over top; cover. Cook over low to medium heat until bottom layer browns; turn with spatula. Brown again.

Jennifer Cutter, Ed. Dir.
Beta Beta No. 4142
Longwood, Florida

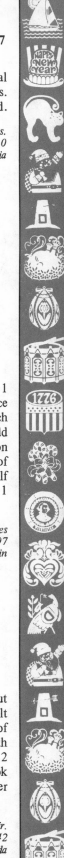

CREAMY AU GRATIN POTATOES

6 to 8 potatoes
2 pt. sour cream
8 oz. Cheddar cheese, shredded
Chopped green onions to taste

Cook potatoes with peelings until tender; cool. Peel potatoes; shred. Combine potatoes, sour cream and 3/4 of the cheese; place in 9 x 13-inch baking dish. Sprinkle top with remaining cheese and green onion. Bake at 350 degrees until hot and bubbly. May substitute 1 can cream of mushroom soup for 1 pint sour cream, if desired.

Connie Oakden, Pres.
Delta Sigma No. 4123
Milwaukie, Oregon

POTATOES DELUXE

1 2-lb. bag frozen hashed brown
   potatoes
1 c. diced onions
1 c. cream of chicken soup
2 8-oz. cartons sour cream
1/2 c. melted margarine
8 oz. sharp cheese, grated

Thaw potatoes for 30 minutes; add remaining ingredients. Turn into greased 9 x 13-inch baking pan. Bake in 350-degree oven for 1 hour. Yield: 8-10 servings.

Mary Scott, Pres.
Alpha Sigma No. 3224
Springdale, Arkansas

SCALLOPED POTATOES

1 2-lb. package frozen hashed brown
   potatoes
1 8-oz. carton sour cream
1 can cream of chicken soup
1 med. onion, chopped
1 c. grated sharp Cheddar cheese
1 1/2 c. Post Toasties, crushed
1/2 c. melted margarine

Combine first 5 ingredients; mix well. Spread in greased 9 x 11-inch baking dish. Combine Post Toasties and margarine; press

on top of potato mixture. Bake at 325 degrees for 1 hour.

Lorraine E. Ross
Alpha Epsilon No. 1565
Paducah, Kentucky

SPINACH AND ARTICHOKES AU GRATIN

2 6-oz. jars marinated artichoke
   hearts, drained
3 10-oz. package frozen chopped
   spinach, thawed
1 8-oz. package cream cheese,
   softened
1/4 c. butter or margarine, softened
6 tbsp. milk
Dash of pepper
1/2 c. grated Parmesan cheese

Place artichoke hearts in shallow 1 1/2-quart casserole. Squeeze moisture from spinach; arrange over artichokes. Beat cream cheese and butter until smooth in small bowl of electric mixer; beat in milk gradually. Spread over spinach. Sprinkle with pepper and Parmesan cheese. Bake, uncovered, at 375 degrees for 40 minutes. This casserole may be covered and refrigerated for as long as 24 hours before baking. Yield: 8 servings.

Dorothy M. Steele, Ed. Dir.
Alpha Theta No. 3918
Honolulu, Hawaii

SPINACH SOUFFLE

1/4 c. butter
1/4 c. all-purpose flour
1/2 tsp. salt
Dash of cayenne paper
1 c. milk
8 oz. sharp American cheese, thinly
   sliced
4 eggs, separated
1 14-oz. can chopped spinach,
   well drained

Melt butter; blend in flour, salt and cayenne pepper. Add milk; cook over medium heat until mixture thickens and bubbles, stirring constantly. Remove from heat; add cheese. Stir until all cheese is melted. Beat egg yolks until thick and light. Add cheese mixture slowly, stirring constantly. Cool slightly. Beat egg whites until stiff peaks form. Fold egg yolk mixture gradually into egg whites. Add spinach; stir just enough to distribute spinach evenly. Pour into ungreased 1 1/2-quart casserole. Trace circle through mixture 1 inch from edge and 1 inch deep. Bake at 300 degrees for 1 hour and 15 minutes. Serve immediately. Yield: 4 servings.

Susie Clesson, V.P.
Eta Omicron No. 4095
Great Bend, Kansas

HARVEST SQUASH

3 acorn squash
2 tbsp. melted butter or margarine
1 1-lb. can or jar applesauce
1/4 c. (firmly packed) brown sugar
2 tsp. grated orange rind
1/8 tsp. nutmeg
1/8 tsp. cinnamon

Halve and seed squash. Place, cut side down, in shallow baking pan. Bake in preheated 350-degree oven for 35 minutes. Turn squash over. Brush insides with butter. Combine remaining ingredients; fill squash centers. Bake for 20 minutes longer. Yield: 6 servings.

Photograph for this recipe on page 46.

SQUASH SUPREME

1/2 c. butter or margarine
2 c. drained cooked squash, mashed
1 can cream of chicken soup
1 med. onion, chopped
1 egg, beaten
1 8-oz. carton sour cream
Stuffing mix or buttered crumbs

Melt butter in casserole. Combine remaining ingredients except stuffing mix in casserole. Top with stuffing mix. Bake at 350 degrees for 30 minutes.

Nancy Woolwine, Sec.
Alpha Nu No. 1596
Wilmington, North Carolina

BAKED YAMS

Parboiled yams
1 sm. can frozen orange juice, thawed
Butter
Honey
Brown sugar

Peel yams; place in baking dish. Cover with orange juice. Dot with butter; drizzle with honey. Sprinkle with brown sugar. Bake, uncovered, at 350 degrees until syrup is bubbly.

Ellen Clark, Treas.
Gamma Omicron No. 3837
Sunland, California

SWEET POTATO CRUNCH

3 c. mashed baked sweet potatoes
1 c. sugar
2 eggs, well beaten
1/2 c. butter
1 c. light cream
1 tsp. Sherry or Bourbon
1 tsp. butter flavoring
1 c. (packed) light brown sugar
1/2 c. soft margarine
1/3 c. self-rising flour
1 c. chopped nuts

Combine first 7 ingredients; beat until well combined. Place in greased baking dish. Combine remaining ingredients; mix well. Sprinkle over top. Bake at 350 degrees for 25 minutes.

Virginia T. Weaver, Historian
Alpha Tau No. 1196
Lake City, Florida

BUTTER DAFFODIL

Butter sticks
Green pepper sticks

Dip butter curler in hot water before making each curl. Draw curler forward lightly and rapidly over 1 stick butter, making a thin shaving which curls up. Drop into ice water; chill until firm. Arrange curls over firm butter stick to resemble flower petals. Add 2 green pepper sticks for leaves. Chill.

Photograph for this recipe on page 88.

SUMMER BARBECUE SAUCE

1 bottle catsup
1/2 c. vinegar
1/2 c. (packed) brown sugar
1/2 c. oil
1 tsp. salt
2 tsp. Worcestershire sauce
1 tsp. dry mustard
1 clove of garlic, chopped
1 med. onion, chopped

Combine all ingredients and 1/2 cup water. Simmer for 20 to 30 minutes. May use on chicken, hamburgers, steak and hot dogs.

Joan Oldham
Beta Iota No. 1972
Longwood, Florida

QUANTITY BARBECUE SAUCE

3   20-oz. bottles catsup
1/2 c. butter
1/2 c. red wine vinegar
1 bay leaf
1 tsp. monosodium glutamate
1/2 tsp. Worcestershire sauce
1/8 tsp. finely rubbed oregano
1/8 tsp. finely rubbed sweet basil
1/8 tsp. finely rubbed rosemary
1/8 tsp. thyme
1/8 tsp. tarragon
1 1/2 c. (packed) brown sugar
1/8 c. tarragon vinegar
3/4 tsp. pepper
1/4 tsp. dry mustard
1/2 tsp. instant minced onion
1/2 tsp. celery salt

Pour catsup into large kettle; add 1 1/2 catsup bottles water. Add remaining ingredients. Simmer for 2 hours and 30 minutes to 3 hours, stirring frequently. Discard bay leaf. Cool and refrigerate in covered jars. This keeps well for 6 months in refrigerator.

Cheryl Wahlenmaier, Reporter
Beta Kappa No. 3124
Arkansas City, Kansas

SPECIAL BARBECUE SAUCE

1/2 c. butter
1/4 c. vinegar
2 tbsp. sugar
1 tsp. prepared mustard
1/2 tsp. pepper
1 1/2 tsp. salt
1/4 tsp. cayenne pepper
1 or 2 thick lemon slices
1 lg. onion, sliced
2 tbsp. Worcestershire sauce
1/2 c. catsup

Combine 1/2 cup water and remaining ingredients except Worcestershire sauce and catsup. Simmer for about 30 minutes. Add remaining ingredients; boil for several minutes longer. May be stored in refrigerator or used immediately. This sauce may be used on pork, chicken, hamburgers or hot dogs. Use only last 30 minutes of cooking time as early basting tends to burn.

Elizabeth Hackbarth, V.P.
Nu Gamma No. 4671
Lakeland, Florida

CRANBERRY CATSUP

2 c. diced onions
2 lb. cranberries
1 lb. light brown sugar
1/2 tsp. ground cloves
1 1/2 tsp. cinnamon
1 tsp. allspice
1/2 tsp. ginger
1 tsp. salt
1/4 tsp. pepper
1 c. red wine vinegar

Place onions, cranberries and 1 1/2 cups water in 4-quart saucepan. Cover tightly; boil for 15 minutes or until cranberries have popped and onions are tender, stirring occasionally toward end of cooking time. Do not overcook. Pour mixture into blender container; puree to make about 5 1/2 cups mixture. Combine remaining ingredients. Stir into puree; mix well. Pour into saucepan; bring to a rolling boil. Pour into hot, sterilized 1/2 pint jars; seal. Process in hot waterbath for 10 minutes to complete seal. Yield: About 7 cups.

Lorri Lassiter
Epsilon Nu No. 3622
Saint Augustine Shores, Florida

CHERRY MARMALADE

    1 29-oz. can crushed pineapple
Juice of 2 lemons
7 1/2 c. sugar
1 9-oz. jar maraschino cherries
1 bottle Certo
Red food coloring

Combine pineapple, lemon juice and sugar. Drain cherries, adding enough water to cherry juice to measure 3/4 cup liquid. Chop cherries; add with liquid to pineapple mixture. Bring to a boil, stirring constantly. Boil for 2 minutes. Remove from heat; add Certo and enough food coloring to tint to desired color. Stir well. Fill hot sterilized jars; seal at once. Process in hot waterbath for 10 minutes to complete seal.
This makes an attractive Christmas gift.

Maxine Talbert
Beta Eta No. 3696
Fairfield, Illinois

EASY PEACH PRESERVES

    5 c. crushed peaches
2 c. crushed pineapple
7 c. sugar
2 sm. boxes strawberry or orange
    gelatin

Cook peaches, pineapple and sugar for 15 minutes. Remove from heat; stir in gelatin until dissolved. Pour into hot sterilized jars; seal. Process in hot waterbath for 10 minutes to complete seal.

Vauda Gaye Emmart, Publ. Chm.
Alpha Omega No. 2065
Winchester, Virginia

HOT PEPPER JELLY

    2 lg. green bell peppers
1 hot red pepper or 2 chili peppers
1 1/2 c. cider vinegar
5 1/2 c. sugar
Green food coloring
1 6-oz. bottle fruit pectin

Wash, core, seed and quarter peppers. Combine 1/2 of the peppers with 1/2 cup vinegar in blender container; process on chop. Repeat with remaining peppers and 1/2 cup vinegar. Rinse blender with remaining 1/2 cup vinegar. Place sugar, peppers and vinegar in large kettle; bring to a full boil, stirring constantly. Boil for 1 minute. Remove from heat; skim off foam. Add several drops of food coloring. Add pectin; stir well. Skim; cool for 5 minutes. Ladle into hot sterilized jars. Seal with paraffin. Cool before moving. May spread over cream cheese and serve with Melba toast or crackers as an appetizer.

Marti Johnson
Gamma Rho No. 2537
Fort Myers, Florida

JOLLY JELLY

    1 1 3/4-oz. box powdered fruit pectin
3 c. Rosé wine
4 c. sugar

Combine fruit pectin and 3/4 cup water in large saucepan. Bring to a boil over high heat; boil for 1 minute, stirring constantly. Reduce heat to medium; add wine and sugar. Cook for about 4 to 6 minutes or until all sugar is dissolved, stirring constantly. Remove from heat; pour quickly into 5 wine, sherbet, Brandy or Champagne glasses. Cover with 1/8-inch hot paraffin.
Tie stem of glass with green yarn; give as a special Merry Christmas gift to an ESA sister.

Pandra D. Warren, Past Pres.
Alpha Sigma No. 3887
Columbia, South Carolina

RHUBARB AND STRAWBERRY JAM

    5 c. diced rhubarb
3 c. sugar
1 3-oz. package strawberry gelatin

Combine rhubarb and sugar; let stand overnight. Boil for 20 minutes. Add gelatin; mix well. Seal in jars. Keep in refrigerator.

Mrs. Jeanne Williamson, Rec. Sec.
Alpha Upsilon No. 3337
Milwaukee, Wisconsin

CANDIED DILL PICKLES

1 1-qt. jar dill pickles, sliced
2 c. sugar
1 tbsp. vinegar
1 chunk of onion

Remove pickles from jar, draining off juice.
Fill jar half full with pickles; add 1 cup
sugar. Add remaining pickles and remaining
sugar. Add vinegar and top with onion. Seal;
let stand in refrigerator for 4 days before
using. May add more vinegar or substitute 1
or 2 cloves of garlic for onion, if desired.

Helen Miller, Pres.
Alpha Omicron No. 440
New Castle, Indiana

SQUASH PICKLES

1 1/2 tbsp. salt
4 c. thinly sliced yellow squash
2 c. chopped onions
2 c. vinegar
4 green peppers, chopped
2 c. sugar
1 tsp. celery seed
1 tsp. mustard seed

Sprinkle salt over squash and onions. Let
stand for 1 hour. Squeeze out and discard
juice. Combine vinegar, peppers, sugar,
celery seed and mustard seed in kettle; bring
to a boil. Boil for 5 minutes. Add squash and
onions; boil for 5 minutes longer. Seal in hot
sterilized jars. Process in hot waterbath for
10 minutes to complete seal.

Barbara S. Wenk, Ed. Dir.
Beta Beta No. 3279
Richmond, Virginia

PEPPERED OLIVES

1 7 1/2-oz. jar stuffed Spanish
   green olives
1/3 c. salad oil
2 tbsp. vinegar
1/2 tsp. crushed red pepper

Drain liquid from olives. Add oil, vinegar
and pepper to olives in jar. Cover tightly;
shake well. Refrigerate for up to 2 weeks.

Photograph for this recipe on page 19.

ANDALUSIAN OLIVE RELISH

1 c. stuffed Spanish green olives
1 4 1/2-oz. jar sliced mushrooms,
   drained
1 c. frozen tiny onions
1/2 c. olive oil
1/4 c. lemon juice
1 clove of garlic, minced
1/2 tsp. chervil
1/8 tsp. pepper

Combine all ingredients in covered container; refrigerate for at least 48 hours
before serving.

Photograph for this recipe on page 19.

CARROT RELISH

6 c. ground carrots
3 green peppers, ground
1 sweet red pepper or pimento, ground
4 c. ground cabbage
4 onions, ground
1 1/2 tbsp. salt
1/2 c. mustard seed
5 c. sugar
1 qt. vinegar

Combine all ingredients; mix well. Cook for
1 hour. Place in hot sterilized pint jars; seal.
Process in hot waterbath for 10 minutes to
complete seal. Serve with hamburgers or hot
dogs.

June Petersen, V.P.
Zeta Chi No. 3878
Fort Collins, Colorado

CORN RELISH

1 can white Shoe Peg corn
1 can French-style green beans
1 can sm. English peas
4 stalks celery, chopped
1/2 green pepper, chopped
1 sm. jar pimento, drained and chopped
1/2 red onion, chopped
1/2 head cauliflower, cut up
1 c. sugar
3/4 c. vinegar
1/2 c. oil

1 tsp. salt
1/4 tsp. pepper

Drain corn, beans and peas. Combine all vegetables. Combine last 5 ingredients for dressing; pour over vegetables. Refrigerate for 24 hours. Pour off excess dressing before serving.

Sharon Peacock
Rho Tau No. 2932
Sedalia, Missouri

CRANBERRY-APRICOT RELISH

3 c. cranberries
1 c. sugar
2 1-lb. cans apricot halves
1/3 c. rum

Place cranberries in 9 x 13-inch baking pan; sprinkle sugar over cranberries. Cover with foil. Bake at 300 degrees for 45 minutes. Drain apricots; reserve 1/2 cup juice. Add apricots and reserved juice to cranberries; cover with foil. Bake for 15 minutes longer. Remove from oven; stir in rum. Cover; chill thoroughly. Yield: 4 cups.

Mary Hoyer, Past Pres.
Beta Kappa No. 345
Estes Park, Colorado

CRANBERRY CHUTNEY RELISH

1 1-lb. can whole cranberry sauce
1/2 c. raisins
1/2 c. unpared chopped cooking apples
1/2 c. chopped celery
1 tsp. ground ginger

Combine all ingredients; mix well. Chill thoroughly before serving. Serve with turkey or ham.

Peggy Sparkman, Ed. Dir.
Kappa Theta No. 4343
Gainesville, Texas

LABOR DAY RELISH

1 c. vinegar
2 c. sugar
1 tbsp. salt
6 c. sliced cucumbers

1 c. sliced onions
1 c. sliced green peppers

Combine vinegar, sugar and salt; add cucumbers, onions and green peppers. Store in 1-gallon container in refrigerator for 5 to 7 days. These will keep well for 6 to 8 weeks.

Velda Adolf, Sec.
Kappa Tau No. 4527
Burlington, Colorado

THANKSGIVING SWEET POTATO CASSEROLE

3 c. mashed sweet potatoes
1/2 c. sugar
Melted butter
2 eggs, beaten
1 tsp. vanilla extract
1/3 c. milk
1 c. (packed) light brown sugar
1/2 c. flour
1 c. chopped pecans

Combine potatoes, sugar, 1/2 cup melted butter, eggs, vanilla and milk; mix well. Spread in buttered 13 x 9-inch baking dish. Combine 1/3 cup melted butter with remaining ingredients; sprinkle over potatoes. Bake at 350 degrees for 25 minutes. Yield: 14 servings.

Brenda Sims
Beta Pi No. 2225
Benton, Arkansas

SCALLOPED PINEAPPLE

1 c. soft margarine
2 c. sugar
4 eggs
1/4 c. milk
6 slices bread, crumbled
1 No. 2 can crushed pineapple,
*   well drained*

Combine margarine, sugar and eggs; beat until light. Blend in milk; add bread. Mix well. Fold in pineapple. Place in baking dish; cover. Bake at 350 degrees for 1 hour.

Gail Boudreaux, Corr. Sec.
Gamma Nu No. 4508
Winter Park, Florida

ZUCCHINI RELISH

10 c. finely chopped zucchini
4 c. finely chopped onions
3 or 4 chopped green bell peppers
1 red bell pepper or 1 sm. jar
*   pimentos, chopped*
5 tbsp. pickling salt
3 c. sugar
3 c. white vinegar
1 tsp. dry mustard
1 tsp. turmeric
2 tbsp. celery seed
2 tbsp. cornstarch
1/2 tsp. pepper

Combine first 4 ingredients in large crock or glass container; sprinkle salt over top. Add 2 trays ice cubes. Cover with upside-down plate; weight down. Let stand for 3 hours or overnight. Drain and rinse with cold water. Place in large kettle; add remaining ingredients. Simmer for 30 minutes. Place in hot sterilized jars; seal. Process in hot waterbath for 10 minutes to complete seal.

Clennie Johnston, Charter Mem.
Beta Beta No. 4096
Leadville, Colorado

SUNDAY BRUNCH CHEESE STRATA

12 slices white bread, trimmed
1/2 lb. sliced Cheddar cheese
4 eggs, well beaten
2 1/2 c. milk
1 tsp. salt
1/8 tsp. pepper
1/4 tsp. prepared mustard
1 tbsp. instant minced onion
1/2 tsp. Worcestershire sauce (opt.)

Arrange bread slices in greased shallow 2-quart baking dish, cutting slices to fit. Place cheese slices over bread. Top with remaining bread slices. Combine eggs, milk and seasonings in a bowl; mix well. Pour over bread and cheese. Refrigerate for at least 1 hour but overnight, if possible. Bake at 350 degrees for 1 hour or until silver knife inserted in center comes out clean. Yield: 6-8 servings.

Kathy Hartsig, Sec.
Zeta Omicron No. 3998
Seminole, Florida

CHEESE LINZERTART

1 11-oz. package pie crust mix
3 eggs
1 c. light cream
1 tsp. salt
1/4 tsp. pepper
1 8-oz. package Swiss cheese,
*   finely diced*

Prepare pie crust mix according to package directions. Roll out dough to fit pizza pan or 9 x 12-inch pan. Beat eggs with cream; add salt and pepper. Sprinkle cheese over pie crust; pour cream mixture over cheese. Roll remaining dough into ropes; crisscross over top. Bake at 325 degrees for 30 minutes. Serve warm or cold.

Jean Watson, Pres.
Lambda Xi No. 2709
San Antonio, Texas

WELSH RAREBIT

1/4 c. butter
8 c. shredded sharp Cheddar cheese
2 tsp. Worcestershire sauce
1 tsp. dry mustard
Dash of cayenne pepper
4 eggs, slightly beaten
1 c. light cream or half and half

Melt butter in 3-quart heavy saucepan over medium-low heat. Add cheese; cook, stirring constantly, until cheese is melted. Stir in Worcestershire sauce, mustard and cayenne. Combine eggs and cream. Remove cheese from heat; stir in egg mixture until well blended. Return to medium heat; cook until thickened, stirring constantly. May serve over toasted, buttered English muffins, buttered toast triangles, hard-cooked egg slices, broiled mushroom caps stuffed with crumbled bacon, shrimp, crab meat, asparagus spears or tomato slices.

Photograph for this recipe on opposite page.

CHEESE GRITS

1 c. grits
1 tsp. salt
1/2 c. butter
1 lb. New York sharp cheese, grated

2 tsp. Lawry's salt
1 tsp. paprika
2 tsp. Worcestershire sauce
3 eggs, beaten

Add grits and salt to 4 cups boiling water; cook for 5 minutes. Combine all ingredients; mix well. Pour in ungreased shallow baking dish. Bake at 300 degrees for 1 hour.

Judy Lester, ESA Found. Chm.
Beta Kappa No. 697
Seymour, Indiana

CHRISTMAS MORNING SOUFFLE

1 lb. sausage links
4 eggs, beaten
2 1/2 c. milk
3/4 tsp. dry mustard
2 c. grated sharp cheese
8 slices bread, cubed

Brown sausage in skillet; drain and cut into bite-sized pieces. Combine eggs, milk and mustard; beat until well blended. Stir in sau-sage, cheese and bread cubes. Pour into 9 x 13-inch pan. Refrigerate, covered, overnight. Bake at 325 degrees for 1 hour. Cut into squares and serve hot.

Carolyn Essley
Gamma Omicron No. 3976
Bellevue, Washington

EASTER OMELET PIE

6 eggs
1/4 tsp. pepper
1/4 tsp. salt
1/2 c. canned chopped mushrooms
1/4 c. milk
1 c. cubed sharp Cheddar cheese
1 unbaked 9 or 10-in. pie shell

Beat eggs until light in medium-sized mixing bowl. Add all ingredients except pie shell; beat slightly until thoroughly mixed. Pour into pie shell. Bake at 375 degrees for about 20 minutes or until filling is set. Yield: 6 servings.

Fran Lanning, Pres.
Beta Gamma No. 4267
Hampton, Virginia

CREAMED EASTER EGGS

1/4 c. butter
3 tbsp. all-purpose flour
1 tsp. salt
1/8 tsp. pepper
1/8 tsp. paprika
1 tsp. grated onion
2 c. milk
6 hard-boiled eggs, chopped
1 tbsp. chopped parsley

Melt butter; stir in flour, seasonings and onion. Cook, stirring, over low heat until bubbly. Add milk; cook until thickened. Add eggs and parsley. Heat through. Serve in noodle nest or over sliced tomatoes or cooked asparagus on toast.

Kathy Horton
Beta Pi No. 2225
Benton, Arkansas

CURRIED EGGS AND SHRIMP

16 hard-boiled eggs
2/3 c. mayonnaise
1 tsp. curry powder
1 tsp. salt
1 tsp. paprika
1/2 tsp. dry mustard
6 tbsp. margarine
1/4 c. flour
1 can cream of shrimp soup
3/4 soup can milk
1/2 c. shredded cheese
1 8-oz. package frozen shrimp, cooked
1 c. soft bread crumbs

Cut eggs lengthwise; remove yolks and mash. Mix yolks with mayonnaise and seasonings. Fill whites; arrange in large baking dish. Melt 4 tablespoons margarine; blend in flour. Stir in soup and milk. Cook, stirring, until sauce thickens. Add cheese; stir until melted. Sprinkle shrimp over eggs; cover eggs and shrimp with sauce. Combine crumbs and 2 tablespoons melted margarine; sprinkle around edge. Bake at 350 degrees for 15 to 20 minutes or until heated through. Garnish with parsley.

Betty Allen, I.C. Philanthropic Chm.
Alpha Chi No. 2055
Stuarts Draft, Virginia

ANNETTE'S EASTER BRUNCH EGGS

8 Cheddar cheese slices
12 eggs
1 c. sour cream
1/2 c. chopped parsley
Paprika
6 English muffins, split and toasted

Place cheese slices on buttered jelly roll pan. Break eggs carefully over cheese; drizzle sour cream over eggs. Sprinkle with parsley and paprika. Bake in 350-degree oven for 20 minutes or until eggs are set. Serve over muffins. Yield: 6 servings.

Joyce Stefanoff, Sec.
Gamma Epsilon No. 2570
Spokane, Washington

EASTER EGG CASSEROLE

4 slices bacon, diced
1/2 lb. chipped beef, coarsely shredded
1/2 c. butter
1 or 2 4-oz. cans sliced mushrooms
1/2 c. flour
Pepper to taste
4 c. milk
16 eggs
3/4 tsp. salt
1 c. evaporated milk
1/4 c. melted butter

Saute bacon until crisp; remove from pan. Add beef, butter and mushrooms; mix well. Sprinkle flour and pepper into pan. Stir in milk gradually; cook, stirring, until thickened. Combine eggs, salt and evaporated milk; beat well. Pour melted butter in large skillet; add egg mixture and scramble. Arrange alternate layers of sauce and eggs in large flat baking dish; cover. Bake at 275 degrees for 1 hour. This may be refrigerated overnight before baking, if desired. Yield: 12-15 servings.

Marge Green, Pres.
Rho Chi No. 2988
Saint Charles, Missouri

Recipes on page 159.

EASTER EGG AND SAUSAGE CASSEROLE

12 slices bread, trimmed
2 lb. lean pork sausage
2 tsp. prepared mustard
6 eggs
1 1/2 c. milk
1 1/2 c. half and half
2 tsp. Worcestershire sauce
1 1/2 c. shredded Swiss cheese

Place bread in 9 x 13-inch baking pan. Cook sausage until crumbly; drain off fat. Add mustard to sausage; mix well. Sprinkle over bread. Beat eggs, milk, half and half and Worcestershire sauce in a mixing bowl; add cheese. Pour over bread and sausage. Let stand in refrigerator overnight. Bake at 350 degrees for 45 minutes. Let stand for 15 minutes before cutting. Yield: 12 servings.

Elsie Clarke, Pres.
Alpha Chi No. 4461
Manchester, Missouri

HEARTY EASTER MORNING BRUNCH

6 slices bread, trimmed
6 slices American cheese
4 eggs
1 3/4 to 2 c. milk
1 tbsp. minced onion
1/4 tsp. salt
1/8 tsp. dry mustard
1 c. diced ham
1/2 10-oz. package frozen chopped broccoli, thawed
1/4 c. shredded cheese

Line 9 x 13-inch baking pan with bread; cover bread with cheese slices. Beat eggs and milk together; add onion, salt and mustard. Stir in ham and broccoli. Pour over bread and cheese slices. Bake at 350 degrees for 50 minutes. Sprinkle shredded cheese over top. Bake for 5 minutes longer. Serve immediately. Yield: 6 servings.

Alanna Levin, Sec.
Beta Kappa No. 4484
Oelwein, Iowa

Recipe on page 86.

LINDA'S BRUNCH EGG CASSEROLE

2 c. plain croutons
1 c. shredded natural Cheddar cheese
4 eggs, slightly beaten
2 c. milk
1/2 tsp. salt
1/2 tsp. prepared mustard
1/8 tsp. onion powder
Dash of pepper
4 slices fried bacon, crumbled

Combine croutons and cheese in greased deep 1 1/2-quart baking dish. Combine next 6 ingredients; mix until well blended. Pour over crouton mixture in casserole. Sprinkle top with bacon. Bake in 325-degree oven for about 1 hour or until eggs are set. Yield: 4 servings.

Linda Rucker
Northern Virginia Dist. Coun. Pres.
Beta Omega No. 4099
Fairfax, Virginia

HOLIDAY OMELET

8 eggs
1/4 c. milk
1/4 c. diced onion
1/4 c. diced bell pepper
1/2 tsp. salt
1/2 tsp. pepper
2 tsp. chopped pimento
3 tbsp. butter
1/2 c. grated cheese

Beat eggs and milk until fluffy. Blend in onion, bell pepper, salt, pepper and pimento. Melt butter in large skillet over medium heat. Pour egg mixture into skillet; cook until underside is done, lifting edge occasionally. Turn over completely. Sprinkle cheese on half of the top side; flip other half over cheese. Turn omelet over; cook for 1 minute longer or until cheese is melted. Yield: 4 servings.

Sandy Bunch, Pres.
Alpha Gamma No. 240
Phoenix, Arizona

CHRISTMAS QUICHE LORRAINE

> 4 eggs, slightly beaten
> 2 c. milk
> 1/2 tsp. salt
> 1/4 tsp. dry mustard
> 1/8 tsp. white pepper
> 2 c. shredded Swiss cheese
> 6 slices bacon, cooked and crumbled
> 2 tbsp. chopped green onion
> 1 unbaked 9-in. pie shell
> 2 tbsp. Parmesan cheese

Combine eggs, milk, salt, mustard and pepper in a bowl. Toss cheese, bacon and onion together; turn into pie shell. Pour milk mixture over cheese mixture. Sprinkle over Parmesan cheese. Bake in preheated 375-degree oven for 35 to 40 minutes or until a knife inserted near center comes out clean. Allow to stand for 10 minutes before serving. Yield: 6 servings.

Photograph for this recipe on page 112.

EASY BAKED RICE

> 1/2 c. margarine or butter
> 1 med. onion, chopped
> 1 1/2 c. long grain rice
> 2 cans beef consomme
> Salt and pepper to taste
> Slivered almonds (opt.)

Melt margarine in skillet; add onion. Saute slightly. Add rice; brown for about 10 minutes. Add consomme. Season with salt and pepper. Stir; pour into greased 2-quart casserole. Bake at 300 degrees for 45 minutes. Sprinkle top with slivered almonds; bake for 15 minutes longer.

> *Jayne Phelps*
> *Alpha Omicron No. 3122*
> *Wellington, Kansas*

RICE AND SOUR CREAM CASSEROLE

> 3/4 lb. Jack cheese
> 3 c. sour cream

> 2 cans chopped green chilies
> 1 1/2 c. rice, cooked
> Salt and pepper to taste
> 1 c. grated Cheddar cheese

Cut Jack cheese into strips. Mix sour cream and chilies thoroughly. Season rice with salt and pepper. Place half the rice in buttered 1 1/2-quart casserole. Add sour cream mixture, then Jack cheese. Add remaining rice. Cover with foil. Bake at 350 degrees for 30 minutes. Top with Cheddar cheese; bake until cheese is melted.

> *Jane Viers*
> *Gamma Kappa No. 3265*
> *Northglenn, Colorado*

WILD RICE CASSEROLE

> 1/4 c. margarine
> 1/2 c. chopped green pepper
> 1/2 c. chopped onion
> 1 pkg. Uncle Ben's wild rice mix
> 1/2 c. long grain rice
> 1 sm. can sliced mushrooms
> 4 1/2 tsp. instant chicken bouillon

Melt margarine in skillet or heavy pan. Add green pepper, onion, wild rice and long grain rice. Saute until rice is slightly brown and onion is transparent. Add remaining ingredients, 4 1/2 cups water and package of spices from box of wild rice mix. Bring to a boil. Cover; cook over low heat for about 45 minutes or until rice is tender.

> *Luetta Neelly, Treas.*
> *Theta Chi No. 4536*
> *Greensburg, Kansas*

DRESSING BALLS

> 4 c. finely diced celery
> 1/2 c. minced onions
> 1/2 c. margarine
> Minced parsley to taste
> 2 tsp. poultry seasoning
> 1 tsp. salt
> 1/2 tsp. pepper
> 1   1 1/2-lb. loaf bread, cubed

Simmer celery in 2 cups boiling water for 20 minutes. Drain and reserve liquid. Cook onions in margarine over low heat until tender but not brown. Combine all ingredients; mix well. Shape into 12 balls. Place on greased baking sheet. Bake at 350 degrees for 1 hour.

Dee Murray, Pres.
Beta Kappa No. 34504
Estes Park, Colorado

STUFFY BREAD STUFFING

1 pkg. corn bread mix
4 slices bread
1 sm. onion, diced
3 eggs, beaten
1 can cream of chicken soup
1 can cream of celery soup
Salt and pepper to taste

Prepare corn bread mix according to package directions; cool. Crumble corn bread and bread into bowl; add onion, eggs, soups, salt and pepper. Stir all together, adding enough water to make soupy. Turn into large greased pan. Bake at 350 degrees for 20 to 25 minutes or until done.

Lani Marie Alderman, Ed. Dir.
Epsilon Tau No. 3653
Kissimmee, Florida

TURKEY GIBLET DRESSING

Giblets and neck from 1 12-lb. turkey
3 qt. dried bread crumbs
1 1/2 tsp. sage
1 1/2 tsp. rosemary leaves, crushed
1/2 c. margarine, melted
1/2 c. chopped celery
1 tsp. thyme
1 1/2 tsp. salt
1/3 to 1/2 c. minced parsley
2 tsp. instant beef bouillon
1/2 c. chopped onions

Add enough water to turkey giblets and neck to cover well; cook for 1 hour and 30 minutes, adding water as needed. Drain and reserve 1 cup liquid. Chop giblets into bread

crumbs. Add remaining ingredients and reserved liquid; mix well. Use as stuffing for turkey or bake as side dish.

Peggy Hiner, Pres.
Alpha Mu No. 944
Rexburg, Idaho

FESTIVE STUFFING BALLS

1/2 c. chopped onion
1/2 c. chopped celery
2 tbsp. butter
1 12-oz. can vacuum-pack golden whole kernel corn, drained
1 8-oz. package seasoned stuffing mix
1/2 tsp. salt
1/4 tsp. pepper
1/2 tsp. marjoram, crushed
2 eggs
1 c. milk
1/2 c. melted butter

Saute onion and celery in butter until tender. Add corn, stuffing mix, seasonings, eggs and milk; mix well. Shape into 1 1/4 to 1 1/2-inch balls. Place in shallow 9 x 13-inch or 10-inch round pan; pour melted butter over stuffing balls. Bake, uncovered, in preheated 375-degree oven for 15 minutes. Yield: 25 to 28 stuffing balls.

Photograph for this recipe below.

Meats

The feature attraction of most menus is the meat entree, whether the meal is designed to please a steadfast budget watcher or to impress a party of formally-dressed dinner guests — including the boss and his wife. But, everyone will agree that meats are really at their best when served for a special occasion and holiday meals. When there is a reason to serve the very best, choose a superb cut of beef, lamb, or pork, and plan a festive meal featuring the best china, finest silver and linens, and the most elegant recipes.

Easter dinner is one holiday meal that is most often served formally with every recipe chosen and prepared with the care of a French chef. The hostess (usually Mom) knows that all the guests will be decked out in their new spring finery to match Mother Nature's spring flowers, budding trees and bright butterflies. What a memorable way to celebrate Easter and usher in Spring! The traditional meat for Easter dinner is lamb. This originated with the Jewish custom of sacrificing the Paschal lamb for Passover, which is observed at this time of year. For Christians, the lamb is symbolic of Christ. But, many families also favor ham, pork roast, prime rib or an eye-of-the-round beef roast as their traditional Easter meats. The arrival of tender, young carrots, green peas, cucumbers, asparagus and spinach are the harbingers of Spring in many European markets, and thus have become the traditional Easter vegetables. The British custom of serving Hot Cross Buns is also popular in America, and for dessert, many cooks choose yellow or white cake iced in springtime pastels and decorated with tinted coconut. Deviled eggs or egg salad have become a traditional part of Easter dinner, as well, to make use of the gaily tinted eggs left by the Easter Bunny.

Decorations are as much a part of an elegantly formal meal as they are at any family meal. Bright spring flowers and gala Easter Eggs make a sparkling centerpiece for the table, and can be complemented with jelly beans, chocolate bunnies and even soft, stuffed toy lambs. Remember to use your cheeriest table linens, and have all the glassware, silver and window panes glistening clean so that the eating area will reflect the brightness and joy that Easter and Spring bring to everyone's heart. The most enjoyable formal meal you ever prepare may be the Easter meal you create for your family each year. Because everyone is relaxed and happy, there will be plenty of talk and laughter. Moreover, each table guest will be thrilled that you have created a beautiful springtime meal to be remembered for years.

Your family's favorite cuts of meat can set the pace for holiday eating all through the year. Father's Day is the perfect time for Mom and the kids to charcoal steaks on the outdoor grill, accompanied by corn on the cob, baked potatoes and a tasty fresh spinach salad. Then, for Mother's Day, Dad and the children can prepare Mom's favorite recipe. Spareribs, hamburgers, lamb chops, shish kabobs, and hot dogs are the menu attractions for outdoor holiday meals from Memorial Day to Labor Day. It is no wonder that Americans have become renowned meat eaters! Modern American agriculture produces an abundant supply of the tenderest, most flavorful and reasonably priced meats to be found anywhere in the world. Moreover, American cooks have become experts at preparing game meats, from squirrel and rabbit to venison and bear, which also make superb holiday fare — casual or formal, indoors or out.

ESA members, among the best cooks and homemakers in the world, have noticed that no food arouses and satisfies the appetites of their families the way meats do. Moreover, they know that meats do not have to take an unreasonable part of the food budget if they are bought and prepared with the care they deserve. Meat cookery also has plenty of room for culinary experimentation and inventiveness. So prepare tasty, nutritious different cuts of meats as often as possible for an everyday is a holiday menu.

BACKPACKER'S BEEF JERKY

5 to 6 lb. flank steak, cut in
    1/4-in. strips
3 3/4 c. Kikkoman teriyaki sauce
2 tbsp. lemon juice
1/4 tsp. minced garlic
1 tsp. Tabasco sauce

Place steak strips in bowl. Combine remaining ingredients; pour over steak strips. Cover. Marinate in refrigerator for 4 hours or longer. Drain. Arrange steak strips on rack over cookie sheet. Bake at 140 degrees for about 12 hours or until dry but not crumbly.

Marjorie Kadlub
Delta Beta Chap.
Windsor, Colorado

BARBECUED FLANK STEAK

1/4 c. soy sauce
3 tbsp. honey
2 tbsp. vinegar
1 green onion, finely chopped
1 1/2 tsp. garlic powder
1 1/2 tsp. ginger
3/4 c. salad oil
1 1 1/2-lb. flank steak

Combine all ingredients except steak for marinade. Place steak in shallow pan; pour marinade over top. Let stand for 4 hours or longer. Grill for 3 to 5 minutes on each side for medium rare steak.

Betty Hajeh, Parliamentarian
Iota Alpha No. 2961
Fremont, California

BEEF POLYNESIAN

2 1/2 lb. beef sirloin tip
1 1/2 tsp. garlic salt
1 tsp. paprika
1/4 c. oil
1 14-oz. can pineapple chunks
1 10 1/2-oz. can beef broth
1/4 c. wine vinegar
1/2 c. sliced celery
1/2 c. sliced green pepper
1 c. sliced onion
2 lg. tomatoes, cut in wedges
1 tbsp. soy sauce
3 tbsp. brown sugar
1 tbsp. (or more) cornstarch

Trim excess fat from beef. Cut beef in large cubes; mix with garlic salt and paprika. Brown in hot oil. Drain off excess oil. Drain pineapple, adding syrup to beef. Stir in beef broth and 2 tablespoons wine vinegar. Cover; simmer over low heat for about 1 hour and 30 minutes or until beef is tender. Add celery and green pepper; cover and cook for 5 minutes. Add onion; cook for 5 minutes longer or until vegetables are just tender. Add tomatoes and pineapple. Blend soy sauce, brown sugar, cornstarch, 1/2 cup water and remaining 2 tablespoons wine vinegar together. Add to sauce around beef, stirring gently to blend. Simmer until clear and thickened. Serve over rice. Yield: 4-5 servings.

Pat Osborne, Pres.
Alpha Kappa No. 1058
Longview, Washington

SPECIAL BEEF BRISKET

1 env. dry onion soup mix
1 2 to 4-lb. beef brisket
2 tbsp. minced garlic
1 c. red wine
1 c. catsup

Line roasting pan with heavy-duty foil. Sprinkle half the onion soup mix on foil. Rinse beef; place on foil. Sprinkle remaining soup mix over beef. Sprinkle garlic over top. Combine wine and catsup; pour around sides of beef. Add 1/2 cup water around side. Cover tightly with foil. Bake at 325 degrees for 3 to 4 hours or until beef is tender. Refrigerate for 1 or 2 days before using. May add sliced carrots and potatoes, if desired. Slice thin to serve. May reheat in gravy.

Carol Kauffman
Zeta Delta Chap.
Arvada, Colorado

EASTER BEEF IN AN EGGSHELL

    1   4 to 5-lb. beef eye-of-round
          roast
    1 tbsp. prepared mustard
    1 tbsp. soy sauce
    Chou Pastry
    Butter
    2 tbsp. flour
    1/3 c. white table wine
    Salt and pepper to taste

Place beef on large sheet of foil; spread with mustard mixed with soy sauce. Fold sides of foil over beef, making double fold, then fold ends upward and double back. Place in shallow pan. Bake at 300 degrees for 3 hours. Chill. Open foil; reserve liquid for sauce. Place beef on flat baking pan. Pat dry with paper towel. Spread with Chou Pastry, covering top, sides and ends of beef. Decorate top as desired. Bake on low shelf of 425-degree oven for about 30 minutes or until browned. Melt any fat left on foil; add butter if needed to make 2 tablespoons.

Blend in flour. Pour wine in measuring cup with reserved beef liquid. Add enough water to make 1 cup liquid. Stir into butter and flour; simmer until thickened. Season with salt and pepper. Yield: 8 servings.

Chou Pastry

    1/4 tsp. salt
    6 tbsp. butter
    3/4 c. sifted flour
    3 eggs

Heat 3/4 cup water, salt and butter to boiling point; add flour. Stir over moderate heat until mixture forms ball and follows spoon. Remove from heat. Cool slightly. Add eggs, one at a time, beating well after each addition.

Photograph for this recipe above.

BEER-BRAISED BEEF

    1   3-lb. chuck roast, cubed
    2 to 3 c. sliced onions

1 tsp. garlic powder
1 c. beef bouillon
2 tbsp. brown sugar
6 sprigs of parsley, chopped
1 12-oz. can beer
2 tsp. thyme
1 bay leaf
1/2 tbsp. cornstarch
2 tbsp. wine vinegar

Brown roast and onions. Place in Crock-Pot. Add remaining ingredients except cornstarch and vinegar. Cook for 6 to 8 hours on High. May bake in 325-degree oven for 4 hours if desired. Thicken pan juices with mixture of cornstarch and vinegar.

Mary Mollenkopf
Gamma Omicron No. 2052
East Palestine, Ohio

GRILLED CHUCK ROAST

1 chuck roast
1 pkg. marinade for meat, prepared

Marinate roast in marinade for about 1 hour. Place on hot grill; cook to desired degree of doneness.

Sharon Van Dyke
MAL
Orange Park, Florida

CHUCK BOURGUINONNE

1 2 1/2-lb. boned beef chuck roast
   2 in. thick
6 slices bacon
Salt to taste
1 can beef broth
1/2 c. dry red wine
2 lg. cloves of garlic, minced
1 lg. bay leaf
1/2 lb. small whole white onions
4 med. carrots
1/2 lb. sliced fresh mushrooms
2 tbsp. flour

Trim fat from beef; cut in 1 1/2-inch cubes. Fry bacon crisp in large heavy pan. Remove bacon from pan; drain. Brown beef chunks in bacon drippings; pour off fat. Sprinkle beef with salt. Add crumbled bacon, broth, 1 cup water, wine, garlic and bay leaf. Cover; simmer for 1 hour, stirring occasionally. Add onions, carrots and mushrooms. Cover; simmer for 1 hour or until tender. Remove bay leaf. Blend 1/4 cup water into flour. Push beef and vegetables to one side; stir flour mixture slowly into sauce. Cook, stirring until thick.

Julie Ann Justice
Beta Omega No. 4263
Peru, Indiana

CORNED BEEF CASSEROLE

2 1/2 c. shell macaroni
1 12-oz. can corned beef, diced
2 c. diced Cheddar cheese
1 can cream of chicken soup
1 c. milk
1/2 c. chopped onion
2 slices bread
2 tbsp. melted butter

Cook macaroni according to package directions; drain. Combine macaroni, corned beef, cheese, soup, milk and onion; mix well. Turn into 2-quart casserole. Trim crust from bread; cut into cubes. Toss in melted butter. Arrange around edge of casserole. Bake in preheated 350-degree oven for 45 minutes or until golden brown. Let stand for 10 minutes before serving.

Chris Wiseman, 1st V.P.
Alpha Chi No. 2055
Waynesboro, Virginia

PADDIE'S CORNED BEEF AND CABBAGE

4 lb. corned beef
1 lg. head cabbage

Place beef in kettle; cover with cold water. Simmer for 3 hours. Cut cabbage into eighths; place in kettle with beef. Cook until tender. Yield: 8 servings.

Pauline Herber, W. and M. Com.
Eta Omega No. 2658
Watsonville, California

FOURTH OF JULY TERIYAKI HAWAIIAN

3 to 4 lb. beef tenderloin, sirloin
*   or round steak 3/4 to 1 in. thick*
1   1-lb. 4 1/2-oz. can pineapple
*   chunks*
1/3 c. soy sauce
1 tsp. ground ginger
1 tsp. sugar
1/2 tsp. garlic salt
Cherry tomatoes
Green pepper chunks

Cut beef into cubes. Drain pineapple; reserve syrup. Combine reserved syrup, soy sauce, ginger, sugar and garlic salt in shallow dish; add beef. Let stand at room temperature for 1 hour, turning once. Drain beef; thread on skewers alternately with pineapple chunks, tomatoes and green pepper chunks. Broil or grill over coals, turning frequently, until beef is brown on all sides and cooked to desired degree of doneness. Yield: 8 servings.

Mary Alice Covelli, Ed. Dir.
Beta Epsilon No. 357
Fort Morgan, Colorado

FOURTH OF JULY MARINATED SHISH KABOB

2 lb. beef sirloin or tenderloin
1/2 c. olive oil
1/4 c. lemon juice
1 tsp. salt
1 tsp. marjoram
1 tsp. oregano
1/2 tsp. pepper
1 clove of garlic, minced
1/2 c. chopped onion
1 lg. can mushrooms
2 green peppers, cut in squares
1 jar boiled onions
4 tomatoes, cut in wedges

Trim fat from beef. Cut into cubes. Combine remaining ingredients except mushrooms, green peppers, boiled onions and tomatoes; pour over beef. Marinate for 6 hours, turning frequently. Add mushrooms and green peppers. Marinate for 2 hours longer. Alternate beef cubes, green peppers, onions, tomatoes

and mushrooms on skewers. Broil or grill for about 20 minutes, turning and basting frequently with marinade.

Mary Aldridge
MAL
De Land, Florida

GRILLED MARINATED STEAK

1 beef chuck steak or sirloin steak
1 tsp. garlic salt
1 tsp. unseasoned meat tenderizer
1/2 c. soy sauce
3 tbsp. wine vinegar
1 tbsp. sugar

Rub steak with garlic salt and meat tenderizer. Pierce with fork; let stand at room temperature for 30 minutes. Combine soy sauce, 1/2 cup water, vinegar and sugar; pour over steak. Let marinate for 30 minutes. Grill on each side over hot coals to desired doneness.

Jean Morris
Gamma Delta No. 2208
Peru, Indiana

NEW YEAR'S PAMPERED BEEF FILLETS

6 lg. fresh mushroom crowns
2 tbsp. butter or margarine
6 beef fillets 1 in. thick
1/2 c. chopped fresh mushroom stems
*   and pieces*
1/4 c. chopped green onions
4 tsp. cornstarch
1 c. Burgundy
2 tbsp. snipped parsley
1 tsp. salt
Dash of pepper

Flute mushroom crowns; set aside. Heat butter in heavy skillet until golden brown and bubbling. Brown fillets in butter quickly over high heat for about 1 minute on each side. Place fillets on squares of heavy foil on baking sheet. Cool slightly. Add mushroom stems and pieces and onions to skillet drippings. Cook until tender but not brown. Blend in cornstarch. Add 1/2 cup water and remaining ingredients; cook, stirring, until thickened and bubbly. Cook for 1 minute longer. Spoon 3 heaping tablespoons sauce over each fillet; top each with mushroom crown. Bring corners of each foil square up over fillet; twist gently and seal. Refrigerate until ready to use. Place packets in baking pan; open tops slightly. Bake at 500 degrees for 14 to 15 minutes for rare or 16 to 18 minutes for medium doneness. Yield: 6 servings.

Pauline Herber, W. and M. Com.
Eta Omega No. 2658
Watsonville, California

CHINESE NEW YEAR CHOP SUEY

> *1   1-lb. beef round steak 1/2 in. thick*
> *2 tbsp. oil*
> *1 beef bouillon cube*
> *1 c. diced celery*
> *1 c. sliced onions*
> *1/4 lb. mushrooms, sliced*
> *1 c. bean sprouts, drained*
> *3 tbsp. cornstarch*
> *1 tsp. soy sauce*
> *2 tbsp. molasses*
> *1 tsp. vinegar*
> *1 tsp. salt*

Cut beef diagonally into 1/2-inch strips. Brown in oil in skillet. Dissolve bouillon cube in 1 1/2 cups hot water; stir into skillet. Add celery, onions and mushrooms. Cover; simmer for 20 minutes. Add bean sprouts. Combine cornstarch, soy sauce, molasses, vinegar and salt; stir into beef mixture. Cook until thick. Serve with Chinese noodles or rice.

Bonnie L. Kreider, V.P.
Epsilon Theta No. 598
North Manchester, Indiana

ROLLED STEAK IN WINE

> *2 carrots, cut in lengthwise strips*
> *2 celery sticks*
> *3 strips bacon*
> *1 whole boneless round steak*
> *1/2 bottle Burgundy*

Place carrots, celery and bacon on steak; roll up, slanting at wide side. Tie or secure with skewers. Place in baking dish. Pour wine over steak. Bake at 325 degrees for at least 1 hour and 30 minutes or until tender. Use pan juices for gravy.

Mary Balkowitsch
Alpha Epsilon No. 414
Vancouver, Washington

SAKE FLANK STEAK

> *1/4 c. soy sauce*
> *1/4 c. Sake or Sherry*
> *1/4 c. salad oil*
> *2 tsp. powdered ginger*
> *1 clove of garlic, halved*
> *1 tbsp. sugar*
> *1   1 1/2-lb. flank steak*

Combine first 6 ingredients; mix well. Place steak in marinade; refrigerate for 24 to 48 hours. Drain well. Grill over charcoal for 4 to 5 minutes on each side. Slice very thin diagonally to serve.

Jeanette Adams, Pres.
Theta Mu No. 2981
Craig, Colorado

STAR-SPANGLED PEPPER STEAK

> *4 chuck steaks 1 in. thick*
> *1/2 c. bottled Italian salad dressing*
> *2 tbsp. lemon juice*
> *Instant unseasoned meat tenderizer*
> *2 tbsp. peppercorns*

Pierce steaks deeply with fork; place in shallow dish. Combine Italian dressing and lemon juice; pour over steaks. Cover. Refrigerate for at least 2 hours, turning several times. Remove from marinade; sprinkle with tenderizer. Crush peppercorns; press onto each side of steaks. Place on grill, 6 inches above hot coals. Grill to desired degree of doneness, turning once.

Carol Serres, Pres.
Delta Tau No. 3684
Creve Coeur, Missouri

BEST BURGUNDY BEEF STEW

5 lb. beef stew meat
Seasoned flour
Butter
1/4 c. olive oil
1/2 lb. bacon, diced
4 cloves of garlic, crushed
2 carrots, chopped
2 leeks, chopped
4 med. onions, chopped
2 tbsp. minced parsley
2 bay leaves
1 tsp. thyme
1 fifth Burgundy
1 tbsp. flour
Small whole potatoes
Small whole onions
Fresh mushrooms, sliced

Dredge beef in seasoned flour; saute in Dutch oven in 1/4 cup butter and olive oil until browned on all sides. Remove beef. Add next 6 ingredients; cook until bacon is crisp. Return beef to Dutch oven; add bay leaves, thyme and Burgundy. Simmer for 1 hour and 30 minutes to 2 hours, adding hot water if needed. Combine 1 tablespoon flour and 1 tablespoon butter to make a smooth paste; stir into beef mixture. Add potatoes, whole onions and mushrooms; simmer for 2 to 3 hours longer. Add more Burgundy, if needed. Serve with hot French bread.

Joanne Van Nortwick
Delta Tau No. 4264
Yakima, Washington

CHUCK WAGON STEW

1 tsp. sugar
1/4 c. flour
2 lb. lean stew beef
2 tbsp. shortening
2 tsp. salt
1/4 tsp. thyme
1 bay leaf
2 tomatoes, quartered
1 can beef broth
3 sm. potatoes, quartered
3 sm. onions, quartered
3 sm. carrots, quartered
3 stalks celery, chopped
1 16-oz. can green peas

1/4 tsp. pepper
1 tsp. chili pepper

Combine sugar and flour; dredge beef in flour mixture. Brown in shortening. Place in Crock·Pot. Add remaining ingredients. Cook on Low for 8 to 10 hours.

Carol Elliott, Treas.
Beta Omega No. 4210
Midland, Texas

HALLOWEEN FIVE-HOUR STEW

2 lb. beef round steak
2 8-oz. cans tomato sauce with cheese
1 1/2 tsp. salt
1/4 tsp. pepper
2 lg. potatoes, cut in eighths
6 carrots, cut into 1-in. pieces
1 c. coarsely chopped celery
1/2 med. green pepper, chopped
1 med. onion, chopped
1 slice white bread with crust, cubed

Trim excess fat from beef; cut into 1-inch squares. Combine beef, 1 cup water and remaining ingredients in Dutch oven; mix thoroughly. Bake, tightly covered, in preheated 250-degree oven for 5 hours. Stir once or twice during cooking period.

Jane Viers
Gamma Kappa No. 3265
Northglenn, Colorado

PARTY BEEF STROGONOFF

1 1/2 lb. round or sirloin steak, cut in strips
Salt and pepper to taste
Garlic salt to taste
1/2 c. flour
1/4 c. cooking oil
1 sm. can mushrooms
1 can beef broth
1 8-oz. package noodles
1 carton sour cream

Season steak with salt, pepper and garlic salt; dredge with flour. Brown on all sides in cooking oil. Pour off excess oil; add mushrooms and beef broth. Simmer until beef is tender. Cook noodles in boiling salted water until tender; drain. Combine with beef mixture. Stir in sour cream 5 minutes before serving. Yield: 8-10 servings.

Billie Stull, Pres.
Alpha Iota No. 3664
Mount Vernon, Illinois

SKILLET STROGANOFF

1 1-lb. thick beef steak,
   thinly sliced
Seasoned flour
Cooking oil
1/2 c. chopped onion
2 tsp. Worcestershire sauce
1 c. sour cream
1 can cream of mushroom soup
1/2 tsp. salt
1/4 lb. sliced fresh mushrooms
2 tbsp. pimentos
1 1/3 c. beef bouillon
1 1/3 c. Minute rice

Dredge beef with seasoned flour; brown in small amount of oil. Add onion; brown lightly. Add Worcestershire sauce, sour cream, mushroom soup, salt, mushrooms and pimentos. Simmer until beef is tender. Make a well in center; add boiling bouillon, then rice. Cover; remove from heat. Let stand for 5 minutes. Yield: 4-6 servings.

Gladys Jones, Pres.
Kappa Psi No. 4538
Helotes, Texas

CORN BREAD-HAMBURGER CASSEROLE

1 lg. onion, chopped
3 tbsp. shortening
1 lb. ground beef
1 c. tomato sauce
2 c. cooked mixed vegetables or
   niblet corn
1 tsp. salt
1/4 tsp. pepper
1 1/2 c. corn bread mix

Saute onion in shortening until tender; stir in ground beef. Brown lightly. Add tomato sauce and vegetables; season with salt and pepper. Bring to a boil; pour into medium-sized casserole. Prepare corn bread mix ac-

cording to package directions; spread over beef mixture. Bake at 375 degrees for about 25 minutes or until golden brown.

Ann Kennedy, Treas.
Alpha Chi No. 2055
Waynesboro, Virginia

BRENDA'S SPECIAL MEAT LOAF

1 8-oz. can tomato sauce
1 egg
1 1/2 tsp. salt
Garlic salt to taste (opt.)
1/2 tsp. pepper
1 onion, quartered
3 slices bread, torn
1/4 lb. Cheddar cheese, cubed
1 1/2 lb. ground beef
8 green olives, sliced

Place all ingredients except beef and olives in blender container; blend thoroughly. Mix in ground beef and olives. Turn into loaf pan. Bake at 350 degrees for 1 hour and 30 minutes.

Brenda Gilbert, Pres.
Beta Beta No. 4686
Andover, Kansas

TOP-OF-THE-STOVE MEAT LOAF

4 slices stale bread
1/2 c. milk
1 1/2 lb. ground beef chuck
1/2 lb. ground pork
2 eggs
1 med. onion, chopped
1 tsp. nutmeg
1 tsp. salt
Pepper to taste

Soak bread in milk. Combine all ingredients with hands or fork until well mixed. Shape into oval or round ball. Brown on all sides in hot fat in Dutch oven or iron skillet. Add 1 1/2 cups warm water. Simmer for 1 hour and 30 minutes, adding more water, if needed.

Louise Muckenstorm, V.P.
Beta Omicron No. 2029
Saint Petersburg, Florida

BEEF IN COSTUME FOR HALLOWEEN

1   4-lb. pumpkin
1 lb. lean ground beef
1 c. chopped onion
Cooking oil
1/3 c. chopped red pepper
1/3 c. chopped green pepper
1 clove of garlic, minced
1 tsp. salt
1/4 tsp. thyme
1/4 tsp. pepper
1   7 1/2-oz. can pitted ripe olives
1   8-oz. can tomato sauce
2 eggs, beaten

Cut top from pumpkin; scrape out seeds and fibers. Simmer in salted water to cover for about 20 to 25 minutes or until almost tender. Drain. Brown beef and onion in 1 tablespoon oil. Add red and green peppers and garlic. Cook for 1 minute longer. Remove from heat; stir in all remaining ingredients. Spoon into pumpkin; place lid on top. Brush pumpkin with oil. Bake at 350 degrees for about 1 hour. Let stand for about 10 minutes, then cut into wedges to serve. May use lettuce basket to lower pumpkin into boiling water and to remove easily without breaking skin. Yield: About 8 servings.

Photograph for this recipe above.

VERSATILE QUICKIE MEAT LOAF

1 lb. ground beef
1 env. dry onion soup mix
2/3 c. evaporated milk

Combine all ingredients; mix well. Shape into 4 individual loaves. Place in ungreased shallow baking pans. Bake at 350 degrees for about 30 minutes or until brown. May shape into meatballs; cook and serve with hot barbecue sauce or shape into patties for an outdoor grill.

Elaine Lass, Pres.
Beta Rho No. 2007
Clinton, Iowa

PINEAPPLE MEATBALLS

1/2 c. milk
1 slice bread, crumbled
1 egg
2 lb. ground beef
2 1/2 tsp. salt
Pepper to taste
Dash of garlic salt
2 tbsp. salad oil
1 can beef bouillon
1 No. 2 can pineapple chunks
1/2 c. chopped green pepper
1/4 c. wine vinegar
1/2 c. sugar
2 tsp. soy sauce
2 tbsp. cornstarch

Pour milk over bread to soften. Combine bread, egg, beef, 2 teaspoons salt, pepper and garlic salt; mix well. Dip fingers in water; shape beef mixture into walnut-sized balls. Brown in hot oil, shaking pan frequently so meatballs will hold rounded shape. Combine bouillon, pineapple with syrup, green pepper, vinegar, sugar, soy sauce and 1/2 teaspoon salt in saucepan; simmer for about 15 minutes. Dissolve cornstarch in small amount of water; stir into pineapple sauce. Simmer until sauce is clear and thickened, stirring frequently. Add browned meatballs; simmer for 10 to 15 minutes. Serve over rice or noodles.

Mrs. Orville Baute, Sec.
Beta Kappa No. 3498
Seymour, Indiana

SWEET AND SOUR MEATBALLS

2 lb. hamburger
1 c. corn flakes
1/3 c. chopped parsley
2 eggs, beaten
2 tbsp. soy sauce
1/4 tsp. pepper
1/3 tsp. catsup
2 tsp. minced onion
1   1-lb. can cranberry sauce
1   12-oz. bottle chili sauce
2 tbsp. brown sugar
1 tsp. lemon juice

Combine first 8 ingredients; mix well. Form into meatballs; place in single layer in baking dish. Combine remaining ingredients; mix until smooth. Pour over meatballs. Bake at 350 degrees for 30 to 45 minutes.

Judy McNeal, Pres.
Beta Xi No. 4334
Ilwaco, Washington

CHILI PIZZERIA

1/2 lb. ground beef
1 med. onion, chopped
1 tbsp. oil
1 can kidney beans
2 c. tomatoes
1 tsp. salt
1/2 tsp. oregano
1/4 tsp. thyme
1 1/2 tsp. chili powder
1 can tomato paste
1 c. shell macaroni

Saute beef and onion in oil until browned. Add remaining ingredients; mix well. Cover; simmer, stirring occasionally, until macaroni is done.

Mrs. Lindy Lybarger
Theta No. 598
North Manchester, Indiana

MEXICAN LASAGNE

1 1/2 lb. ground beef
1 sm. onion, chopped

1 pkg. taco seasoning mix
2 pkg. frozen spinach, thawed and
   well drained
1/2 c. taco sauce
10 corn tortillas
3 c. shredded Monterey Jack cheese
1 c. sour cream

Brown ground beef and onion; add taco seasoning mix, 1 cup water and 1 package spinach. Pour 1/4 cup taco sauce into 3-quart casserole. Overlap 5 tortillas in bottom of casserole. Spoon half the beef mixture over tortillas; top with 1/2 of the cheese. Cover with remaining tortillas; spread with remaining taco sauce. Spread remaining beef mixture over top. Spread with sour cream. Place remaining spinach over sour cream and top with remaining cheese. Bake, covered, at 375 degrees for 30 minutes; uncover. Bake for 20 minutes longer.

Helen Linn, Ed. Dir.
Gamma Kappa No. 3265
Denver, Colorado

GLORIFIED MACARONI

2 tbsp. bacon drippings
2 lg. onions, chopped
2 med. green peppers, chopped
1/4 lb. mushrooms, thinly sliced
3/4 lb. ground beef round
1/4 lb. bulk sausage
1 tbsp. chili powder
3/4 tsp. salt
1/8 tsp. pepper
1   1-lb. can whole tomatoes
1/2 lb. shell or elbow macaroni,
   cooked and drained

Heat bacon drippings in a large kettle or Dutch oven; add onions and green peppers. Stir-fry until tender. Add mushrooms; stir-fry for 5 minutes. Add beef and sausage; stir-fry for about 5 minutes or until no longer pink, breaking up lumps with spoon. Stir in chili powder, salt and pepper. Add tomatoes; simmer, uncovered, for about 30 minutes or until slightly thickened. Stir in macaroni; heat just until bubbly.

Bernita Faye Scott
Lambda No. 1029
Indianapolis, Indiana

SOUPER SKILLET PASTA

1 lb. hamburger
1 env. dry onion-mushroom soup mix
1 1/2 tsp. oregano
2 16-oz. cans whole tomatoes
3 c. shell macaroni
1/3 c. grated Parmesan cheese
Shredded mozzarella cheese

Brown hamburger in large skillet; drain. Add soup mix, oregano, undrained tomatoes and 2 cups water. Bring to a boil; stir in macaroni. Simmer, covered, for 20 minutes or until macaroni is tender, stirring occasionally. Stir in Parmesan cheese. Top with mozzarella cheese. Yield: 6 servings.

Mrs. Dina James
Alpha Tau Chap.
LaPorte, Indiana

HAMBURGER STEAK WITH MUSHROOMS

1/2 lb. fresh mushrooms, chopped
3/4 c. margarine
1/2 env. dry onion soup mix
4 hamburger steaks

Saute mushrooms in margarine in skillet. Add onion soup mix and hamburger steaks; cook until steaks are done on both sides, stirring mushroom mixture occasionally.

Janice Kemp, Awards and W. and M. Chm.
Theta Phi No. 1620
Denton, Texas

PATIO SPANISH DELIGHT

2 lb. ground beef
2 cloves of garlic, chopped
1 green pepper, chopped
2 med. onions, chopped
Cooking oil
3 tbsp. chili powder
2 cans tomato sauce
1 can whole kernel corn
1 1-lb. package wide noodles, cooked
Chopped pitted black olives to
*   taste (opt.)*
Chopped mushrooms to taste (opt.)
Salt to taste
1/2 lb. Cheddar cheese, grated

Brown beef; pour off excess fat. Set aside. Cook garlic, green pepper and onions in small amount oil until tender; add beef, chili powder, tomato sauce, corn, noodles, olives, mushrooms, salt and 2/3 of the cheese. Turn into casserole; top with remaining cheese. Bake at 350 degrees for 30 minutes.

Marybeth Savage, W. and M. Co-Chm.
Omicron No. 116
Santa Barbara, California

FOURTH OF JULY GIANT STUFFED BURGER

1 egg, beaten
1 1/4 c. herb-seasoned stuffing mix,
*   crushed*
1 4-oz. can chopped mushrooms,
*   drained*
1/3 c. beef broth
1/4 c. sliced green onions with tops
1/4 c. snipped parsley
2 tbsp. melted margarine
1 tsp. lemon juice
2 lb. ground beef
1 tsp. salt

Combine egg, stuffing mix, mushrooms, beef broth, green onions, parsley, margarine and lemon juice; set aside. Combine beef and salt; divide mixture in half. Pat each half to an 8-inch circle on sheets of waxed paper. Spoon stuffing mixture over 1 circle to within 1 inch of edge. Top with second circle of beef; peel off top sheet of paper. Seal edges together. Invert beef patty onto well-greased wire grill basket; peel off remaining paper. Grill over medium coals for 10 to 12 minutes. Turn and grill for 10 to 12 minutes longer or to desired doneness. Cut patty into wedges; serve with warmed catsup, if desired. Yield: 8 servings.

Nancy Bowman, Pres.
Eta Beta No. 2676
Liberal, Kansas

HALLOWEEN CHEESY BURGER PIE

2 lb. ground beef
2 tsp. salt

3/4 tsp. oregano
1/4 tsp. pepper
3/4 c. dry bread crumbs
1 8-oz. can tomato sauce
1 garlic clove, minced
2 tbsp. instant minced onion
1 c. minced celery
1 med. green pepper, minced
1 c. chili sauce
2 unbaked pie shells
2 eggs, beaten
1/3 c. milk
3/4 tsp. garlic salt
3/4 tsp. dry mustard
1 tsp. Worcestershire sauce
3/4 lb. Cheddar cheese, shredded

Brown beef, drain off excess fat. Add next 10 ingredients; mix well. Pour into pie shells. Combine remaining ingredients; spread topping over fillings. Bake at 400 degrees for 40 minutes.

Katherine Alexander, Treas.
Theta Kappa No. 4650
Kennewick, Washington

PIZZA MEAT PIE

1 can crescent dinner rolls
1 lb. ground beef
1 sm. onion, chopped
1 8-oz. can mushroom pieces
2 tsp. Italian seasonings
1 6-oz. can tomato paste
Salt to taste
1 8-oz. package shredded mozzarella
   cheese
1 8-oz. can tomato sauce

Spread crescent roll triangles in 10-inch pie plate to make crust. Brown ground beef and onion; drain off excess fat. Mix ground beef, mushrooms, 1 teaspoon Italian seasonings and tomato paste together; season with salt. Spoon mixture into crust; cover with mozzarella cheese. Bake at 350 degrees for 15 minutes. Heat tomato sauce and remaining 1 teaspoon Italian seasonings just before serving; spoon over top of each pie wedge.

Martha C. Sherlock, V.P.
Zeta Omicron No. 3998
Seminole, Florida

TRUE CORNISH PASTIES

1/4 lb. peeled potatoes, grated
1/2 lb. lean ground beef
1 med. onion, finely chopped
1 tsp. salt
1/2 tsp. pepper
3/4 lb. shortcrust pastry dough
Milk

Combine potatoes, 3 tablespoons water, beef, onion, salt and pepper in large bowl; mix well. Roll out pastry thin; cut into 5-inch rounds, using saucer as guide. Place 1 tablespoon beef mixture on each round; dampen edges with cold water. Fold pastry over to form a ridge. Press edges together; flute with fingers. Stand pasties upright on greased cooking sheet; snip slit in top for steam vents. Brush with milk. Bake at 375 degrees for 45 minutes to 1 hour.

Peggy Gifford
Gamma Beta Chap.
Burlington, Washington

STAR-STUDDED CASSEROLE

1 lb. ground beef
1 1-lb. can sliced carrots
1 env. French's brown gravy mix
1/4 c. catsup
1 tbsp. brown sugar
1 tbsp. French's prepared yellow
   mustard
2 or 3 slices bread, lightly buttered

Brown ground beef in large skillet, stirring to crumble; drain off excess fat. Drain liquid from carrots into measuring cup; add enough water to make 1 cup liquid. Stir into ground beef; add gravy mix, carrots, catsup, brown sugar and mustard. Bring to a boil over medium heat, stirring occasionally. Spoon into 1 1/2-quart shallow casserole. Trim crusts from bread. Cut stars, using a small star-shaped cookie cutter; arrange over casserole. Bake at 400 degrees for 15 to 20 minutes. Yield: 4-6 servings.

Photograph for this recipe on page 2.

SAVORY HERO SANDWICH

1 lb. ground beef
1 6-oz. can tomato paste
2 tbsp. chopped onion
1 tsp. salt
Dash of pepper
1 loaf Vienna bread, cut in half
lengthwise
American cheese slices
Tomato slices
Green pepper rings

Combine beef, tomato paste, onion and seasonings; mix until well blended. Spread half the beef mixture on each half of bread. Place on ungreased cookie sheet. Bake at 450 degrees for 20 minutes. Top with layers of cheese slices, tomato slices and green pepper rings. Bake until cheese melts. Yield: 8 servings.

Barbara Reeves, Pres.
Gamma Omicron No. 2052
East Palestine, Ohio

SLOPPY JOES

1 to 2 lb. hamburger, seasoned
1 sm. can red kidney beans
1 sm. can pork and beans
1 sm. can tomato sauce

Brown hamburgers; add remaining ingredients. Simmer until thickened. Serve over hamburger buns.

Shirley Sailsbey
Alpha Iota No. 4360
Fort Morgan, Colorado

BARBECUED PORK FOR SANDWICHES

1 3-lb. pork Boston butt, cooked
2 c. (or more) broth
1/4 tsp. nutmeg
1/4 tsp. allspice
1/2 tsp. ground cloves
1 tsp. cinnamon
1/4 tsp. chili powder
1/4 bottle Worcestershire sauce
1/2 bottle chili sauce

Shred pork. Combine remaining ingredients in large saucepan; bring to a rapid boil. Add pork; reduce heat. Simmer for 2 hours, stirring frequently. May add a small amount of brown sugar, if desired.

Edith Collins, Treas.
Alpha Mu No. 346
Muncie, Indiana

FOURTH OF JULY BARBECUED PORK CHOPS

1 c. cola drink
3 cloves of garlic, minced
1/2 c. (scant) soy sauce
4 to 6 loin pork chops 1 in. thick

Combine cola drink, garlic and soy sauce; pour over chops. Marinate chops in refrigerator for about 6 hours. Grill chops over charcoal fire to desired doneness, brushing with marinade each time chops are turned.

Sharon Bradley
MAL
Elkhart, Indiana

NEW YEAR'S PORK CHOP CASSEROLE

Potatoes
6 pork chops
1/8 tsp. (or more) oregano
Salt and pepper to taste
1 sm. onion, chopped
1 can stewed tomatoes

Slice enough potatoes to cover bottom of greased large baking dish generously. Place pork chops on potatoes; sprinkle with oregano, salt and pepper. Top with onion slices and stewed tomatoes. Cover. Bake in 350-degree oven for 1 hour. Remove cover. Bake for 30 minutes longer.
This can be cooking while watching New Year's parades and bowl games. Serve with traditional black-eyed peas.

Shirley Brice, Soc. Chm.
Alpha Xi No. 1610
Virginia Beach, Virginia

PORKFEST PLATTER

3 pork blade steaks 3/4 in. thick
1 1/2 tsp. salt

1/8 tsp. pepper
1 med. head cabbage
1 lg. Idaho-Oregon Sweet Spanish
    onion
1/2 c. vinegar
2 tbsp. brown sugar
2 tsp. caraway seed
1 to 1 1/2 lb. smoked Polish sausage,
    cooked
4 Washington Golden Delicious apples,
    cored
6   1/2-in. thick slices hot cooked
    smoked pork shoulder roll

Cut each pork steak in half diagonally along
bone. Brown lightly in large Dutch oven;
pour off drippings. Sprinkle 1 teaspoon salt
and pepper over steaks; add 2 tablespoons
water. Quarter cabbage lengthwise; cut each
portion in thin slices. Slice onion crosswise
into rings. Place cabbage and onion on top
of steaks. Cover tightly; cook slowly for 15
minutes. Remove steaks. Combine vinegar,
brown sugar, caraway seed and 1/2 teaspoon
salt; pour over cabbage mixture, tossing
lightly. Cook for 5 minutes. Reserve 1/3 of
the cabbage mixture. Place steaks on top of
remaining cabbage in Dutch oven; cover with
reserved cabbage. Place sausage on top of
cabbage; cook slowly, covered, for 20 minutes. Cut each apple crosswise in 1/2-inch
rings. Place apple rings on top of sausage;
cook, covered, for 6 to 8 minutes or until
apples are just tender. Remove apple rings,
sausage and pork steaks to warm platter. Stir
cabbage; remove to platter, using slotted
spoon. Cook down liquid in Dutch oven to
1/2 cup. Place hot smoked pork shoulder
slices on platter; pour liquid over pork.
Yield: 6 servings.

Photograph for this recipe on page 68.

CRANBERRY-BURGUNDY
GLAZED HAM

1   10 to 14-lb. bone-in fully cooked
    ham
Whole cloves
1   1-lb. can whole cranberry sauce
1 c. (packed) brown sugar
1/2 c. Burgundy
2 tsp. prepared mustard

Place ham, fat side up, in shallow roasting
pan. Score fat in diamond pattern; stud with
whole cloves. Insert meat thermometer; do
not let tip touch bone. Bake in 325-degree
oven for 2 hours and 30 minutes to 3 hours
or until meat thermometer registers 130 degrees. Combine remaining ingredients in
saucepan; simmer, uncovered, for 5 minutes.
Spoon half the cranberry glaze over ham
during last 30 minutes baking time. Serve
remaining sauce with ham.

Lucy Davis
Jr. Past Pres., Virginia State Council
Beta Tau No. 3953
Woodbridge, Virginia

LIMERICK HAM DINNER

1   3-lb. smoked boneless ham
    shoulder butt
1 tsp. Tabasco sauce
6 whole cloves
1 clove of garlic, peeled
1 bay leaf
1 tsp. celery seed
1 lg. green cabbage
2   1-lb. cans whole white potatoes
1/2 c. minced parsley

Place ham in large kettle; add water to cover.
Stir in Tabasco sauce, cloves, garlic, bay leaf
and celery seed. Cover tightly; bring to a
boil. Reduce heat; simmer until tender,
allowing 35 minutes per pound. Remove to
platter; keep warm. Wash cabbage; cut into 6
wedges. Boil, covered, in ham cooking liquid
for about 8 to 10 minutes or until just tender. Heat potatoes. Drain; roll in parsley.
Arrange with ham and cabbage on serving
platter. Yield: 6 servings.

Erin Horseradish Sauce

1/4 c. prepared horseradish
1/4 tsp. Tabasco sauce
1/4 tsp. salt
1/2 c. heavy cream, whipped
1 tbsp. chopped chives (opt.)

Combine horseradish, Tabasco sauce and salt
in small bowl. Fold in whipped cream. Turn
into serving dish; sprinkle with chives. Serve
with ham. Yield: 1 1/3 cups.

Photograph for this recipe on page 72.

Place ham and yams in baking pan. Combine remaining ingredients, using beater; pour over ham and yams. Bake at 350 degrees for 30 minutes. May be baked in electric skillet, if desired.

Sue Lain, Historian
Alpha Lambda Chap.
Columbus, Indiana

CREAMY HAM CASSEROLE

1 med. head cauliflower
2 c. cubed cooked ham
1 3-oz. can sliced mushrooms,
*   drained*
1/4 c. butter or margarine
1/3 c. all-purpose flour
1 c. milk
1 c. cubed sharp process
*   American cheese*
1/2 c. sour cream
1 c. soft bread crumbs
1 tbsp. melted butter or margarine

Break cauliflower into buds; cook, covered, in boiling salted water for 10 to 12 minutes or until tender. Drain. Combine ham and mushrooms. Melt butter in medium saucepan; stir in flour. Add milk; cook, stirring, until thickened. Add cheese and sour cream to sauce; stir until cheese melts. Combine with cauliflower and ham. Turn into 2-quart casserole. Combine crumbs and melted butter; sprinkle over top. Bake, uncovered, at 350 degrees for 40 minutes or until heated through. Yield: 6 servings.

Elaine Butterfield
Gamma Phi No. 2561
Auburndale, Florida

APRICOT-PEANUT HAM SLICE

1   3 to 3 1/2-lb. fully cooked
*   smoked ham slice 1 1/2 inch thick*
Whole cloves
1/2 c. (firmly packed) brown sugar
1 tbsp. vinegar
1 tsp. prepared mustard
1/2 c. apricot preserves
1/3 c. flaked or shredded coconut
1/4 c. chopped peanuts
2 tbsp. finely chopped candied ginger

Remove rind from ham slice; score fat. Stud with cloves. Place ham on a rack in shallow baking pan. Combine brown sugar, vinegar and mustard. Spread over top of ham. Bake in preheated 325-degree oven for 1 hour and 30 minutes, basting occasionally. Combine preserves, coconut, peanuts and ginger. Spread over ham slice. Bake for 15 minutes longer.

Photograph for this recipe above.

SOUTHERN-GLAZED HAM

1 ham steak
1 1-lb. 13-oz. can whole yams,
*   drained*
1 8-oz. can tomato sauce
3/4 jar fruit preserves
2 tsp. prepared mustard
2 tsp. vinegar
1/2 tsp. ground cloves

HAM LOAF WITH SOUR CREAM SAUCE

1 3/4 lb. ground ham
3/4 lb. ground lean pork
1 c. (about) bread crumbs
2 eggs, beaten
1 c. milk

2 tsp. chopped celery
1/2 tsp. onion
1 tbsp. catsup
1/4 tsp. paprika
1 c. (packed) brown sugar
1/4 to 1/2 c. vinegar
2 tsp. mustard
1/2 c. sour cream
1/4 c. horseradish
1/2 c. mayonnaise
1 c. unsweetened applesauce

Combine ham, pork, crumbs, eggs, milk, celery, onion, catsup and paprika; mix well. Shape into loaf; place on shallow baking pan. Combine brown sugar, 1/2 cup water, vinegar and mustard in saucepan; bring to a boil. Boil for 5 minutes; pour over loaf. Bake at 325 to 350 degrees for 1 hour and 30 minutes, basting every 20 minutes. Combine remaining ingredients for sauce; serve with loaf.

Martha Heflin, Photographer
Beta Eta No. 3696
Fairfield, Illinois

EASTER PINEAPPLE-HAM LOAF

1 lb. ground smoked ham
1 lb. lean ground fresh pork
2 eggs, beaten
2 tbsp. catsup
3/4 c. soft bread crumbs
3/4 c. milk
8 pineapple slices
1 c. (packed) brown sugar
1/4 c. pineapple syrup
2 tbsp. vinegar
1 tsp. prepared mustard

Combine first 6 ingredients; mix well. Shape into 9 patties. Stand on end in loaf pan with slices of pineapple between, beginning and ending with patties. Heat remaining ingredients for glaze, stirring until sugar is dissolved. Bake loaf in 325-degree oven for 30 minutes; baste with glaze. Bake for 1 hour longer, basting with glaze every 20 minutes.

Mary A. Recker, Pres.
Beta Kappa No. 4484
Arlington, Iowa

HAM SOUFFLE

8 slices bread with crusts removed
2 c. diced ham
1 c. diced celery
1 c. diced onion
1/2 c. mayonnaise
3 eggs
3 c. milk
1 can cream of mushroom soup
1/2 to 1 c. shredded Cheddar cheese
Paprika

Cut bread slices into cubes; place half the cubes in 9 x 13-inch pan. Combine next 4 ingredients; spread over bread cubes. Beat eggs and milk together. Place remaining bread cubes over ham mixture; pour egg mixture over top. Refrigerate for 3 to 4 hours or overnight. Combine soup and cheese; pour over bread cubes, covering well. Sprinkle with paprika. Bake at 350 degrees for 1 hour or until heated through and bubbly.

Trish Morgan
Omicron No. 374
Tacoma, Washington

EASTER PORKIES

1 lb. ground cured ham
1 1/2 lb. ground pork
1 c. quick-cooking oats
2 eggs, beaten
1 c. milk
Salt and pepper to taste
1 1/2 c. (packed) brown sugar
1/2 c. vinegar
1 tbsp. mustard

Grind ham and pork together; add next 4 ingredients. Mix well. Shape into 12 individual meat loaves. Place in baking pan. Combine remaining ingredients and 1/2 cup water; heat until sugar is dissolved. Bake loaves at 350 degrees for 1 hour and 30 minutes, basting frequently with brown sugar mixture.

Jean Connelly, Sec.
Alpha Kappa No. 4404
Fort Wayne, Indiana

GLAZED HAM BALLS IN PINEAPPLE SLICES

1/2 lb. ground ham
3/4 lb. ground pork
1/2 c. oats
1 egg, beaten
1/2 tsp. salt
3 tbsp. brown sugar
1 tbsp. flour
1/3 tsp. dry mustard
1/2 c. fruit juice
1 tbsp. vinegar
4 whole cloves
2 1/2 tbsp. dark corn syrup
1 can (or more) sliced pineapple

Combine ham, pork, oats, egg and salt; mix well. Chill. Shape into small balls; place in shallow pan. Bake at 300 degrees for 1 hour. Drain off drippings. Combine brown sugar, flour and mustard in saucepan. Add fruit juice, vinegar, cloves and corn syrup. Cook, stirring, until slightly thickened; pour over ham balls. Bake for 15 minutes longer. Place pineapple slices on platter; place ham ball in each ring. Spoon sauce over top.

Sharon R. Oaks, Pres.
Delta Xi No. 3984
Crawfordsville, Indiana

DANISH PORK AND PEAS

3 lb. finely ground pork
1/2 lb. ground beef
1 c. milk
1 tsp. salt
1/2 tsp. pepper
1 can early June peas
Butter

Combine first 5 ingredients; mix well. Place in tube pan. Steam for 3 to 4 hours. Turn out onto platter. Season peas with butter and thicken as desired. Spoon hot peas into pork ring.

Irene Alexander
Alpha Beta No. 165
Lincoln, Nebraska

KOREAN KABOBS

1 1-lb. pork tenderloin
1/2 c. unsweetened pineapple juice
1/4 c. soy sauce
1/4 c. chopped onion
1 tbsp. brown sugar
4 tsp. sesame seed
1 clove of garlic, minced
1/8 tsp. pepper
Green pepper chunks
Pineapple slices, cut in thirds
1 tsp. cornstarch

Cut tenderloin into 1/3-inch slices. Combine next 7 ingredients for marinade. Add pork slices; marinate, covered, for 2 hours or up to 2 days in refrigerator. Thread pork on 4 skewers alternately with green pepper chunks and pineapple pieces. Dissolve cornstarch in 2 tablespoons water; thicken marinade with cornstarch mixture. Grill kabobs over charcoal fire, turning and brushing with thickened marinade. Yield: 4 servings.

Gale Craske
Alpha Lambda No. 1482
Durham, North Carolina

SAUSAGE CASSEROLE

1 20-oz. can pineapple chunks
1 18-oz. can sweet potatoes, sliced
   1 in. thick
1 12-oz. package smoked link
   sausage, slashed at 1 in.
   intervals
3 tbsp. brown sugar
2 tbsp. cornstarch
1/4 tsp. salt
1 tbsp. butter or margarine

Drain pineapple, reserving juice. Add enough water to reserved juice to measure 1 1/4 cups liquid. Arrange pineapple chunks, sweet potatoes and sausage in 10 x 6 x 1 3/4-inch baking dish. Combine brown sugar, cornstarch and salt in small saucepan; blend in pineapple juice mixture gradually. Cook and stir until thickened and bubbly; cook for 1 minute longer. Remove from heat; stir in butter. Pour over sausage mixture in baking dish; cover. Bake at 350 degrees for 35 to 40 minutes or until heated through. Yield: 4-6 servings.

Ruthe Hollodick, Fin. Chm.
Alpha Nu No. 1596
Wilmington, North Carolina

BARBECUED SPARERIBS

4 lb. spareribs
1 onion, quartered
2 tsp. salt
1/4 tsp. pepper
1/2 c. cider vinegar
1/2 c. (packed) light brown sugar
1/2 c. catsup
1/4 c. chili sauce
1/4 c. Worcestershire sauce
2 tbsp. chopped onion
1 tbsp. lemon juice
1/2 tsp. dry mustard
1 clove of garlic, crushed
Dash of cayenne pepper

Place spareribs, quartered onion, salt, pepper and 3 quarts water in large kettle. Bring to a boil. Reduce heat; simmer, covered, for 1 hour and 30 minutes or until very tender. Drain. Combine remaining ingredients in medium saucepan; simmer, uncovered, for 1 hour, stirring occasionally. Arrange spareribs on rack in broiler pan. Brush with sauce. Broil 5 inches from source of heat for 10 minutes on each side, basting frequently with sauce. Yield: 6 servings.

Marlene Bellendir
Kappa Chi No. 4457
Brush, Colorado

FOURTH OF JULY CHUCK WAGON RIBS

6 lb. spareribs
2 tsp. salt
3/4 c. molasses
3/4 c. catsup
1/4 c. vinegar
1 med. onion, minced
1 clove of garlic, crushed
1 tbsp. prepared mustard
1 tbsp. Worcestershire sauce
1/2 tsp. cayenne pepper
1 lemon, thinly sliced

Cut spareribs into serving pieces; place in foil-lined shallow pan. Sprinkle with salt. Bake at 350 degrees for 1 hour. Blend molasses, catsup and vinegar together; stir in remaining ingredients except lemon slices. Bring to a boil; simmer for 15 minutes, stirring occasionally. Place spareribs on outdoor grill. Brush with sauce. Cook for 30 minutes, turning frequently and brushing with sauce. Top with lemon slices just before spareribs are done. Yield: 6 servings.

Barbara B. Threatt, Publ. Dir.
Alpha Beta No. 1408
Roanoke, Virginia

ROAST VENISON WITH SOUR CREAM GRAVY

3 c. dry red wine
1/2 c. apple cider
3 bay leaves
4 peppercorns
1 6-lb. venison roast
Salt
1/4 c. butter
1 1/2 tbsp. all-purpose flour
1 c. sour cream

Combine 2 1/2 cups wine and apple cider in shallow dish; add bay leaves and peppercorns. Place venison in marinade; cover and refrigerate overnight, turning occasionally. Place venison on rack in roasting pan, fat side up; sprinkle with salt. Insert meat thermometer in center of thickest part of venison not touching bone or resting in fat. Strain and reserve 1 cup marinade. Melt butter in 1-quart saucepan; add reserved marinade. Bake venison in preheated 325-degree oven for about 25 minutes per pound for medium rare or to desired degree of doneness, basting occasionally with marinade mixture. Remove roast to warmed platter. Combine flour and 1/2 teaspoon salt in 1 1/2-quart saucepan. Add 3/4 cup pan drippings gradually, stirring until smooth. Add remaining 1/2 cup wine. Cook over medium heat until thickened, stirring constantly. Reduce heat to low; stir in sour cream. Heat to serving temperature. Yield: 6-8 servings.

Photograph for this recipe on page 135.

Poultry and Seafood

There are 2 foods that everyone considers to be the most festive . . . poultry
and seafood. In fact, for the tastiest holiday meals, there is no better choice.
Each has a distinctively delicate and delectable flavor that blends with all
manner of sauces, vegetables, side dishes and fruits. Poultry is as American as
the flag and as traditional as the Thanksgiving turkey. Also, American waters
abound with a variety of fish and seafood to please almost every palate.
These two foods have been customary holiday entrees for generations, with
turkey most often associated with that most original American holiday feast,
Thanksgiving.

Much has been made in the history books of the turkey, corn, cranberries,
beans and squash served at the first Thanksgiving dinner (and rightly so!);
but, those books usually fail to mention that oysters, clams and lobsters
were an integral part of that meal, as well as the Pilgrim's use of ducks, geese,
and game birds. Make this the year that your Thanksgiving celebration more
truly reflects the spirit of the original. If you are not careful, you may start a
family tradition that will be followed for generations!

First of all, invite as many people as you can think of — family, friends, neighbors, or anyone you know who might otherwise have to spend Thanksgiving alone. Plan your menu so that there will be enough food for everyone, with plenty left over to snack on between games on the lawn and television programs. If the celebration gets large enough, consider using the fellowship hall of a convenient church. Or, if you live in a region where the weather permits, have your Thanksgiving feast outdoors. Even though they lived on the chilly New England coast, that's what the Pilgrims and Indians did! Your holiday menu should include turkey or any of the other birds of similar delectableness — such as duck, Cornish hen, quail or dove. Oysters can be used in the stuffing, while crab, lobster, shrimp and other seafood favorites can be used in souffles, pies, salads or as appetizers. Of course, this same menu can be scaled down for smaller family use, as well.

Thanksgiving and all of its favorite traditions generate a host of decorating ideas. If the guest list is to be large, send out invitations announcing your plans for an Authentic Thanksgiving. Have the decorations reflect our New England Puritan heritage, as well as an Indian motif. Have centerpieces of Pilgrim hats, Indian corn, turkey feathers, acorns, autumn leaves and cornucopias of the many fall fruits and vegetables.

Poultry and seafood are just as much at home in other settings as they are at a sumptuous Thanksgiving meal. Seafood, of course, tastes its very best when cooked over a fire and eaten right on the beach. But, in any city or in front of a cozy fire in the winter, almost nothing is as refreshing as chilled shrimp or raw oysters eaten with crackers and a piquant seafood sauce. Poultry is an anytime-anywhere palate pleaser, as well. Cornish hens are excellent company fare, while Sunday doesn't seem complete in many homes if fried or baked chicken is not the featured entree for the midday meal. Families lucky enough to have a hunter or sports fisherman in their midst well know what delectable meals can be built around pheasant, quail, and waterfowl, as well as trout, bass and perch.

If ESA members had to give still another reason why homemakers should spotlight poultry and seafood regularly on their everyday is a holiday menus, it would be because both are packed with protein and are very low in calories. Moreover, each is an asset to any budget. Make more use of poultry and seafood in your meal planning, and before you know it, you'll be making the best use of your creative cooking skills, as well.

CHICKEN AND YELLOW RICE

1 7-oz. package yellow rice mix
1 green pepper, diced
1 tomato, diced
2 tsp. salt
1 bay leaf
1/4 c. butter
6 chicken breasts
1 onion, chopped
2 cloves of garlic, finely diced
1 can chicken broth
1 can Ro-Tel tomatoes

Combine rice, green pepper, tomato, salt and bay leaf in 1 1/2-quart oblong baking dish; set aside. Melt butter in skillet; brown chicken breasts, turning once. Place chicken over rice mixture. Stir onion and garlic into pan drippings; saute until soft. Add chicken broth, Ro-Tel tomatoes and 1 cup water; bring to a boil. Pour over chicken and rice; cover with foil. Bake at 350 degrees for 1 hour. Yield: 6 servings.

Bette Hendrickson, Philanthropic Chm.
Sigma Chi No. 4689
New Orleans, Louisiana

CHICKEN KIEV

4 lg. chicken breasts, boned
Salt to taste
1 tbsp. chopped green onion
1 tbsp. snipped parsley
1 1/4-lb. stick butter, chilled
All-purpose flour
1 egg, beaten
1/2 c. fine dry bread crumbs

Remove skin and bones from chicken; cut in half lengthwise. Place chicken pieces, boned side up, between 2 pieces of clear plastic wrap. Pound, working out from center, to form cutlets not quite 1/4 inch thick. Peel off wrap; sprinkle with salt, onion and parsley. Cut stick of chilled butter into 8 sticks; place stick at end of each cutlet. Roll as for jelly roll, tucking in sides. Press end to seal well. Coat each roll with flour; dip in mixture of 1 tablespoon water and beaten egg. Roll in crumbs. Chill for at least 1 hour. Fry chicken in deep fat at 375 degrees for about 5 minutes or until golden brown.

Gertrude Kamphaus, Pres.
Gamma Tau No. 811
Canute, Oklahoma

EASTER CHICKEN AND ASPARAGUS CASSEROLE

4 lg. chicken breasts
1 stalk celery, chopped
1 can cream of mushroom soup
1 can asparagus, drained
Grated cheese
Bread crumbs
2 tbsp. melted butter

Cook chicken in water with celery until tender. Drain and remove skin and bones; shred chicken. Arrange alternate layers of chicken, soup and asparagus in 1-quart baking dish. Bake at 350 degrees until bubbly. Sprinkle grated cheese and bread crumbs over top. Drizzle with melted butter. Return to oven to brown. Yield: 6 servings.

Gloria Gardner, Pres.
Alpha Iota No. 1098
Jackson, Tennessee

CHICKEN CONTINENTAL

1 pkg. dried beef
6 or 8 chicken breasts or thighs, boned
1/4 lb. bacon
1 can cream of mushroom soup
1/2 c. white wine
1 4-oz. can mushroom buttons, well drained
1 c. sour cream

Arrange dried beef over bottom of greased baking pan. Wrap chicken in bacon; place over beef. Combine remaining ingredients; pour over chicken. Bake at 300 degrees for 1 hour and 30 minutes to 2 hours. May be cooked in Crock-Pot on Low for 8 hours, if desired.

Lucille Eastin
Epsilon Epsilon No. 1896
Englewood, Colorado

CHICKEN AND SPROUTS ORIENTAL

6 whole chicken breasts with breast
bones cracked
Soy sauce
Salt
2/3 c. chopped onion
1 lb. carrots, peeled and cut in
strips
2 10-oz. packages frozen California
Brussels sprouts
1 1/2 c. cold chicken broth or bouillon
4 tsp. cornstarch
1/8 tsp. pepper
2 tbsp. dry Sherry
1 9 1/2-oz. can water chestnuts,
drained and sliced

Remove skin and excess fat from chicken pieces and discard. Brush chicken breasts with soy sauce; sprinkle with 1/2 teaspoon salt. Place chicken in large shallow roasting pan. Bake, uncovered, at 325 degrees for 30 minutes. Sprinkle onion around chicken; bake for 15 minutes longer. Cook carrots in small amount of water until crisp tender; drain. Cook Brussels sprouts according to package directions; drain. Blend chicken broth, cornstarch, pepper, Sherry, 2 tablespoons soy sauce and 1/4 teaspoon salt together in large saucepan. Bring to a boil, stirring constantly. Simmer for 3 minutes, stirring occasionally. Add water chestnuts, carrots and Brussels sprouts; toss gently until mixed. Spoon vegetables and sauce over chicken. Bake for 15 minutes or until heated through. Serve with rice, if desired. Yield: 6 servings.

Photograph for this recipe on page 92.

CHICKEN ROYALE

2 c. dressing mix
1/4 c. finely diced onion
1/3 c. finely diced celery
Melted butter
1/2 c. flour
1 tsp. salt
1/2 tsp. paprika
Dash of pepper
4 chicken breasts, boned

Combine dressing mix, onion, celery, 1/3 cup melted butter and 1/2 cup water. Combine flour, salt, paprika and pepper in paper bag; add chicken breasts. Shake until chicken is well coated. Fill cavity of each breast with stuffing; skewer with toothpicks to hold stuffing. Melt 1/2 cup butter; dip chicken in butter. Place in baking dish. Drizzle remaining butter over chicken. Bake at 325 degrees for 1 hour.

Sour Cream-Mushroom Sauce

1/2 lb. mushrooms, cut in half
1/4 c. minced onion
2 tbsp. butter
2 tbsp. flour
1/2 c. heavy cream
1/2 c. sour cream
1/2 tsp. salt
1/4 tsp. pepper

Saute mushrooms and onion in butter; remove from frying pan. Stir flour into butter. Add cream, sour cream, salt and pepper. Cook until sauce is smooth, stirring constantly. Add mushrooms and onion. Heat thoroughly. Serve over Chicken Royale.

Barbara Moneymaker, Parliamentarian
Beta Theta No. 4270
Stuarts Draft, Virginia

CHICKEN AND SHRIMP ROSE´

6 tbsp. flour
1 1/2 tsp. salt
1/4 tsp. pepper
1/4 tsp. ground ginger
6 boned chicken breasts
2 tbsp. salad oil
4 tbsp. butter or margarine
4 green onions with tops, sliced
1 c. chicken bouillon
1 1/4 c. Rosé wine
1 c. sliced fresh mushrooms
1 3 1/2-oz. can pitted black olives
12 (or more) shrimp

Combine 3 tablespoons flour, salt, pepper and ginger; dredge chicken with flour mixture. Heat oil and 2 tablespoons butter in skillet; brown chicken. Remove from skillet; set aside. Cook and stir onions in skillet until wilted; set aside. Drain off fat. Stir in bouillon and wine, scraping up brown particles. Shake 3 tablespoons flour and 1/2 cup water in covered jar until smooth; stir into wine mixture gradually. Reduce heat; cook, stirring, for about 5 minutes or until sauce is smooth and thick. Return onions to sauce. Place chicken in baking dish; pour sauce over top. Cover with foil. Bake at 350 degrees for 30 to 40 minutes, turning chicken once. Saute mushrooms in remaining 2 tablespoons butter. Arrange chicken on serving dish. Stir olives and shrimp into sauce; cook until shrimp turns pink. Pour over chicken. Cover with mushrooms. Garnish with parsley. Yield: 6 servings.

Helen Forbis, Pres.
Mu No. 119
Oakland, California

CHICKEN BREASTS BAKED IN WINE

1 c. red wine
1/4 c. soy sauce
1/4 c. salad oil
1 clove of garlic, peeled and sliced
1 tsp. powdered ginger
1 tbsp. brown sugar
3 to 4 c. cooked wild rice
3 chicken breasts, split

Combine all ingredients except rice and chicken; mix well. Place chicken in large casserole. Pour wine mixture over chicken; cover. Bake in preheated 375-degree oven for 1 hour and 30 minutes or until chicken is tender. Uncover last 15 minutes of baking if pan juices have not cooked down. Serve at once, surrounded by mounds of hot cooked wild rice. Yield: 6 servings.

Jane Bowyer, Philanthropic Chm.
Alpha Tau No. 2046
Richmond, Virginia

PARTY CHICKEN

8 slices bacon
4 lg. chicken breasts, boned
1 pkg. chipped beef
1 can cream of mushroom soup
1 c. sour cream

Wrap 2 slices bacon around each chicken breast. Cover bottom of greased baking dish with chipped beef. Arrange chicken over beef. Mix soup and sour cream together; pour over chicken. Bake at 275 degrees for 3 hours.

Pat Meriedth, State Coun. Jr. Past Pres.
Epsilon Delta No. 2618
Champaign, Illinois

ELEGANT CHICKEN

1 pkg. Uncle Ben's quick-cooking
*   wild rice*
1 can mushroom soup
1 can mushrooms
1 can water chestnuts, sliced
6 chicken breast halves
Salt and pepper to taste
Slivered almonds

Combine rice, soup, 1 1/4 cups water, mushrooms and water chestnuts. Place in 9 x 13-inch pan. Top with chicken breasts; sprinkle with salt, pepper and almonds. Cover. Bake at 350 degrees for 1 hour and 20 minutes. Uncover; brown, if desired.

Edith Butler, V.P.
Epsilon Beta No. 2955
Bradenton, Florida

MAIN DISH CASSEROLE

1 can mushroom soup
2/3 c. milk
3 c. long grain rice
1   4-oz. can mushroom stems and pieces
1 env. dry onion soup mix
3 chicken breasts, split in half
Paprika

Combine soup and milk; reserve 1/2 cup mixture. Combine remaining soup mixture with rice, mushrooms and liquid and onion soup mix; pour into a 2-quart baking dish. Arrange chicken breasts over top. Pour reserved soup mixture over chicken breasts; sprinkle with paprika. Cover. Bake in 325-degree oven for 1 hour. Uncover; bake for 15 minutes longer. Yield: 4 servings.

Christine Wiseman, 1st V.P.
Alpha Chi No. 2055
Waynesboro, Virginia

VERA JEAN'S CHICKEN CASSEROLE

1 sm. box Uncle Ben's wild rice mix or
*   1 c. long grain rice*
1 can cream of celery soup
1 box frozen mixed vegetables, thawed
1 pkg. dry onion soup mix
Chicken breasts
Minced parsley

Place rice in 9 x 15-inch casserole; stir in celery soup and 1 soup can water. Sprinkle vegetables, then onion soup mix evenly over rice. Top with chicken. Sprinkle with parsley. Cover tightly with foil. Bake at 350 degrees for 2 hours.

Helen M. Curry, Sec.
Beta Mu No. 2126
Muncie, Indiana

CHICKEN CUTLETS IN WHITE WINE

1 lb. chicken cutlets
2 tbsp. butter
1/2 lb. fresh mushrooms, sliced
1 c. white wine
1/2 tsp. tarragon
1/2 tsp. salt
1 tbsp. flour

Saute chicken in hot butter in a large heavy skillet until brown on both sides. Saute mushrooms for 1 minute. Add 3/4 cup wine, tarragon and salt. Reduce heat; simmer, covered, for 15 minutes or until chicken is tender. Stir flour into remaining 1/4 cup white wine until well blended; stir in chicken mixture. Cook until thick and smooth. Yield: 4 servings.

Betty Burkholder, Rec. Sec.
Alpha Alpha No. 911
Victoria, Texas

CHICKEN ENCHILADAS

12 tortillas
1 can cream of mushroom soup
1 can cream of chicken soup
1 can green chili peppers
1 med. onion, chopped
1 2-lb. chicken, cooked and boned
1 lb. Cheddar cheese, grated

Tear tortillas in quarters; combine soups, peppers and onion. Arrange tortillas, soup mixture, chicken and cheese in alternate layers in casserole. Bake, uncovered, at 350 degrees for 45 minutes. Turn oven off; let casserole stand in oven for 30 minutes longer. This may be prepared ahead of time and refrigerated, if desired.

Ina Harrison, Pres.
Beta Pi No. 433
Miami, Oklahoma

CHICKEN CURRY

1 fryer, disjointed
Salt and pepper to taste
1 bouillon cube
2 tbsp. (heaping) tomato paste
1 1/2 tsp. (about) curry powder
1/4 tsp. sugar
1/3 c. sour cream
1 tsp. monosodium glutamate
Shredded coconut

Season chicken with salt and pepper; brown in hot fat. Place chicken in shallow baking pan. Stir 1/2 cup hot water into frying pan; add bouillon cube, tomato paste, curry powder, sugar, sour cream and monosodium glutamate. Mix well. Pour over chicken; sprinkle with shredded coconut. Cover with aluminum foil. Bake at 350 degrees for about 1 hour to 1 hour and 30 minutes.

Gerri Pearson, V.P.
Gamma Phi No. 2561
Auburndale, Florida

CHERRIES AND CHICKEN

1/3 c. flour
1 1/2 tsp. salt
1/2 tsp. paprika
1/4 tsp. garlic salt
3 lg. chicken breasts, halved
1/4 c. butter or margarine
1 1-lb. can pitted dark sweet
*   cherries, drained*
1 c. white wine

Combine flour and seasonings in paper or plastic bag; add 2 or 3 pieces of chicken at a time and shake. Melt butter in large skillet. Brown chicken slowly. Add cherries. Pour wine over all. Cover; simmer for about 35 minutes or until well done.

Bernadette T. Irwin, Pres.
Alpha Tau No. 4340
York, Pennsylvania

CHICKEN IN YELLOW BARBECUE SAUCE

1/4 c. vinegar
1/4 c. syrup
Dash of Tabasco sauce
1/8 c. catsup
1/4 c. oil
1/4 c. prepared mustard
1 tsp. salt
3 fryers, halved

Combine first 7 ingredients; mix until well blended. Place chicken, skin side up, on grill at highest point above coals. Cook for 1 hour and 30 minutes or until tender, turning frequently and brushing with sauce.

Beverly S. Pittman, Rec. Sec.
Beta Epsilon No. 3915
Lake City, Florida

ASPARAGUS-CHICKEN CASSEROLE

1 1-lb. can asparagus spears
1 c. cubed cooked chicken
1 c. cubed cooked ham
1 can Cheddar cheese soup
1/4 c. sour cream
2 tbsp. chopped chives
2 tbsp. grated Parmesan cheese

Drain asparagus spears; arrange in a shallow baking dish. Cover with chicken and ham. Mix soup with sour cream and chives; spoon over chicken and ham. Sprinkle with freshly grated Parmesan cheese. Bake at 350 degrees until bubbly. Yield: 4 servings.

Alice M. Tyner, Pres.
Epsilon No. 118
Los Angeles, California

BAKED CHICKEN AND DRESSING

1 7 or 8-oz. package herb-seasoned
*   stuffing mix*
2 c. chicken broth
1 can cream of mushroom soup
2 eggs, well beaten
2 1/2 c. diced cooked chicken
1/2 c. milk
2 tbsp. chopped pimento (opt.)

Toss stuffing mix with broth, 1/2 of the soup and eggs; turn into 11 x 7 x 1 1/2-inch pan or square baking dish. Top with chicken. Combine remaining soup with milk and pimento; pour over chicken. Cover with foil. Bake at 350 degrees for 45 minutes. Yield: 6-8 servings.

Patricia Reed
Alpha Iota No. 3365
Stuarts Draft, Virginia

CHICKEN AND HAM IMPERIAL

1/2 c. butter
1/2 c. flour
1 qt. milk
1 lb. fresh mushrooms, sliced
*   lengthwise*
1 1/2 c. diced chicken
1 1/2 c. diced ham
1/2 c. Sherry
1 1/2 c. grated processed sharp cheese
2 tsp. minced onion
2 tsp. salt
1/2 tsp. pepper
Slivered almonds

Melt butter in saucepan. Add flour; stir to make a smooth paste. Stir in milk; cook until thick and smooth. Saute mushrooms. Stir chicken, ham and mushrooms into sauce; add Sherry, cheese, onion and seasonings. Mix well. Place in chafing dish; sprinkle almonds over top. Serve in noodle nests or over rice.

Pat Rhinehart
Gamma Gamma No. 4030
Mount Prospect, Illinois

CHICKEN AND PEAS CASSEROLE

2 pkg. frozen peas
3 to 4 c. cooked cubed chicken
2 cans cream of mushroom soup
1/2 c. mayonnaise
1 can mushrooms
1 tbsp. paprika
1 c. grated cheese
1 c. bread crumbs

Cook peas in salted water for 2 to 3 minutes; drain. Place in buttered 9 x 13-inch pan. Cover with chicken. Combine soup, mayonnaise and mushrooms; add paprika. Pour over chicken. Sprinkle with cheese; cover with crumbs. Bake at 350 degrees until bubbly and brown. Serve over Chinese noodles, if desired.

Doris Parker
Beta Eta No. 3696
Fairfield, Illinois

CHICKEN AND WILD RICE

1 1/2 to 2 c. diced cooked chicken
1 can mushrooms, drained
3 c. cooked wild rice
2 tbsp. flour
1 1/4 c. chicken broth
1/2 c. blanched slivered almonds

Place layer of chicken in greased pan. Sprinkle mushrooms over chicken; top with rice. Combine flour and chicken broth; mix until smooth. Pour over rice; sprinkle almonds over top. Bake at 350 degrees for 1 hour to 1 hour and 15 minutes. Yield: 6-8 servings.

Della Cunningham, Treas.
Alpha Kappa No. 3750
Schuyler, Nebraska

CURRY IN A HURRY

1/4 c. butter
2 tbsp. curry powder
1/4 c. chopped onion
1 tbsp. instant chicken bouillon
2 1-lb. cans applesauce
3 c. diced cooked chicken

Melt butter in large saucepan; stir in curry powder. Cook for 3 or 4 minutes over low heat. Add onion; simmer for 2 or 3 minutes. Dissolve bouillon in 2 cups hot water; add to curry. Add remaining ingredients; cook until heated through. Serve on bed of hot rice with condiments of chopped tomatoes, chopped onion, shredded coconut, crumbled bacon and chopped hard-boiled eggs. Yield: 4-6 servings.

Sandra Somers, V.P.
Alpha Phi Chap.
Staunton, Virginia

DEEP-FRIED CHICKEN

1 chicken, disjointed
1 egg
1 c. flour
1 tsp. salt
1/2 tsp. pepper
1 tbsp. paprika
1/2 c. (about) milk
Cooking oil for frying

Remove skin from chicken. Beat egg slightly with fork; stir in flour, seasonings and milk. Dip chicken into batter; drain off excess. Fry in deep hot oil until brown.

Rose Reller, V.P.
Iota Alpha No. 2961
Fremont, California

EASY OVEN CHICKEN

1 frying chicken, disjointed
1/4 env. dry onion soup mix
2 tbsp. dry Sherry

Place chicken in large casserole. Sprinkle with soup mix. Pour Sherry over top. Cover. Bake at 375 degrees for 1 hour. May uncover last 10 minutes of cooking time to brown, if desired.

Virginia M. Johnson
MAL
Denver, Colorado

Recipes on pages 154 and 156.

EASY CHICKEN DIVAN

2   10-oz. packages frozen broccoli
2 c. sliced cooked chicken
2 cans cream of chicken soup
1 c. mayonnaise or salad dressing
1 tsp. lemon juice
1 tsp. curry powder
1/2 c. shredded shapr Cheddar cheese
1/2 c. soft bread crumbs
1 1/2 tsp. melted butter

Cook broccoli in boiling salted water until tender; drain. Arrange broccoli in greased 9 x 13-inch pan. Place chicken on top. Combine soup, mayonnaise, lemon juice and curry powder; pour over chicken. Sprinkle with cheese. Combine bread crumbs and butter; sprinkle on top. Bake at 350 degrees for 25 to 30 minutes until thoroughly heated and bubbling. Yield: 8 servings.

Ann Riley, Ed. Dir.
Gamma Eta No. 3416
Farmington, New Mexico

JAPANESE CHICKEN WINGS

16 to 20 chicken wings, cut in
   3 pieces
Garlic powder
Cornstarch
2 eggs, well beaten
Sweet and Sour Sauce

Boil wing tips in water to cover to make stock. Reserve 1/2 cup stock. Soak remaining wing pieces in salted water for 30 minutes. Rinse; sprinkle damp wings with garlic powder. Let stand for 30 minutes. Dip in cornstarch, then in eggs. Brown in hot fat. Place in baking dish in single layer; cover with Sweet and Sour Sauce. Bake at 325 degrees for 1 hour, turning once after 40 minutes. Arrange wings on platter; spoon sauce over wings to serve.

Sweet and Sour Sauce

1/2 c. sugar
1/2 c. vinegar
1/2 c. reserved chicken stock

Recipes on pages 148, 149 and 180.

3 tbsp. soy sauce
3 tbsp. catsup
1/2 tsp. garlic powder

Combine all ingredients; mix well.

Pauline G. Magnuson, Pres.
Alpha Beta No. 186
Walla Walla, Washington

LEMONADE CHICKEN

1   6-oz. can frozen lemonade
   concentrate, thawed
1/3 c. soy sauce
1 tsp. seasoned salt
1/2 tsp. celery salt
1/8 tsp. garlic powder
2   2 to 3-lb. fryers, disjointed

Combine lemonade concentrate, soy sauce and seasonings in jar; cover. Shake vigorously to blend. Pour into small bowl. Dip chicken pieces in lemonade mixture. Place on grill over medium coals; cook for 45 to 50 minutes, brushing with lemonade mixture and turning frequently. Garnish with lemon twists and parsley, if desired. Yield: 8 servings.

Cheryl Weaver
Eta Rho No. 2957
Derby, Kansas

LUNCHEON CHICKEN CASSEROLE

2 c. rice
1 can chicken gumbo soup or cream
   of chicken soup
1 can cream of mushroom soup
Chicken breasts, thighs and legs
1/2 pkg. dry onion soup mix

Combine rice, soups and 1 cup water; pour into 7 x 11-inch casserole. Add chicken. Sprinkle onion soup over top. Bake, uncovered, at 350 degrees for 1 hour and 30 minutes. Cover with foil. Bake for 30 minutes longer.

Coleen Hanchett, Pres.
Zeta Lambda No. 2395
Salina, Kansas

FIESTA MEXICAN CHICKEN

1 lg. fryer, disjointed
Flour
2 1/4 tsp. chili powder
1 tsp. salt
1/4 c. vegetable oil
2 tbsp. butter
1 can tomatoes
1 1/2 tsp. sugar
2 tbsp. instant minced onions
1/2 c. sliced stuffed olives
2 cans yellow corn, drained

Wash and dry chicken. Place 1/2 cup flour, 1/4 teaspoon chili powder and 1/2 teaspoon salt in a bag. Add chicken to bag, a few pieces at a time; shake to coat evenly. Heat oil in skillet; cook chicken over moderate heat until brown on all sides. Drain. Heat butter in saucepan; blend in 2 tablespoons flour, remaining 2 teaspoons chili powder and remaining 1/2 teaspoon salt. Add tomatoes, sugar and onions; cook over moderate heat, stirring constantly, until thickened. Remove from heat; stir in olives. Spoon corn into 2 1/2-quart casserole. Place chicken over corn. Cover with tomato mixture. Cover. Bake in preheated 375-degree oven for 40 minutes. Uncover; bake for 30 minutes longer. Serve tomato-corn mixture over rice, if desired.

Susan Atria
Alpha Sigma Chap.
Columbia, South Carolina

MEXICAN CHICKEN CASSEROLE

12 tortillas
1 can green chilies
1 can cream of chicken soup
1 can cream of mushroom soup
3 sm. cans Swanson's chicken
1 lg. onion, chopped
2 c. sliced Cheddar cheese

Cut each tortilla into 8 pieces; line baking dish with half the tortillas. Combine chilies, soups, chicken and onion; spoon half the soup mixture over tortillas. Top with half the cheese. Repeat layers. Bake in 325-degree oven for 40 minutes. Let stand in

oven for about 1 hour after turning off heat. Yield: 10 servings.

Veda Murphy, Ed. Dir.
Alpha Pi No. 815
Gallup, New Mexico

NO-LABOR CHICKEN DINNER

1/2 c. margarine
1 med. onion, thinly sliced
1 3-lb. fryer, disjointed and skinned
Seasoned salt to taste
1/2 c. white Chablis
2 10-oz. packages frozen Italian
* vegetables*
1 c. sour cream

Melt margarine in skillet; saute onion until transparent. Sprinkle chicken pieces with seasoned salt; brown in margarine. Add Chablis. Cover; cook over low heat for 30 minutes or until chicken is tender. Remove chicken. Add vegetables to skillet; cook over medium heat until thawed. Add sour cream to vegetable mixture; return chicken to skillet. Bring to a boil. Serve immediately.

Cynthia Clanton
Delta Nu No. 3541
Orlando, Florida

POLLY'S SUPER CHICKEN ENCHILADAS

1 chicken, cooked
1 can cream of chicken soup
1 can cream of mushroom soup
1 soup can milk
1 or 2 cans mild green chilies
Salt and pepper to taste
Flour tortillas
1/4 lb. Monterey Jack cheese, grated
1 sm. carton sour cream

Remove skin and bones from chicken; dice. Combine chicken and soups in saucepan. Heat at low temperature. Add milk and chilies. Season with salt and pepper. Stir until hot and bubbly. Place a small amount of chicken and sauce on each tortilla; roll up. Secure with toothpick. Place tortillas in shallow casserole; cover with remaining sauce. Top with cheese. Bake at 350 degrees for 30 to 35 minutes or until cheese is melted. Serve topped with dab of sour cream.

Polly Renard, Pres.
Kappa Omega No. 2615
Plano, Texas

SPECIAL CHICKEN DELIGHT

1 1/2 c. chopped boned chicken
4 hard-boiled eggs, chopped
3/4 c. diced celery
3/4 c. chopped almonds
1 1/2 cans cream of chicken soup
3/4 c. mayonnaise
1 1/2 pkg. potato chips, crumbled

Combine chicken, eggs, celery and almonds; stir in soup and mayonnaise. Turn into greased casserole. Top with potato chips. Bake at 450 degrees for 12 to 15 minutes.

Jackie Jackson, State Coun. 2nd V.P.
Alpha Tau No. 2046
Richmond, Virginia

THANKSGIVING CHICKEN CASSEROLE

1/2 c. margarine
1 pkg. herb-seasoned stuffing mix
1 chicken, stewed
2 c. chicken broth
1 can mushroom soup
1 can chicken soup

Melt margarine; stir in stuffing mix. Line bottom of baking pan with 1/2 of the stuffing mixture. Remove bones from chicken; place chicken over stuffing mixture. Combine chicken broth and soups; pour over chicken. Sprinkle remaining stuffing over top. Bake at 350 degrees for 45 minutes.

Elaine Wood, Ed. Dir.
Delta Kappa No. 4717
Roanoke, Virginia

ROAST DUCKLING WITH OLIVE-SHERRY SAUCE

2   4 to 5-lb. ducklings
Salt
1 med. onion
1/2 bay leaf
1 rib of celery
1/4 c. butter or margarine
1/4 c. flour
1/3 c. dry Sherry
3/4 c. sliced stuffed Spanish green
   olives
Dash of pepper

Remove giblets and necks from duck cavities; set aside. Rub inside of each duckling with salt; place on rack in shallow roasting pan. Bake in 350-degree oven for 2 hours and 15 minutes, draining off fat after 1 hour. Combine 2 cups water, giblets, necks, onion, bay leaf and celery in saucepan; bring to a boil. Cover; simmer for 45 minutes or until giblets are tender. Strain and measure broth; add enough water to measure 2 cups liquid. Discard onion, celery and bay leaf; chop giblets. Melt butter in saucepan over medium heat; blend in flour. Add liquid and Sherry gradually; cook until sauce boils, stirring constantly. Add giblets, olives, 1/4 teaspoon salt and pepper; cook over low heat for 5 minutes. Serve sauce with ducklings. Yield: 6-8 servings.

Photograph for this photograph on page 34.

CHRISTMAS CORNISH HENS

2 c. red wine
1/2 c. currant jelly
1 No. 2 can white grapes
1 tbsp. chicken base or 1 No. 2 can
   chicken stock
Cornstarch
Salt and pepper to taste
2 game hens

Boil wine in saucepan until alcohol has evaporated. Stir in next 3 ingredients; thicken with cornstarch to desired thickness. Season with salt and pepper. Bake hens in 400-degree oven for 30 minutes or until tender, basting frequently with wine sauce.

Dorothy Steele, Ed. Dir.
Alpha Theta No. 3918
Honolulu, Hawaii

CORNISH HENS WITH ONIONS

4 sm. onions
5 or 6 cloves for each onion
4 Cornish hens
2 tsp. curry powder
1/2 c. butter, melted
Salt and pepper to taste or Season
*   All*

Stud onions with cloves. Insert 1 onion in each Cornish hen. Stir curry powder into melted butter; brush over hens using all the butter. Sprinkle with salt and pepper. Wrap individually in foil. Bake at 350 degrees for 1 hour. Uncover. Bake for 15 minutes longer.

Teresa Hupp
Alpha Phi No. 2051
Staunton, Virginia

CORNISH HENS WITH WILD RICE STUFFING

1 box Uncle Ben's wild rice mix
3/4 lb. ground hot sausage
1 lg. onion, chopped
2 stalks celery, chopped finely
4 Cornish hens
Salt and pepper to taste
1/3 c. melted butter or margarine

Cook wild rice according to package directions, using 1/4 cup less water. Brown sausage in hot skillet; remove sausage from fat with slotted spoon. Saute onion in fat until soft; remove from fat. Combine rice, sausage, onion and celery; let cool. Wash Cornish hens well; sprinkle cavity with salt and pepper. Fill cavity of each hen with wild rice stuffing; tie legs together with string. Place on broiling pan; brush with melted butter. Bake in preheated 375-degree oven for 1 hour and 30 minutes.

Susan Atria
Alpha Sigma No. 3887
Columbia, South Carolina

HARVEST DINNER

1 10-lb. turkey
Salt and pepper

1/4 c. butter or margarine
6 to 8 med. Louisiana yams
1 16-oz. jar spiced crab apples
2 tbsp. cornstarch
1/2 c. Rhine wine
1 6-oz. can unsweetened pineapple
*   juice*
1/2 c. dark corn syrup
1 1/2 tsp. lemon juice

Sprinkle inside of turkey with salt and pepper. Place on rack in shallow roasting pan. Melt butter in saucepan; brush turkey with part of the butter. Bake at 325 degrees for 2 hours. Cook yams in boiling salted water until almost done; drain. Peel and cut in half. Drain crab apples, reserving syrup. Blend cornstarch and wine; stir into remaining butter. Add reserved crab apple syrup, pineapple juice, corn syrup, lemon juice and 1/4 teaspoon salt. Cook, stirring constantly, until sauce boils for 30 seconds. Drain fat from roasting pan. Arrange yams around turkey; brush both with sauce. Bake for 30 minutes longer or until meat thermometer registers 185 degrees, brushing once with sauce. Heat crab apples in remaining sauce. Arrange turkey, yams and crab apples on platter. Serve with hot sauce. May use two 23-ounce cans Louisiana yams. Drain and bake for 15 minutes with turkey.

Photograph for this recipe above.

HELEN'S FAVORITE TURKEY PIE

2 c. cubed turkey
1 tbsp. flour
1 c. sliced carrots
1 c. diced onions
1/4 c. sliced celery
1/2 tsp. thyme leaves, crushed
1/8 tsp. pepper
1/4 c. butter or margarine
1 can golden mushroom soup
1 c. cooked cut green beans
Pastry for 2-crust pie
Milk

Toss turkey with flour in bowl. Cook carrots, onions and celery with thyme and pepper in butter in saucepan until tender. Stir in soup, turkey mixture and green beans. Pour into 9-inch pastry-lined pan. Roll out remaining pastry. Cut into 1/2-inch wide strips. Crisscross strips over filling to form lattice top. Brush pastry with milk. Bake at 350 degrees for 45 minutes or until crust is lightly browned.

Mrs. Helen Davis
Beta Xi Chap.
Ocean Springs, Mississippi

TURKEY CROQUETTES

3 tbsp. shortening
1/3 c. flour
1 tsp. salt
1 c. milk
2 1/2 c. ground cooked turkey
1 tbsp. minced onion
2 tbsp. minced parsley
2 eggs
2 tbsp. lemon juice
1/3 c. fine dry bread crumbs
Oil for frying

Melt shortening; blend in flour and salt. Stir in milk. Cook over low heat until smooth and thick, stirring constantly. Add turkey, onion and parsley; spread in greased shallow pan. Chill thoroughly. Shape into 8 logs. Beat eggs and lemon juice together lightly with fork. Roll turkey logs in crumbs. Dip in egg mixture; roll again in crumbs. Fry croquettes in deep oil at 375 degrees, turning to brown evenly. Drain on absorbent paper. A delicious way to use leftover turkey.

Martha Heflin, Photographer
Beta Eta No. 3696
Fairfield, Illinois

TURKEY CREOLE

1/2 c. chopped onion
1 green pepper, chopped
1 clove of garlic, crushed
2 tbsp. salad oil
1 16-oz. can tomatoes
2 tsp. chili powder
1 1/2 tsp. salt
1 tsp. sugar
3/4 tsp. oregano
1 c. long grain rice
3 c. chopped cooked turkey

Cook onion, green pepper and garlic in oil in 12-inch skillet over medium heat until tender. Add 2 cups water, tomatoes and seasonings; bring to a boil. Stir in rice. Reduce heat to low; cover and simmer for 25 minutes. Stir in turkey; heat through. Yield: 4 servings.

Sharon Wilson, Publ. Chm.
Delta Iota No. 4396
Wray, Colorado

TURKEY LOAF

3 to 4 c. ground turkey
1 egg, well beaten
1/8 tsp. thyme
1/8 tsp. sage
Salt and pepper to taste
1/2 to 3/4 c. cracker crumbs
1/4 c. wheat germ
1 can cream of chicken soup

Combine turkey, egg, seasonings, cracker crumbs, wheat germ and 1/4 cup chicken soup in large bowl; mix well. Shape into loaf; place in loaf pan. Cover with remaining soup. Bake at 350 degrees for about 1 hour or until done. Yield: 6-8 servings.

Vatricia J. Sprouse, Rec. Sec.
Alpha Eta No. 230
Denver, Colorado

BEER BATTER-FRIED FISH

2 12-oz. packages frozen fish
    fillets or 1 1/2 lb. fresh fish
    fillets
2 eggs, separated
1/2 c. beer
1/4 c. milk
1 c. all-purpose flour
1/2 tsp. seasoned salt
1/4 tsp. seasoned pepper

Thaw frozen fillets enough to separate. Cut into 3 x 1 1/2-inch pieces. Place on paper towels to dry. Beat egg yolks until thick and light; blend in beer, milk, flour and seasonings. Mix until smooth. Beat egg whites until stiff but not dry; fold into beer mixture. Pat fillets dry. Dip into batter; lift out with fork or slotted spoon. Drain slightly. Fry in deep fat at 375 degrees for 2 to 3 minutes or until golden brown and puffed. Drain on absorbent paper. Yield: 6 servings.

Lorene Johnstone, V.P.
Alpha Beta No. 165
Lincoln, Nebraska

BAKED FISH WITH MUSHROOMS

1 lb. perch or catfish fillets
2 tbsp. melted butter
3 tbsp. lemon juice
1/4 c. minced onion
1/2 lb. mushrooms, washed and sliced
2 tbsp. margarine or butter
2 tbsp. flour
1/4 tsp. salt
1/8 tsp. pepper
3/4 c. milk
1/8 c. red wine

Place fish in an ungreased 11 1/2 x 7 1/2 x 1 1/2-inch baking dish. Combine melted butter, lemon juice and onion; pour over fish. Turn fish to coat both sides; place, skin side up, in dish. Bake in preheated 350-degree oven for 20 to 30 minutes until fish flakes easily with fork. Cook mushrooms in margarine until tender; stir in flour, salt and pepper. Cook over low heat for several minutes, stirring frequently. Remove from heat. Stir in milk. Return to heat; cook, stirring constantly, until mixture begins to boil. Add wine; cook until mixture thickens slightly. Pour over fish just before serving. One 6-ounce can sliced drained mushrooms may be substituted for fresh mushrooms, if desired. Yield: 3-4 servings.

Linda Crow, Past Pres.
Gamma Beta No. 4122
Hartselle, Alabama

TROUT MEUNIERE

4 4-oz. trout fillets
1/2 tsp. salt
2 tbsp. flour
6 tbsp. butter
2 tbsp. fresh lemon juice
1 tbsp. Worcestershire sauce

Sprinkle trout with salt; dredge with flour. Melt 2 tablespoons butter in large skillet; add trout. Saute over moderate heat for about 2 minutes on each side or until golden. Remove to platter; keep warm. Melt remaining butter in small skillet; add lemon juice and Worcestershire sauce. Simmer for about 2 minutes. Pour over trout. Garnish with lemon wedges and parsley. Yield: 2-4 servings.

Diana E. Henderson
Alpha Omega No. 4060
Largo, Florida

SALMON LOAF

1 can cream of celery soup
1/3 c. mayonnaise or salad dressing
1 egg, beaten
1/2 c. chopped onion
1/4 c. chopped green pepper
1 tbsp. lemon juice
1 1-lb. can salmon, drained, boned
    and flaked
1 c. cracker crumbs

Combine all ingredients; mix well. Place in greased 9 x 5 x 3-inch loaf pan. Bake at 350 degrees for 1 hour. Unmold; slice to serve. Yield: 6-8 servings.

Alice Otto
Alpha Omicron No. 1827
Burlington, Iowa

JAMBALAYA

1/2 c. chopped green onions
1/2 c. chopped white onions
1 lg. green pepper, cut in strips
1/2 c. chopped celery and leaves
1 tsp. minced garlic
1/3 c. butter
1 lb. shrimp, shelled and deveined
2 doz. oysters or 1 c. cubed ham
1   1-lb. can tomatoes
1 c. chicken broth
Salt to taste
1/4 tsp. cayenne pepper
1 c. rice

Saute onions, green pepper, celery and garlic in butter until tender but not brown. Add shrimp and oysters; cook for 5 minutes. Add tomatoes, chicken broth, salt, cayenne pepper and rice. Cook for 25 to 30 minutes over low heat or until rice is tender. Add tomato juice or V-8 juice if mixture becomes too dry. May cook in electric skillet at 275 to 300 degrees, if desired. Yield: 6-8 servings.

Darlene Scott, Pres.
Beta Psi No. 4150
Cincinnati, Ohio

COLUMBUS DAY STUFFED FILLETS

1/3 c. chopped onion
6 tbsp. butter or margarine

1/3 c. slivered almonds
1/2 c. chopped stuffed Spanish green
    olives
Pepper
3 c. fresh bread crumbs
8 sm. flounder fillets
1/4 c. melted butter or margarine
2 tbsp. lime juice

Saute onion in butter until golden; add almonds. Cook for 3 minutes longer, stirring frequently. Remove from heat; stir in olives and 1/4 teaspoon pepper. Pour over bread crumbs; toss to mix well. Season fish lightly with salt and pepper; place 4 fillets in shallow buttered baking pan. Spread stuffing on fillets; top with remaining fillets. Combine melted butter and lime juice; pour over fish. Bake in 350-degree oven for 20 minutes, basting once with pan liquids. Yield: 4 servings.

Photograph for this recipe on this page.

CREAMY KING CRAB OVER ASPARAGUS AND TOAST

1   7-oz. can king crab
2 tbsp. butter
2 tbsp. flour
1 c. half and half
1/2 c. milk
2 egg yolks, beaten
3 tbsp. dry Sherry
1 1/2 tbsp. lemon juice
1/2 tsp. salt
Toast points
2 lb. cooked fresh asparagus

Drain crab; slice. Melt butter; blend in flour. Add half and half and milk. Cook, stirring, until sauce is thickened. Stir a small amount of hot sauce into egg yolks. Return to hot sauce mixture. Cook over low heat, stirring constantly, for 1 or 2 minutes. Add crab, Sherry, lemon juice and salt; heat through. Arrange toast on individual serving plates; top with several asparagus spears and creamed crab. Frozen crab and canned asparagus may be used, if desired. Yield: 5-6 servings.

Ann Krupkat, Treas.
Alpha Upsilon No. 3337
South Milwaukee, Wisconsin

CRAB IMPERIAL CASSEROLE

1 lb. crab meat
1 tsp. chopped onion
Salt and pepper to taste
1/4 c. chopped green pepper
1/2 c. salad dressing or mayonnaise

Combine all ingredients; mix well. Place in 1-quart casserole. Bake at 350 degrees until golden brown.

Carolyn B. King, Sec.
Gamma Phi No. 2561
Winter Haven, Florida

CRAB MEAT MUFFINS

1/2 c. butter
1/2 lb. Velveeta cheese, sliced
1 pkg. frozen or canned crab
1 tbsp. grated onion
3 tsp. lemon juice
2 tsp. Worcestershire sauce
8 English muffins

Melt butter in double boiler; add cheese. Cook, stirring, until cheese is melted. Add remaining ingredients except muffins; stir to blend. Spread mixture over English muffin halves. Bake at 325 degrees for 20 minutes.

Mary Lou Mulch, Reg. Coun. Past Pres.
Epsilon Sigma No. 3896
Fairfield, California

SEAFARER'S NEWBURG

1/4 c. margarine
1/4 c. flour
1/8 tsp. salt
1 3/4 c. milk
1/4 c. dry Sherry
1 can cream of chicken or celery soup
1 c. chopped celery
1   4 1/2-oz. can crab or shrimp
1/4 c. grated Cheddar cheese

Melt margarine in medium skillet; add flour and salt. Blend until smooth. Add milk, Sherry and soup gradually; cook, stirring,

until sauce is thickened and smooth. Add celery, crab and cheese; heat just to boiling point, stirring frequently. Serve over rice.

June Johnson, Parliamentarian
Lambda XI No. 311
Seattle, Washington

DEVILED SHELLFISH

1/4 c. finely chopped green pepper
1/4 c. finely chopped onion
1/4 c. finely chopped celery
1 c. mayonnaise
1 tsp. Worcestershire sauce
1/2 tsp. salt
1 c. cooked shrimp
1 c. crab meat
2 c. herb-seasoned stuffing mix,
  crushed

Combine all ingredients until well blended. Spoon into shallow 1-quart casserole or ovenproof shells. Bake at 350 degrees for 30 minutes or until browned.

Melba Rilott
MAL
Dunedin, Florida

CRUNCHY SEAFOOD CASSEROLE

1 can mushroom soup
1/3 c. mayonnaise
1/3 c. evaporated milk
1 can shrimp
1 can crab
1 can water chestnuts, sliced
1 c. chopped celery
2 tbsp. minced parsley
2 tbsp. chopped onions
1/2 can pimento, chopped
2 c. cooked shell macaroni
1 tbsp. lemon juice or 2 tbsp. Sherry

Combine all ingredients; mix well. Place in greased casserole. Bake at 350 degrees for 30 to 35 minutes.

Judy A. Fishback
Delta Tau No. 4264
Yakima, Washington

MOTHER'S DAY SEAFOOD CASSEROLE

2 cans cream of shrimp soup
1/2 c. mayonnaise
1 sm. onion, grated
3/4 c. milk
1/4 tsp. salt
1/8 tsp. white pepper
1/8 tsp. nutmeg
1/8 tsp. cayenne pepper
1/4 tsp. seasoned salt
3 lb. shrimp, cooked and cleaned
1   7 1/2-oz. can crab meat, drained
1   5-oz. can water chestnuts,
    drained and sliced
1 1/2 c. diced celery
3 tbsp. minced parsley
1 1/3 c. long grain rice
Slivered almonds

Blend soup into mayonnaise in large bowl; stir until smooth. Add onion and then milk. Add all ingredients except rice and almonds. Cook rice according to package directions; stir into seafood mixture, adding more milk if mixture is too dry. Turn into buttered large casserole; sprinkle slivered almonds over top. Garnish with paprika. Bake, uncovered, at 350 degrees for 30 minutes or until bubbly. Freezes well. Yield: 8-10 servings.

Sharon Baggs, Corr. Sec.
Delta Tau No. 3684
Manchester, Missouri

OYSTER HOT DISH

2   1-pt. jars oysters
1/2 c. butter
1 bunch parsley, chopped
1 c. half and half
2 c. Waverley cracker crumbs
Salt and pepper to taste

Drain oysters; reserve juice. Melt butter; mix with parsley. Heat half and half with reserved oyster juice until just warm. Combine all ingredients; mix well. Turn into oblong baking dish. Bake at 350 degrees for 30 to 45 minutes.

Azele Bennett
Omicron No. 374
Tacoma, Washington

BARBECUED SHRIMP

4 lb. jumbo shrimp with shells
1 lb. butter
Garlic powder
Paprika
Pepper
Salt

Rinse shrimp. Place about 1 pound shrimp in single layer in 9 x 12-inch baking dish. Slice 1 stick butter over shrimp. Cover with garlic powder until white, then cover with paprika until red. Cover with pepper. Sprinkle with salt. Repeat layers 3 times, ending with butter. Bake in preheated 400-degree oven for 20 to 30 minutes. Peel shrimp; dip in butter mixture.

Cece Coon, Pres.
Gamma Nu No. 4508
Winter Park, Florida

SPANISH GREEN OLIVE PAELLA

1/2 lb. Italian sausage, cut in 1/2-in. slices
1 med. onion, chopped
1 clove of garlic, minced
4 c. chicken broth
1/4 tsp. saffron
1/8 tsp. pepper
1 c. rice
2 c. diced cooked chicken
1/2 c. halved stuffed Spanish green
    olives
1 med. green pepper, cut in strips
6 sm. clams in shells
1/2 lb. cooked shrimp, peeled and
    deveined
6 lemon wedges

Brown sausage in large skillet over medium heat; drain off fat. Add onion and garlic; saute until golden. Add chicken broth, saffron, pepper and rice; heat to boiling point. Cover tightly; simmer for 15 minutes. Stir chicken, olives and green pepper into rice mixture; arrange clams on top. Cover; simmer for 10 minutes or until clams open. Add shrimp; simmer just until shrimp are heated through. Garnish with lemon wedges; serve immediately. Yield: 6 servings.

Photograph for this recipe on page 34.

Breads

Holidays, especially Christmas, bring to mind gift giving. And truly, there is no gift that says "from the heart" any more sincerely than homemade breads. There may be more lasting gifts to choose from, but certainly none that are any more appreciated. In fact, you can give almost everyone on your gift list some kind of bread and no two gifts will ever be the same. From A to Z, you can choose a distinctive flavor to highlight your bread such as apricots, carrots, honey, molasses, onion, raisins or zucchini. Even herbs, spices, cheeses, and nuts can add interesting flavors and textures too.

Breads are also an unmistakable part of all Holiday food plans, and intrinsic to the traditions that families build over the years. How many people associate waking on Christmas morning, not only to the thrill of anticipation, but also to the aroma of grandma's special holiday bread warming in the oven? A fancy bread is still the perfect Christmas breakfast because it can be festive and tasty without jading appetites for the Yule feast to come. And, it can be eaten and enjoyed by the family while opening packages.

Christmas Eve is a somewhat quiet time during the Yule festivities. Activities for this night often include visits between close friends and relatives to exchange gifts, or families adding a few last minute touches to their Christmas tree, then for a conclusion, attending midnight church services. It is a good time to arrange a tantalizing array of specialty breads in a convenient spot where everyone can help themselves. Include savory herb and cheese breads, as well as apricot, banana and nut breads, and your favorite spicy coffee cakes glazed with confectioners' sugar icing. Also include various spreads: soft butter, cranberry and other jellies, cream cheese, soft cheese spreads, and so forth. The only other accompaniment you might need is a hot holiday beverage of your choice. Simple, satisfying and not much to clean up on Christmas Eve!

Only a generation or two in the past, bread making was a regular item on the list of the homemaker's weekly chores. But, as "store-bought" bread became a status symbol, homemakers stopped practicing this creative art. Recently though, modern cooks have rediscovered just how satisfying the results of their bread making efforts can be. There is hardly a menu, festive or not, that is truly complete without one recipe or another for bread, rolls, or muffins. For a formal meal, make your own flaky, delicate croissants. On a cold and wintry night, treat the whole family to a meal of freshly-baked Boston brown bread served with baked beans and a hearty vegetable soup. You will find that it's easy to serve your family a more nutritious breakfast when you make your own biscuits or waffles — and for an occasional special treat, try your hand at making doughnuts. Really bring out the country flavor of your next Labor Day Barbecue by serving cornmeal muffins or pancakes.

ESA members believe that there is nothing quite as special as breads baked in your own oven. Not only does it fill the entire house with a wonderful aroma, but it keeps alive an art that has nourished mankind for thousands of years. Moreover, homemade breads can be a natural plus for the homemakers who are becoming more and more concerned about the quality of her family's nutrition. Whether you live in a small apartment in the city, a house in the suburbs, or on a farm in the rural areas, bread making should be a regular part of your kitchen creativity. You will find that you agree as you read over the following recipes for old-fashioned breads, coffee cakes, biscuits, buns, rolls and muffins. You may never want to buy bread again, and your family will be delighted.

BREAKFAST WHOLE WHEAT BISCUITS

1 c. all-purpose flour
4 tsp. baking powder
3/4 tsp. salt
1 c. whole wheat flour
1/4 c. shortening
3/4 c. milk

Sift first 3 ingredients together; stir in whole wheat flour. Cut in shortening until mixture resembles coarse crumbs. Make a well in center; add milk all at once. Stir just until dough clings together. Turn onto lightly floured surface. Knead gently 10 or 12 strokes. Roll or pat out dough 1/2 inch thick. Dip biscuit cutter into flour; cut biscuits. Place on ungreased baking sheet. Bake at 450 degrees for 12 to 15 minutes. Yield: 16 biscuits.

Carol Elliott, Treas.
Beta Omega No. 4210
Midland, Texas

BEER BISCUITS

2 c. Bisquick
1/2   12-oz. can or bottle of beer at
room temperature

Combine Bisquick and beer; mix until smooth. Spoon into muffin pan. Bake in preheated 450-degree oven for 25 minutes.

Pat Reinhold
Alpha Nu No. 1069
Meridian, Mississippi

CHRISTMAS ANGEL BISCUITS

1 pkg. yeast
3/4 c. Crisco
5 c. flour
5 tsp. baking powder
1 tsp. soda
2 tsp. salt
3 tbsp. sugar
2 c. buttermilk

Dissolve yeast in 5 tablespoons lukewarm water; set aside. Blend Crisco with dry ingredients, using pastry cutter. Combine yeast mixture with buttermilk; add dry ingredi-

ents, mixing to make stiff dough. Place in covered container; store in refrigerator. Pinch off dough as needed; place biscuits on cookie sheet in cold oven. Turn oven temperature to 450 degrees. Bake until browned.

Mrs. Garnet A. Hampton, Ed. Dir.
Gamma Chi No. 834
Comanche, Oklahoma

HUSH PUPPIES

1 onion, chopped
1 c. cornmeal
6 tbsp. sugar
1 c. flour
1/2 tsp. salt
2 tsp. (heaping) baking powder
4 eggs, lightly beaten
Milk

Combine onion and dry ingredients; mix well. Add eggs and enough milk to make a thick batter. Drop by spoonfuls into deep fat at 300 degrees. Cook until golden brown on all sides.

Rusty Farrelly
Beta Mu No. 606
Lawton, Oklahoma

JALAPENO CORN BREAD

2 c. yellow cornmeal
3 tsp. baking powder
3/4 c. flour
1 tsp. sugar
1 tsp. salt
2/3 c. cooking oil
3 eggs, slightly beaten
1 c. cream-style corn
1 c. sour cream
3 finely chopped jalapeno peppers
1 c. grated cheese

Sift first 5 ingredients together. Add oil, eggs, corn, sour cream and peppers; mix well. Pour half the batter into greased baking pan; sprinkle half the grated cheese over top. Pour remaining batter over cheese, then sprinkle with remaining cheese. Bake at 450 degrees for 30 minutes.

Gerda Anderson, Rec. Sec.
Beta Zeta No. 3149
Canon City, Colorado

HOLIDAY DILL BREAD

> 1 pkg. hot roll mix
> 1 tbsp. butter or margarine, melted
> 1 c. chopped dill pickles
> 1/3 c. chopped parsley
> 1/2 tsp. fines herbes
> 1 c. grated Cheddar cheese
> 1 egg, beaten

Prepare hot roll mix according to package directions. Let dough rise until doubled in bulk. Roll out on lightly floured surface to an 18 x 11-inch rectangle. Brush with butter. Combine pickles, parsley and fines herbes; sprinkle over dough. Sprinkle cheese on top. Roll up from long end; seal edges and place roll on greased baking sheet. Form into a ring; join edges and seal. Make cuts 3/4 of the way through ring at 1-inch intervals with scissors or sharp knife. Turn each section on its side. Cover; let rise in warm place for about 25 minutes or until doubled in bulk. Brush with beaten egg. Bake in 375-degree oven for 25 minutes or until golden brown. Serve with butter or cream cheese, if desired.

Photograph for this recipe above.

FISH BREAD

> 1 box hot roll mix
> 1/2 c. olive oil
> 2 cans sardines
> 1 can anchovies
> 1/2 c. Parmesan cheese

Prepare hot roll mix according to package directions; place in greased pan. Top with olive oil. Crumble sardines and anchovies; press into dough. Sprinkle Parmesan cheese over top. Let rise according to package directions. Bake at 350 degrees for 10 to 25 minutes. Serve with spaghetti dinner.

Diana Dworsky, Pres.
Beta Zeta No. 3048
Houston, Texas

EASTER MONDAY BREAD

> 2 c. Bisquick
> 1 c. chopped cooked ham
> 3 tbsp. minced onion
> 2 eggs
> 2/3 c. milk

2 tbsp. salad oil
1/2 tsp. prepared mustard
1 1/2 c. shredded cheese
2 tbsp. sesame seed
3 tbsp. melted butter

Combine Bisquick, ham, onion, eggs, milk, oil, mustard and 3/4 cup cheese; mix well. Spread dough in greased 10-inch pie pan. Sprinkle with remaining cheese and sesame seed. Pour butter evenly over top. Bake at 375 degrees for 35 to 40 minutes. Serve warm.

Joanne Chadwick, Pres.
Alpha Theta No. 1616
Fargo, North Dakota

SAINT PATRICK'S DAY IRISH SODA BREAD

3 c. flour
1/3 c. sugar
1 tbsp. baking powder
1 tsp. soda
1 tsp. salt
1 egg, slightly beaten
2 c. buttermilk
1/4 c. melted butter or margarine

Combine flour, sugar, baking powder, soda and salt in large mixing bowl; mix well. Blend egg and buttermilk; add, all at one time, to flour mixture. Mix until dry particles are moistened. Stir in melted butter, mixing well. Pour into greased 9 x 5 x 3-inch loaf pan. Bake at 325 degrees for 1 hour and 5 minutes to 1 hour and 15 minutes or until toothpick inserted in center comes out clean. Do not underbake. Remove from pan; cool on wire rack. Place in airtight wrap; store for at least 8 hours before slicing.

Joyce Kirchner, Pres.
Delta Lambda No. 2469
Grandview, Missouri

IRISH FRECKLE BREAD

4 3/4 to 5 3/4 c. unsifted flour
1/2 c. sugar
1 tsp. salt
2 pkg. Fleischmann's dry yeast
1 c. potato water or water

1/2 c. Fleischmann's margarine
2 eggs at room temperature
1/4 c. mashed potatoes at room temperature
1 c. seedless raisins

Mix 1 1/2 cups flour, sugar, salt and dry yeast thoroughly in a large bowl. Combine potato water and margarine in a saucepan. Heat over low heat until liquid is warm; margarine does not need to melt. Add to dry ingredients gradually; beat for 2 minutes at medium speed of electric mixer, scraping bowl occasionally. Add eggs, potatoes and 1/2 cup flour or enough flour to make a thick batter. Beat at high speed for 2 minutes, scraping bowl occasionally. Stir in raisins and enough additional flour to make a soft dough. Turn out onto lightly floured board; knead for about 8 to 10 minutes or until smooth and elastic. Place in greased bowl, turning to grease top. Cover; let rise in warm place for about 1 hour and 15 minutes or until doubled in bulk. Punch dough down; turn onto lightly floured board. Divide dough into 4 equal pieces. Shape each piece into a slender loaf, about 8 1/2 inches long. Place 2 loaves, side by side, in each of 2 greased 8 1/2 x 4 1/2 x 2 1/2-inch loaf pans. Cover; let rise in warm place for about 1 hour or until doubled in bulk. Bake in preheated 350-degree oven for about 35 minutes or until done. Remove from pans; cool on wire racks.

Photograph for this recipe below.

FREEZER WHOLE WHEAT BREAD

  6 c. (about) flour
  1 c. cornmeal
  6 c. whole wheat flour
  4 pkg. dry yeast
  1/4 c. soft margarine
  3 tbsp. sugar
  2 tbsp. salt
  1/3 c. honey
  1 egg white

Combine 5 cups flour, cornmeal and whole wheat flour in large bowl. Combine yeast, margarine, sugar, salt and 2 cups flour mixture in large mixer bowl. Beat in 4 cups medium hot water and honey gradually. Beat for 2 minutes. Beat in 2 1/2 cups more flour mixture gradually; beat for 2 minutes longer. Stir in enough remaining flour mixture to make soft dough. Beat for 10 minutes longer or knead on floured surface. Let dough rest for 15 minutes. Cut dough into 4 parts. Place in greased 9 x 5-inch pans. Cover with plastic wrap; freeze until firm. Remove from pans; wrap tightly. Return to freezer. Remove from freezer 5 hours before ready to use. Unwrap; place in pan. Thaw completely. Brush with egg white; let rise for 2 hours. Bake at 375 degrees for 35 minutes; cool on wire rack.

Patricia Kilpatrick
Alpha Epsilon Chap.
Fort Collins, Colorado

REFRIGERATOR BRAN MUFFINS

  1 15-oz. box Raisin Bran
  3 c. sugar
  5 c. flour
  5 tsp. soda
  1 tsp. pumpkin pie spice
  2 tsp. salt
  4 eggs
  1/2 c. melted margarine
  1/2 c. melted shortening
  2 tbsp. vanilla extract
  1 qt. buttermilk

Combine bran, sugar, flour, soda, spice and salt in large bowl; mix well. Add eggs, margarine, shortening, vanilla and buttermilk; mix well. Store in covered container in refrigerator. Use as needed for muffins. Fill greased muffin pan 3/4 full. Bake in preheated 400-degrees oven for 15 to 20 minutes.

Betty J. Webber, Past Pres.
Beta Mu No. 2126
Muncie, Indiana

NEW YEAR'S EVE SCONES

  4 c. flour
  2 tsp. (heaping) baking powder
  1 tsp. soda
  1 tsp. salt
  6 tbsp. sugar
  1/4 c. margarine
  Buttermilk

Sift dry ingredients together; blend in margarine and enough buttermilk to make a soft dough. Roll out on a floured board to 1/8 to 1/4-inch thickness. Cut in wedges; fry on electric griddle at 350 degrees until golden but not brown. Serve with butter and jelly or meat spread. Yield: About 28 scones.

Carole Sherrill, Treas.
Gamma Sigma No. 4220
Marshall, Illinois

ALMOND BUNS

  4 to 4 1/2 c. all-purpose flour
  1/2 c. sugar
  1 tsp. salt
  2 pkg. dry yeast
  1 c. milk
  1/2 c. butter
  2 eggs
  1/2 c. ground almonds
  Almond Filling
  Confectioners' sugar

Combine 2 cups flour, sugar, salt and dry yeast in large mixing bowl. Heat milk and butter together until very warm. Add to dry ingredients gradually; beat for 2 minutes on medium speed of mixer, scraping bowl occasionally. Add eggs and 1/2 cup flour. Beat for 2 minutes at high speed, scraping bowl occasionally. Add almonds, stirring to blend well. Stir in enough additional flour to make a soft dough. Turn out on a lightly floured surface; knead for about 5 minutes or until smooth and elastic. Place in buttered large bowl, turning to butter top. Cover; let rise in warm place for about 1 hour or until doubled in bulk. Punch dough down. Divide into 24 equal parts. Shape each ball of dough around 1 ball of filling, sealing edges well. Place on cookie sheets, 2 inches apart. Let rise in warm place for 30 to 45 minutes or until almost doubled in bulk. Bake in pre-heated 375-degree oven for 10 to 12 minutes. Remove to wire racks to cool. Sprinkle lightly with confectioners' sugar before serving.

Almond Filling

    1   8-oz. can almond paste
    1/2 c. confectioners' sugar
    1/4 c. butter

Cream almond paste, confectioners' sugar and butter together until thoroughly blended. Divide into 24 equal parts; shape into balls. Cover and set aside.

Photograph for this recipe on page 88.

CHRISTMAS MORNING PINCH-ME CAKE

    1 c. milk
    1 tsp. salt
    1 1/4 c. sugar
    1/4 c. butter
    4 1/2 c. flour
    2 eggs, lightly beaten
    1 cake yeast, crumbled
    1/2 c. melted butter
    1/2 c. chopped nuts
    3 tsp. cinnamon

Scald milk; add salt, 1/4 cup sugar and butter; add 1/2 of the flour. Stir in eggs and yeast; mix well. Add remaining flour. Let rise until doubled in bulk; punch down. Let rise again. Shape into walnut-sized balls; roll balls in melted butter. Combine remaining sugar, nuts and cinnamon; roll balls in sugar

mixture. Place in angel food pan. Let rise again. Bake in 350-degree oven for 45 minutes. Let cool slightly, then invert onto plate.

Leora Walton, I.C. News Bulletin Chm.
Alpha Beta No. 219
Davenport, Iowa

NUMBER ONE COFFEE CAKE

    1 box light brown sugar
    1/2 c. butter
    1 egg
    1 c. buttermilk
    2 c. flour
    1 tsp. soda
    1/4 tsp. salt
    1 tsp. vanilla extract
    1 c. chopped pecans

Cream brown sugar and butter. Remove 1 cup; reserve for topping. Add egg, buttermilk, flour, soda, salt and vanilla to remaining brown sugar mixture. Beat for 2 minutes. Pour into 2 greased 9-inch cake pans; crumble reserved topping over batter. Sprinkle pecans over top. Bake at 350 degrees for 35 minutes.

Glenda McCoy
Beta Phi No. 3212
Rockville, Indiana

RAISIN COFFEE CAKE

    2 c. sugar
    3/4 c. shortening
    3 c. flour
    1/2 tsp. nutmeg
    1/2 tsp. cinnamon
    1/2 c. raisins
    1/2 c. chopped nuts (opt.)
    2 c. buttermilk
    2 tsp. soda

Cream sugar and shortening together; add flour, nutmeg and cinnamon. Mix well. Reserve 1/2 cup mixture for topping. Add remaining ingredients to remaining flour mixture; mix well. Spoon into greased 9 x 15-inch pan. Sprinkle reserved topping over batter. Bake at 350 degrees for 45 minutes.

Jennie Rose Reeves, Past State Pres.
Alpha Phi Golden No. 327
Lakewood, Colorado

SOUR CREAM YEAST DOUGH

4 1/4 to 4 3/4 c. all-purpose flour
1/3 c. sugar
2 tsp. salt
2 pkg. dry yeast
1/2 c. butter
1 c. sour cream
2 eggs
1 tbsp. grated lemon peel
1 tbsp. grated orange peel

Mix 1 1/2 cups flour, sugar, salt and dry yeast thoroughly in large mixer bowl. Combine 1/2 cup water, butter and sour cream. Heat until very warm. Mixture will have a separated appearance. Add to dry ingredients gradually. Beat for 2 minutes at medium speed, scraping side of bowl occasionally. Add eggs, lemon and orange peels and 1/2 cup flour. Beat at high speed for 2 minutes, scraping side of bowl occasionally. Stir in enough additional flour to make a soft dough. Turn dough out onto lightly floured surface; knead for about 5 minutes or until smooth and elastic. Place in buttered bowl, turning to butter top. Cover; let rise in warm place for about 1 hour or until doubled in bulk. Punch dough down; turn out onto lightly floured surface. Divide dough in half. Prepare Schnecken from half the dough and Orange Crown from other half.

Schnecken

Butter
1/2 c. (firmly packed) brown sugar
Pecan halves
Red candied cherries
1/2 recipe Sour Cream Yeast Dough
1/4 c. sugar
2 tsp. cinnamon
1/4 c. raisins

Heat 1/2 cup butter and brown sugar together until butter is melted and ingredients are well blended. Spoon about 2 teaspoons butter mixture into each of 18 well-buttered muffin cups. Place 2 or 3 pecan halves and 1 cherry over butter mixture. Roll out dough to form a 13 1/2 x 9-inch rectangle; spread with 2 tablespoons butter. Combine sugar and cinnamon; sprinkle over rectangle. Sprinkle with raisins. Roll up, beginning at wide side. Pinch edge of dough to seal well.

Cut into 18 slices. Press 1 slice in each muffin cup over pecans. Cover; let rise for about 30 minutes or until doubled in bulk. Bake in preheated 375-degree oven for 20 to 25 minutes. Turn out immediately onto large tray, leaving pan over rolls for about 1 minute for caramel topping to drizzle over rolls.

Orange Crown

1/2 c. sugar
2 tbsp. grated orange peel
2 tbsp. orange juice
4 tbsp. butter
1/2 recipe Sour Cream Yeast Dough

Combine 1/4 cup sugar, 1 tablespoon orange peel, orange juice and 2 tablespoons butter in saucepan. Boil for 2 minutes. Cool. Pour into well-buttered 9-inch fluted tube pan or ring mold. Shape dough to form 1 1/2-inch balls. Melt remaining 2 tablespoons butter; combine remaining sugar and remaining orange peel. Dip balls into melted butter, then into sugar mixture. Arrange balls in 2 layers in prepared pan. Cover; let rise for about 30 minutes or until doubled in bulk. Bake in preheated 350-degree oven for 35 to 40 minutes. Turn out immediately onto large tray, leaving pan over cake for about 1 minute for glaze to drizzle over cake.

Photograph for this recipe on page 4.

PEACH KUCHEN

2 c. sifted flour
1/2 tsp. baking powder
1/2 tsp. salt
1 c. sugar
1/2 c. butter or margarine
12 fresh or canned peach halves
1 tsp. cinnamon
2 egg yolks, slightly beaten
1 c. heavy cream or sour cream

Sift flour, baking powder, salt and 2 tablespoons sugar together in mixing bowl. Cut in butter with 2 knives or pastry blender until mixture resembles coarse cornmeal. Pat an even layer of crumbly pastry over bottom and halfway up sides of 8-inch square baking pan, pressing firmly with hands. Arrange peaches over bottom pastry; sprinkle with mixture of remaining sugar and cinnamon.

Bake in preheated 400-degree oven for 15 minutes. Combine egg yolks and cream; pour over top. Bake for 30 minutes longer. Serve warm or cold. Yield: 6 servings.

Lois Mathias
Alpha Phi No. 1261
Rochester, Indiana

BAKED PANCAKE

1/4 c. butter
3 eggs
3/4 c. milk
3/4 c. flour

Place butter in round cake pan. Place pan in 425-degree oven. Mix batter quickly while butter melts. Place eggs in blender container; process at high speed for 1 minute. Pour in milk gradually, while blender is running; add flour slowly. Continue processing for 30 seconds. Remove pan from oven; pour batter into hot melted butter. Return to oven. Bake for 20 to 25 minutes or until puffy and well browned. Serve at once with desired topping.

Elizabeth Dyer, Sec.
Beta Phi No. 2199
Kennewick, Washington

HOT CROSS BUNS FOR EASTER

1 pkg. dry yeast
1 c. milk, scalded
1/4 c. sugar
1 1/2 tsp. salt
1/2 tsp. cinnamon
3/4 c. raisins
2 eggs, well beaten
4 c. sifted flour
1/2 c. melted butter
Powdered sugar frosting

Soften yeast in 2 tablespoons warm water. Combine next 5 ingredients; cool to lukewarm. Add yeast mixture and eggs. Add 2 cups flour; mix well. Add butter; beat well. Add remaining 2 cups flour gradually; mix but do not knead. Place in greased bowl; turn to grease top. Cover; chill until firm enough to handle. Divide dough into 18 to 20 portions; shape into buns. Let rise until doubled in bulk. Place on greased cookie sheet. Bake at 400 degrees for 10 to 15 minutes. Form a cross on each bun with powdered sugar frosting.

Dianne G. Metzinger
Kappa Nu No. 4415
Newton, Kansas

HALLOWEEN WITCHCRAFT DOUGHNUTS

4 c. Bisquick
1/2 c. sugar
2/3 c. milk
2 tsp. vanilla extract
2 eggs
1 to 2 tbsp. grated orange rind

Combine all ingredients; beat vigorously for 25 to 30 strokes. Turn dough onto floured surface; knead for about 10 times. Roll out 3/8 inch thick. Cut with floured doughnut cutter. Fry in deep fat at 375 degrees for 1 to 2 minutes on each side or until golden brown. Remove from fat; drain on absorbent paper. Glaze with thin chocolate icing, if desired. Yield: 24 doughnuts.

Beverly Barnes
Beta Psi No. 3520
Evansville, Indiana

FANCY BLUEBERRY MUFFINS

2 c. flour
3 tsp. baking powder
1 tsp. salt
1/3 c. instant dry milk
1 1/4 c. sugar
1/3 c. salad oil
1 c. orange juice
2 eggs, beaten
1 c. blueberries

Combine flour, baking powder, salt, milk and 1 cup sugar; blend in oil, orange juice and eggs. Do not stir more than 30 strokes. Fold in blueberries carefully. Pour into greased muffin pans or cupcake liners. Bake in preheated 350-degree oven for remaining 25 minutes. Cool slightly; sprinkle 1/4 cup sugar over top of muffins. Batter will keep for 2 to 3 days in an airright container in refrigerator. Yield: 18 muffins.

Martha Brough, Pres.
Delta Tau No. 4264
Yakima, Washington

APRICOT SURPRISE BREAD

6 oz. cream cheese, softened
1/3 c. sugar
1 tbsp. flour
2 eggs
1 tsp. grated orange peel
1/2 c. orange juice
1   17-oz. package quick apricot nut
*   bread mix*

Combine cream cheese, sugar and flour. Beat in 1 egg and orange peel. Set aside. Combine remaining slightly beaten egg, orange juice and 1/2 cup water. Add bread mix, stirring only until moistened. Turn 2/3 of the batter mixture into greased and floured 9 x 5 x 3-inch loaf pan. Pour cream cheese mixture over top; spoon on remaining batter. Bake in preheated 350-degree oven for 1 hour. Cool for 10 minutes; remove from pan. Cool completely. Wrap in foil; refrigerate until ready to serve.

Lorna Jost, Pres.
Beta Alpha No. 2322
Norwalk, California

COCONUT-PUMPKIN BREAD

1 1/3 c. oil
5 eggs
2 c. pumpkin
2 c. flour
1 tsp. salt
2 c. sugar
1 tsp. cinnamon
1 tsp. nutmeg
1 tsp. soda
2   3-oz. packages coconut pudding
*   and pie filling mix*
1 c. chopped walnuts (opt.)

Beat oil, eggs and pumpkin together. Sift next 6 ingredients together; stir in pudding mix and walnuts. Add to pumpkin mixture; mix until well moistened. Place batter in well-greased 8 1/2 x 4 1/2-inch loaf pans. Bake in preheated 350-degree oven for 1 hour or until bread tests done.

Suzan Atkin, Treas.
Alpha Delta No. 1711
Milford, Utah

CRANBERRY CHRISTMAS BREAD

2 c. flour
1 c. sugar
1/2 tsp. salt
1 1/2 tsp. baking powder
1/2 tsp. soda
1/2 c. orange juice
2 tbsp. butter
Grated rind of 1 orange
1 egg, well beaten
1 c. cranberries, halved
1/2 c. chopped nuts

Sift dry ingredients together; add remaining ingredients except cranberries and nuts. Mix well. Stir in cranberries and nuts; pour into greased loaf pan. Bake at 350 degrees for 1 hour.

Bonnie Resteiner
Delta Omega No. 4369
Alamosa, Colorado

LUCIA BRAID

5 to 5 1/3 c. all-purpose flour
2 pkg. dry yeast
1/2 c. sugar
1 1/2 tsp. salt
1 1/3 c. milk
1/2 c. butter
Pinch of saffron
3 eggs
1/4 tsp. almond extract
1/2 c. chopped blanched almonds
4 tsp. grated lemon peel
Whole blanched almonds
Sugar cubes, crushed

Combine 2 cups flour, yeast, sugar and salt in a large mixing bowl. Combine milk, butter and saffron in a 1-quart saucepan; heat until warm. Add gradually to flour. Beat for 2 minutes at medium speed, scraping bowl occasionally. Add 1 cup flour, 2 eggs and almond extract; beat for 2 minutes at high speed, scraping bowl occasionally. Stir in chopped almonds and lemon peel. Stir in enough remaining flour to make a soft dough. Turn onto lightly floured surface. Knead for 8 to 10 minnutes or until smooth and satiny. Place in buttered bowl, turning once to butter top. Cover bowl. Let rise on a rack over hot water for 1 hour to 1 hour and 30 minutes or until doubled in bulk. Punch down; let rest for 10 minutes. Divide dough into 3 parts. Use 2 parts for base of 2 breads. Set aside remaining dough to be used for braids. Roll each base portion into 7-inch circle. Place on buttered baking sheet. Divide remaining dough into 6 parts for braids. Roll each piece into 20-inch strand with hands. Braid 3 strands together. Place a braid on each dough base, forming circle. Secure ends by pinching dough together. Insert whole almonds into braid. Cover; let rise over warm water for 45 to 60 minutes or until doubled in bulk. Beat remaining egg and 1 tablespoon water; brush on dough. Sprinkle with crushed sugar. Bake in preheated 350-degree oven for 25 to 30 minutes. Remove to wire rack to cool. Place four 3-inch red candles in candle holders; insert in braid. Light candles just before serving. Yellow food coloring may be substituted for saffron. Yield: 2 loaves.

Photograph for this recipe on page 112.

DATE NUT TIFFIN LOAF

3/4 c. sifted flour
1/8 tsp. salt
3/4 c. sugar
1/2 tsp. baking powder
1/2 lb. pitted dates, quartered
2 c. chopped walnuts
2 eggs, separated
1/2 tsp. vanilla extract
Melted butter

Sift dry ingredients together; add dates and walnuts. Mix with fingers until dates and walnuts are coated. Add beaten egg yolks and vanilla; blend with fingers. Fold in stiffly beaten egg whites. Brush 9 x 5 x 3-inch loaf pan with butter; sprinkle lightly with additional flour. Spoon stiff batter in pan, spreading evenly. Cover pan with foil. Bake at 275 degrees for 1 hour and 45 minutes. Remove foil. Increase temperature to 325 degrees. Bake for 10 to 15 minutes longer or until top is brown. Cool in pan for 5 minutes. Turn out on rack; cool completely. Wrap in waxed paper or foil. This keeps well. May substitute figs for dates and 1 cup candied fruit for 1 cup walnuts, if desired.

Fran Ashley, V.P.
Alpha Lambda No. 3592
Arlington, Virginia

DELICIOUS DATE NUT LOAF

4 eggs
1 c. sugar
1 c. flour
2 tsp. baking powder
Pinch of salt
1 lb. whole pitted dates
1 lb. English walnut halves
1/2 c. Bourbon

Beat eggs until light and lemon colored; add sugar. Beat until sugar is dissolved. Add flour, baking powder and salt; mix until well blended. Add dates and walnuts. Stir until well mixed. Add Bourbon; mix thoroughly. Batter will be thick. Grease loaf pan; line with brown paper and grease again. Spoon batter into pan. Bake at 325 degrees for 1 hour.

Thelma Waggoner
State Coun. Jr. Past Pres.
Alpha Delta No. 1138
Hopkinsville, Kentucky

HOLIDAY BANANA BREAD

4 c. flour
2 tsp. soda
2 c. sugar
2 eggs
1 c. shortening, softened
6 ripe bananas, mashed
2 tsp. vanilla extract
1 c. chopped dates
1 c. chopped red and green maraschino
* cherries*
1 c. chopped nuts

Sift flour, soda and sugar together; add eggs, shortening and bananas. Mix until smooth. Stir in vanilla, dates, cherries and nuts. Turn into 2 or 3 large loaf pans. Bake at 375 degrees until bread tests done.

Doris Sutherland
Beta Tau No. 472
Grand Junction, Colorado

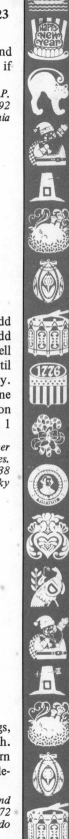

FRUITED LEMON LOAF

1 lb. margarine
1 lb. brown sugar
6 eggs
1 2-oz. bottle pure lemon extract
4 c. sifted flour
1 1/2 c. chopped pecans
1 8-oz. package candied cherries,
    chopped
1 8-oz. package candied
    pineapple, diced

Combine margarine and brown sugar; let stand overnight. Beat in eggs, one at a time, until well mixed. Add lemon extract. Combine flour, pecans and candied fruits; add to egg mixture, a small amount at a time, blending well after each addition. Turn into 5 small loaf pans. Bake at 275 degrees for 1 hour and 30 minutes.

Dorothy Boyd, Treas.
Zeta Lambda No. 2395
Salina, Kansas

PEACHY PECAN BREAD

1 16-oz. can sliced peaches
6 tbsp. butter
2 eggs
1 tbsp. lemon juice
2 c. all-purpose flour
3/4 c. sugar
3 tsp. baking powder
1 tsp. salt
3/4 c. chopped pecans
2 tbsp. peach preserves

Drain peaches, reserving 1/4 cup syrup. Chop 1 cup peaches fine; set aside. Combine remaining peaches, butter, eggs, reserved peach syrup and lemon juice in blender container; cover. Blend just until smooth. Stir dry ingredients together; add egg mixture. Stir just until moistened. Fold in reserved peaches and pecans. Turn into greased 8 x 4 x 2-inch loaf pan. Bake at 350 degrees for 45 to 60 minutes. Spread with peach preserves. Cool in pan for 10 minutes; remove from pan. Cool on rack.

Bev Reinecker
Kappa Tau No. 4527
Burlington, Colorado

POPPY SEED BREAD

3 eggs
2 1/4 c. sugar
1 1/2 c. cooking oil
1 1/2 tsp. salt
1 1/2 tsp. baking powder
1 1/2 tsp. poppy seed
3 c. flour
1 1/2 c. milk
1 1/2 tsp. almond flavoring
1 1/2 tsp. butter flavoring
1 1/2 tsp. vanilla extract

Cream eggs and sugar until light; add oil. Beat well. Combine salt, baking powder, poppy seed and flour; add to creamed mixture alternately with milk, beating well after each addition. Add flavorings; mix well. Pour batter into 2 greased and floured loaf pans. Bake at 350 degrees for 1 hour or until done.

Corinne Schur, Historian
Beta Xi No. 4649
Minneapolis, Kansas

HOLIDAY CRANBERRY-CHEESE BREAD

2 c. all-purpose flour
1 c. sugar
1 1/2 tsp. baking powder
1/2 tsp. salt
1/2 tsp. soda
2 tsp. grated orange peel
2 tbsp. shortening
Juice of 1 orange
1 1/2 c. shredded Cheddar cheese
1 egg, beaten
1 c. cranberries, halved
1/2 c. finely chopped walnuts

Combine flour, sugar, baking powder, salt, soda and orange peel in bowl; cut in shortening. Add enough water to orange juice to measure 3/4 cup; mix with cheese and egg. Stir into flour mixture until just moistened. Blend in cranberries and walnuts. Pour into greased 9 x 5-inch loaf pan. Bake in preheated 350-degree oven for 1 hour to 1 hour and 10 minutes or until wooden pick inserted in center comes out clean. Remove from pan; let stand for 8 hours before serving.

Sandi Smith, Charter Pres.
Omega Theta Chap.
El Paso, Texas

SOUTHERN CRANBERRY NUT BREAD

Flour
1 c. sugar
1 1/2 tsp. baking powder
1 tsp. salt
1/2 tsp. soda
1/4 c. shortening
1 egg, beaten
3/4 c. orange juice
1 tbsp. grated orange rind
1 c. coarsely chopped cranberries
1/4 c. chopped pecans

Sift 2 cups sifted flour, sugar, baking powder, salt and soda together in bowl. Cut in shortening until mixture resembles coarse cornmeal. Combine egg, orange juice and orange rind in small bowl; add to dry ingredients all at once. Stir just until moistened. Combine cranberries, pecans and 1 tablespoon flour; stir into batter. Pour into greased and waxed paper-lined loaf pan. Bake in 350-degree oven for 1 hour or until bread tests done. Cool for 10 minutes; remove from pan. Cool completely.

Wanda L. Sturgill, V.P.
Alpha Chi No. 3268
Lexington, Kentucky

ALL-SOULS BREAD

5 1/2 to 6 1/2 c. unsifted flour
1/2 c. sugar
1/2 tsp. salt
2 pkg. Fleischmann's dry yeast
1/2 c. milk
2/3 c. Fleischmann's margarine
4 eggs at room temperature
1 tsp. anise extract
1 tsp. orange extract
1 egg, beaten

Mix 1 cup flour, sugar, salt and dry yeast in a large bowl thoroughly. Combine milk, 1/2 cup water and margarine in a saucepan. Heat over low heat until liquids are warm. Margarine does not need to melt. Add to dry ingredients gradually; beat for 2 minutes at medium speed of electric mixer, scraping bowl occasionally. Add eggs, anise and orange extracts and 1 cup flour or enough flour to make a thick batter. Beat at high speed for 2 minutes, scraping bowl occasionally. Add enough additional flour to make a soft dough. Cover; let rise in warm place for about 1 hour or until doubled in bulk. Stir down. Turn out onto lightly floured board. Divide in half. Shape each piece into a ball, reserving about 1/4 cup dough from each piece for trim. Place balls in 2 well-greased 8-inch round cake pans. Form four 3-inch bone shapes, four 1 1/2-inch tears and 1 round ball, about 1 inch in diameter, from each piece of reserved dough. Place ball in top center of dough. Arrange tears and bones around side. Cover; let rise in warm place for about 1 hour or until doubled in bulk. Brush lightly with beaten egg, keeping egg from dripping onto sides of cake pan. Sprinkle with additional sugar. Bake in preheated 375-degree oven on lowest rack position for about 25 to 30 minutes or until done. Remove from baking pans; cool on wire racks.

Photograph for this recipe below.

SCOTTISH BREAD

1 lg. box raisins
1/2 c. margarine
2 tsp. soda
4 c. flour
1/2 tsp. salt
2 c. sugar
1 tsp. cinnamon
2 eggs, beaten
1 c. diced maraschino cherries
1 c. chopped nuts

Combine first 3 ingredients in airtight container; pour 2 cups hot water over mixture. Cover. Let soak overnight. Combine remaining ingredients in large mixing bowl; fold in raisin mixture. Grease and flour four 1-pound coffee cans or 6 large soup cans. Fill cans only 1/2 full with batter. Bake at 325 degrees for 1 hour. Remove from cans; cool. Drizzle confectioners' sugar frosting over top, if desired.

Valerie Priebe
State Jr. Past Pres.
Beta Omicron No. 2997
Madison, Wisconsin

SPRINGTIME COFFEE RHUBARB BREAD

1 1/2 c. (packed) brown sugar
2/3 c. cooking oil
1 c. sour milk or buttermilk
1 egg
1 tsp. vanilla extract
2 1/2 c. flour
1 tsp. soda
1 1/2 c. diced rhubarb
1/2 c. chopped walnuts
1/2 c. sugar
1 tsp. cinnamon
1 tbsp. melted butter

Combine first 9 ingredients; mix until well combined. Turn into 3 greased and floured loaf pans. Combine sugar, cinnamon and butter; sprinkle over top. Bake at 350 degrees for 45 minutes.

Cynthia Derrig, Treas.
Alpha Theta No. 1616
Fargo, North Dakota

TOMATO BREAD

1 1/3 c. milk
2/3 c. Grape Nuts
2 1/4 c. flour
3/4 c. sugar
3 tsp. baking powder
1 1/2 tsp. salt
1/4 c. soft shortening, melted
2 eggs, well beaten
1 c. chopped tomato

Heat milk in small saucepan until bubbles form around edge. Remove from heat. Pour warm milk over Grape Nuts. Sift flour with sugar, baking powder and salt in large bowl. Stir shortening, eggs and tomato into Grape Nuts. Add to flour mixture; stir until all ingredients are moistened. Turn batter into greased 9 x 5 x 3-inch loaf pan. Bake in preheated 375-degree oven for 1 hour or until done. Cool. Wrap in waxed paper. Refrigerate overnight.

Catherine Garst
Beta Zeta No. 2556
Madison, Wisconsin

NEVER-FAIL CAN BREAD

1 1/2 c. raisins
2 tbsp. butter
1 tsp. vanilla extract
1 tsp. soda
1 c. sugar
1 egg
2 c. flour
1/2 c. chopped walnuts

Pour 1 cup boiling water over raisins; add butter. Let stand until cool. Add remaining ingredients; mix until well blended. Spoon into 3 greased number 303 cans. Bake at 350 degrees for 1 hour.

Lola L. Bridge, Sec.
Alpha Delta No. 1711
Milford, Utah

ZUCCHINI BREAD

3 eggs, well beaten
1 c. cooking oil
2 c. sugar

3 tsp. vanilla extract
2 c. grated zucchini
3 1/2 c. flour
1 tsp. salt
1 tbsp. soda
1/4 tsp. baking powder
1 tsp. cinnamon
3/4 tsp. nutmeg
1/2 c. chopped nuts

Beat eggs until light; add oil, sugar, vanilla and zucchini. Mix lightly. Add flour, salt, soda, baking powder, cinnamon, nutmeg and nuts. Mix until well combined. Spoon batter into greased and waxed paper-lined loaf pan. Bake at 350 degrees for 1 hour or until done.

Darlene Wallace, Past State Pres.
Theta Zeta No. 2781
Meeker, Colorado

SAINT TIMOTHY'S COFFEE CAKE

1 c. butter
2 c. sugar
1/2 tsp. vanilla extract
2 eggs
2 c. flour
1 tsp. baking powder
1 tsp. cinnamon
1/4 tsp. salt
1 c. chopped nuts
1/2 c. golden raisins
1 c. sour cream
Cinnamon sugar

Cream butter until fluffy; add sugar gradually, beating constantly. Blend in vanilla. Add eggs, one at a time, beating well after each addition. Combine next 6 ingredients; add to butter mixture alternately with sour cream. Mix until well blended. Turn into greased and floured bundt pan; sprinkle top with cinnamon sugar. Bake at 350 degrees for 1 hour. Cool for at least 1 hour before turning out. Sprinkle top again with cinnamon sugar.

Ruth Cummings, Rec. Sec.
Alpha Phi No. 327
Denver, Colorado

CHRISTMAS TREE COFFEE CAKES

4 1/2 to 5 c. all-purpose flour
1/2 c. sugar
1 tsp. salt
2 pkg. dry yeast
1 c. milk
1/2 c. butter
2 eggs
2 tbsp. grated lemon peel
1 tsp. crushed cardamom seed
1/2 c. chopped mixed candied fruits
1/2 c. golden raisins
Eggnog Glaze

Mix 2 cups flour, sugar, salt and dry yeast thoroughly in large mixer bowl. Combine milk and butter. Heat until very warm. Add to dry ingredients gradually; beat for 2 minutes at medium speed, scraping sides of bowl occasionally. Add eggs, lemon peel, cardamom and 1/2 cup flour. Beat at high speed for 2 minutes, scraping sides of bowl occasionally. Stir in enough additional flour to make a soft dough. Turn out onto lightly floured surface; knead for about 5 minutes or until smooth and elastic. Place in buttered bowl, turning to butter top. Cover; let rise in warm place for about 1 hour or until doubled in bulk. Punch dough down; turn out onto lightly floured surface. Knead in fruits and raisins. Divide dough in half. Divide each half into 4 pieces; shape each to form an 18-inch rope. Shape ropes together on a buttered cookie sheet to form a tree by looping dough back and forth in a figure 8 pattern. Pinch ends together. Use a small ball of dough for trunk. Let rise in warm place for about 30 minutes or until doubled in bulk. Bake in preheated 350-degree oven for 25 to 30 minutes. Drizzle with Eggnog Glaze; decorate with candied cherries and pineapple. Yield: 2 coffee cakes.

Eggnog Glaze

1 c. sifted confectioners' sugar
2 tbsp. eggnog

Combine sugar and eggnog; blend well.

Photograph for this recipe on page 4.

Desserts

Desserts can turn an ordinary day into a special day, and add the crowning touch to a gala holiday celebration. In fact, desserts are the cook's own personal holiday because they offer such an opportunity for creating dishes with color, excitement and fun. There is no holiday that can not have its own particular dessert because the real wonder of favorite confections — cakes, cookies, pies, candies, and other sweets — is that they can be flavored, shaped, tinted, and trimmed to fit the occasion.

Valentine's Day is a perfect holiday for your "love-liest" desserts, such as a heart-shaped white cake tinted to a deep pink and iced with fluffy, white frosting. For a children's Valentine's party, the same cake can be topped with heart-shaped redhots. Then again this same cake recipe can be featured at a romantic dinner for two, placed on a silver cake plate and topped with a single red rose. On St. Patrick's Day, this cake can be shaped like a shamrock and tinted green with Creme de Menthe. More shamrocks shaped from green fondant can serve as a decorative holiday topping. A chocolate, apple or gingerbread cake can be decorated with candy corn for Halloween and served on a plate covered with bright fall leaves. Of course, any flavor of cake can be used for any holiday; it's the choice of decoration and trimming that makes it the center of attraction. The same is true for your favorite cookies, which can be shaped, iced with gay colors, or decorated with sugar sprinkles to reflect the holiday theme just as you wish.

There are some holidays, The Fourth of July for example, that open up a world of creative ideas for desserts. An ordinary cheesecake or cream pie recipe can be turned into a red, white, and blue specialty with a topping of cherries or strawberries, blueberries and whipped cream for a dessert the troops will call for year after year. A patriotic parfait is another idea, or you can use green and white layers for St. Patrick's Day. For George Washington's Birthday, make chocolate-covered cherries, cherry cobbler, cherry cookies or a cherry pie. Children of all ages look forward to the celebration of their birthday — the presents, the attention, the singing all work together to make it a happy occasion. But, in their heart of hearts, it's the cake that is baked in their honor that really makes the day. For that reason, a birthday cake should be prepared and decorated with extra care for a truly memorable effect on the honoree. Choose their favorite flavor then write their name and the birth date on the top in their favorite color with piped icing — be sure to include birthday candles, because no one ever outgrows making wishes!

The unmistakable aroma of sweets being prepared in the kitchen spells HOLIDAY. The shared preparation of holiday cakes, cookies, pies, and candies has become a tradition in many homes because it is the rewarding blend of togetherness, cooperation, and fun. Another holiday plus for homemade desserts and confections is that they make excellent gifts — the perfect way to share holiday cheer with friends and family members everywhere. Everyone loves to receive packages in the mail, especially when the box contains a kaliedoscope of homemade goodies from a loved one. Moreover, many desserts can be frozen, either before or after cooking, then thawed when needed. This can be a real timesaver for the busy homemaker during the holidays.

ESA families love holiday desserts, anyday — and so will your family. It is not just the personal touch that makes your desserts so flavorful, but also the fact that they are made with fresh and wholesome ingredients. In fact, desserts in the menu plan provide endless ways to use eggs, dairy products, fresh fruits, and nuts in the family's diet. As most every cook has surely discovered, diners always look forward to a tantalizing dessert, even when it's not a holiday. On the following pages you will find some of the best recipes for favorite holiday desserts, and you can be sure that from now on, you will use every opportunity to serve these favorites as often as possible.

CARAMEL ICING

1 c. (packed) brown sugar
1/3 c. butter
1/4 c. milk
1 c. powdered sugar
1/2 c. chopped nuts

Combine first 3 ingredients in saucepan; bring to a boil. Boil for 1 minute. Add powdered sugar and nuts. Ice cake as desired.

Thelma Taylor, Pres.
Beta Rho No. 730
Muncie, Indiana

CREME KUCHEN

1/3 c. cornstarch
1/4 c. flour
1 1/2 tsp. baking powder
Dash of salt
1/4 c. margarine
1/2 c. sugar
2 eggs, separated
1/2 tsp. vanilla extract
1/2 tsp. grated lemon rind
Creme Patisserie
Pastel Kuchen Frosting
Chocolate Glaze

Sift cornstarch, flour, baking powder and salt together; set aside. Beat margarine and sugar together in large bowl until well mixed. Add egg yolks, one at a time, beating well after each addition. Stir in vanilla and lemon rind. Add flour mixture about 1/3 at a time, beating well after each addition. Beat egg whites until stiff peaks form; fold batter gently into egg whites. Turn batter into 12 greased and lightly floured 2 1/2-inch muffin cups, filling about 1/4 full. Bake in 375-degree oven for 15 minutes or until golden and cake springs back when touched. Loosen edges with spatula; cool on wire rack. Slice off 1/2 inch from top of each cupcake, using a sharp knife; reserve caps. Hollow out centers of cupcakes, leaving a 3/8-inch shell. Reserve crumbs for future use. Fill each hollow with about 2 tablespoons Creme Patisserie; replace caps. Chill for at least 1 hour. Turn filled cupcakes upside down on racks placed on cookie sheets. Spread sides of 4 cupcakes with Pastel Kuchen Frosting. Pour remaining frosting over tops. Spread sides of remaining 8 cupcakes with warm Chocolate Glaze; pour remaining glaze over tops. Sprinkle chocolate-glazed cupcakes with chopped pistachios or let glaze set and decorate with icing from decorator tubes following manufacturer's instructions, if desired. Chill in refrigerator until serving time.

Creme Patisserie

1/4 c. sugar
1 1/2 tbsp. cornstarch
1/4 tsp. salt
1 c. milk
1 egg, well beaten
1 tsp. vanilla extract
1/4 c. whipping cream, whipped

Combine sugar, cornstarch and salt in small heavy saucepan. Stir in milk gradually until smooth. Cook over medium heat until mixture comes to boil, stirring constantly; boil for 1 minute. Remove from heat. Stir about half the hot mixture gradually into well-beaten egg until blended; stir egg mixture into hot mixture in saucepan. Heat for 1 to 2 minutes, stirring constantly; do not boil. Remove from heat; stir in vanilla. Chill. Fold whipped cream into chilled custard mixture.

Pastel Kuchen Frosting

2 tbsp. margarine
2 tbsp. light corn syrup
1 c. confectioners' sugar
2 drops of almond extract
1 drop of yellow food coloring

Combine margarine and syrup in small bowl; stir in confectioners' sugar. Add 1 tablespoon water, almond extract and yellow food coloring; stir until mixture is smooth.

Chocolate Glaze

1 6-oz. package semisweet chocolate
*   pieces*
1/4 c. light corn syrup
1 tbsp. vanilla extract

Combine chocolate pieces, syrup and vanilla in small saucepan. Cook over low heat, stirring constantly, until chocolate is melted. Cook for 3 minutes or until smooth, stirring occasionally. Use warm.

Photograph for this recipe on page 136.

BUTTERMILK CHOCOLATE CAKE

2 c. flour
2 c. sugar
1/2 tsp. salt
1 tsp. soda
1/4 c. cocoa
1 c. margarine
1 c. buttermilk
2 eggs, beaten
1 tsp. vanilla extract

Combine flour, sugar, salt and soda; set aside. Combine cocoa, margarine and 1 cup water in saucepan; bring to a boil. Pour over flour mixture immediately; mix well. Stir in buttermilk, eggs and vanilla. Turn into 9 x 13-inch pan. Bake at 350 degrees for 35 minutes.

Cocoa Frosting

1/2 c. cocoa
6 tbsp. milk
1/2 c. margarine
1 box powdered sugar
1 tsp. vanilla extract

Combine cocoa, milk and margarine; bring to a boil. Add powdered sugar and vanilla. Mix until smooth. Frost warm cake.

Nancy Kite, Ed. Dir.
Beta Tau No. 472
Grand Junction, Colorado

CHOCOLATE CHIP-OATMEAL CAKE

1 c. oatmeal
1 c. (lightly packed) brown sugar
1 c. sugar
1/2 c. margarine
2 lg. eggs, beaten
1 3/4 c. flour
1 tsp. soda
1 tsp. salt
1 tbsp. cocoa
1 pkg. semisweet chocolate chips
1 c. chopped walnuts

Pour 1 3/4 cups boiling water over oatmeal; let stand at room temperature for 10 minutes. Add sugar and margarine; stir until margarine melts. Add eggs; mix well. Sift flour, soda, salt and cocoa together. Add to oatmeal mixture; mix well. Stir in about half the chocolate chips and half the walnuts; pour into 11 x 13-inch pan or tube pan. Sprinkle remaining chocolate chips and walnuts on top. Bake at 350 degrees for 40 minutes or until cake tests done.

LaVera Boedeker, Pres.
Beta Alpha No. 4068
Dubois, Wyoming

RED CHRISTMAS CAKE

1/2 c. shortening
1 1/2 c. sugar
2 eggs
1 c. buttermilk
1 1/2 oz. red food coloring
2 tbsp. cocoa
1 tsp. (scant) salt
1 tsp. soda
2 1/2 c. cake flour

Cream shortening and sugar together; add eggs and buttermilk. Mix until blended. Combine food coloring and cocoa; add to creamed mixture. Sift salt, soda and flour together; fold into creamed mixture until well blended. Turn into 2 layer cake pans. Bake at 350 degrees for 30 to 35 minutes. Cool; remove from pans.

Special Christmas Frosting

3 tbsp. flour
1 c. sugar
1/2 c. butter
1 tsp. vanilla extract

Place flour in saucepan; add 1 cup water gradually to make smooth paste. Cook until thickened. Cool for 2 hours. Cream sugar, butter and vanilla together until fluffy; add flour mixture. Beat with electric beater until light and fluffy. Fill and frost cake.

Arlene Wedebrook, Past State Pres.
Gamma Beta No. 3939
Dayton, Ohio

CHRISTMAS PECAN CAKE

2 c. butter
2 c. sugar

6 eggs
1 tbsp. lemon juice
1 tsp. grated lemon rind
1 tbsp. vanilla extract
4 c. chopped pecans
1 1/2 c. golden raisins
3 c. all-purpose flour
1/2 tsp. salt
1 tsp. baking powder

Cream butter and sugar together until fluffy. Add eggs, one at a time, beating well after each addition. Add lemon juice, rind and vanilla; mix well. Combine pecans and raisins with 1/4 cup flour. Sift remaining flour, salt and baking powder together. Fold into creamed mixture alternately with pecan mixture. Spoon into greased and waxed paper-lined 10-inch tube pan. Bake at 300 degrees for about 1 hour and 50 minutes or until done. Let cool; remove from pan. A syrup made of 1/4 cup orange juice, 1/4 cup lemon juice and 1/4 cup sugar may be poured over hot cake, if desired.

Irene Hubbard, Pres.
Alpha Theta No. 1457
Charlotte, North Carolina

CHRISTMAS BRANDY FRUIT NUT CAKE

3 c. chopped walnuts
1 1/2 c. halved maraschino cherries
1 c. light raisins
1/2 c. dark raisins
3/4 c. all-purpose flour
3/4 c. sugar
1/2 tsp. baking powder
1/2 tsp. salt
3 eggs
Apricot Brandy

Combine walnuts and fruits. Sift flour, sugar, baking powder and salt together; add to fruit mixture, tossing to coat well. Beat eggs until frothy; add 2 tablespoons Brandy. Pour egg mixture over fruit mixture; mix well. Pour batter into greased and floured 9 x 5 x 3-inch loaf pan. Bake in 300-degree oven for 1 hour and 45 minutes. Let cool in pan. Moisten several layers of cheesecloth with 1/4 cup Brandy. Wrap cake in cheesecloth, then in foil. Store in refrigerator for 2 or 3 days. Moisten cheesecloth again with

1/4 cup Brandy. Rewrap cake; store in refrigerator until ready to use.

Karen Rebik
Delta Alpha No. 2664
Kissimmee, Florida

HOLIDAY POUND CAKE

2 c. butter, softened
4 c. sifted confectioners' sugar
6 eggs
2 tsp. vanilla extract
1 tsp. almond extract
4 c. sifted cake flour
1/2 tsp. salt
2 c. whipping cream, whipped

Cream butter. Add sugar gradually; beat until well blended. Add eggs, one at a time, beating well after each addition. Blend in flavorings. Combine flour and salt; add to creamed mixture gradually, beating until thoroughly combined. Spread evenly in buttered and floured 10-inch tube pan; cut through batter with knife. Bake in preheated 350-degree oven for about 1 hour and 10 minutes or until cake tests done. Cool in pan on wire rack for 10 minutes. Remove from pan; let cool completely. Frost cake with whipped cream; chill until ready to serve. Garnish with red and green candied cherries, chopped candied pineapple and pecan halves.

Photograph for this recipe below.

CHRISTMAS PLUM CAKE

2 c. self-rising flour
1 tsp. cloves
1 tsp. cinnamon
1 c. oil
2 c. sugar
3 eggs
2 sm. jars baby food plums

Combine flour, cloves and cinnamon. Combine oil and sugar; beat in eggs. Add to flour mixture, mixing well. Blend in plums. Turn into greased tube or bundt pan. Bake at 350 degrees for 50 minutes to 1 hour.

Jane McCoy, V.P.
Alpha Nu No. 4710
Waynesboro, Virginia

CHRISTMAS REFRIGERATOR FRUITCAKE

1 lb. candied cherries
1 lb. dates
1 lb. candied pineapple slices
1 lb. pecans
3 9-oz. packages vanilla wafers
2 cans sweetened condensed milk

Chop fruit and pecans. Crush wafers; add to fruit mixture. Add milk; mix well. Divide mixture into 4 parts. Shape into rolls; wrap each roll in foil. Store in refrigerator until well chilled. Slice with sharp knife to serve.

Eula Wells
Gamma Omega No. 2910
North Vernon, Indiana

DELICIOUS CHRISTMAS FRUITCAKE

2 c. sifted flour
1 1/2 c. sugar
1 1/2 tsp. soda
1 1/2 tsp. salt
1/2 tsp. cloves
1/2 tsp. cinnamon
1/2 tsp. nutmeg
1/2 tsp. allspice
1/2 c. Wesson oil
1 1/2 c. applesauce

2 eggs
3/4 c. finely cut dates
3/4 c. finely cut raisins
1/2 c. mixed candied fruit
1 c. chopped walnuts
2 tbsp. brown sugar

Sift first 8 ingredients together into large bowl. Add oil and applesauce; beat at low speed of electric mixer for 2 minutes. Add eggs; beat for 2 minutes longer. Add fruits and 3/4 cup walnuts; mix thoroughly. Pour into greased and floured 9-inch tube pan. Combine remaining walnuts and brown sugar; sprinkle over top of batter. Bake at 350 degrees for 35 minutes.

Marjorie Fuller
State Membership Dir.
Delta Tau No. 4264
Yakima, Washington

GAMMA DELTA FRUITCAKE

1/2 lb. vanilla wafers
3/4 c. evaporated milk
2 eggs, well beaten
1/2 c. sugar
1/4 tsp. cinnamon
1/2 tsp. nutmeg
1/2 tsp. allspice
1/4 tsp. salt
2 c. diced mixed candied fruit
1 c. chopped nuts
2 tbsp. flour

Crush wafers to make fine crumbs; soak in milk. Add eggs, sugar, spices and salt; mix thoroughly with electric mixer. Dredge fruit and nuts in flour; stir into batter. Pour into greased and floured loaf pan. Bake at 325 degrees for 1 hour and 20 minutes. Brush top with additional evaporated milk to glaze; bake for 10 minutes longer or until done.
This is Gamma Delta's annual Ways and Means cake and have standing orders for 300. Recipe dates back to 1936.

Norma Northrop, Pres.
Gamma Delta No. 3615
Topeka, Kansas

Recipe on page 91.

LEMON PECAN FRUITCAKE

1 lb. butter
2 1/2 c. sugar
6 eggs
4 c. sifted flour
2 tsp. baking powder
1/4 tsp. salt
1/4 c. lemon extract
1 lb. pecans, chopped
1 lb. dates, chopped
1/2 lb. candied cherries, cut in half
1/2 lb. candied pineapple, diced

Cream butter and sugar together until light and fluffy. Add eggs, one at a time, beating well after each addition. Sift flour, baking powder and salt together; add to creamed mixture. Stir in flavoring; beat thoroughly. Fold in pecans and fruits. Turn into well-greased foil-lined 10-inch tube pan, distributing evenly. Place pan of water on lower rack of oven. Bake fruitcake at 325 degrees for 2 hours and 30 minutes to 3 hours. Remove from pan; cool on rack. Freeze or store in refrigerator until ready to use.

Jean Merrill
State Coun. Pres.-Elect
Gamma Epsilon No. 2570
Spokane, Washington

OLD-FASHIONED FRUITCAKE

3 c. all-purpose flour
1 1/3 c. sugar
2 tsp. salt
1 tsp. baking powder
2 tsp. cinnamon
1 tsp. nutmeg
1 c. orange juice
1 c. salad oil
4 eggs
1/4 c. dark molasses
1 pkg. raisins
1 pkg. golden raisins
1   8-oz. package dates, pitted and
*   halved*
1 lb. mixed candied fruit
1 2/3 c. chopped nuts

Combine first 10 ingredients in large mixing bowl. Blend at low speed of electric mixer for 30 seconds, scraping bowl constantly. Beat at high speed for 3 minutes. Stir in fruits and nuts. Spread batter evenly into 3 or 4 well-greased and floured small bread pans. Place a small pan of water in bottom of oven for moisture. Bake fruitcakes in preheated 275-degree oven for 2 hours and 30 minutes to 3 hours or until a toothpick inserted in center of cake comes out clean. Cool in pans for 5 minutes; turn out on rack to cool. Can be wrapped in foil and frozen to ripen.

Peggy Herren, Pres.
Alpha Beta No. 734
Lawrenceville, Georgia

FELLOWSHIP CAKE

1 1/2 c. sugar
2 c. sifted flour
2 eggs, beaten
2 tsp. soda
3/4 tsp. salt
2 tsp. lemon flavoring
1 tsp. vanilla extract
1 No. 303 can fruit cocktail
1/2 c. (packed) brown sugar
1/2 c. flaked coconut

Combine first 8 ingredients in bowl; mix by hand until well blended. Pour into 13 x 9-inch baking dish. Combine brown sugar and coconut; sprinkle over top. Bake at 350 degrees for 30 to 40 minutes or until cake tests done.

Coconut Topping

3/4 c. sugar
1 tsp. vanilla extract
1/4 c. evaporated milk
1/2 c. margarine
1/2 c. chopped nuts
1/2 c. coconut

Combine all ingredients in a saucepan; bring to a boil. Pour over hot cake. Cover tightly with foil. Serve warm or cold.

Shirley Smith, Pres.
Iota Alpha No. 2961
Fremont, California

Recipes on pages 130, 156 and 157.

CHANUKAH ORANGE-CARROT CAKE

1 c. pareve polyunsaturated margarine
2 c. sugar
1 tbsp. grated orange rind
1 tsp. cinnamon
1/2 tsp. nutmeg
1 c. cholesterol-free egg substitute
1 1/2 c. grated carrots
2/3 c. finely chopped walnuts
3 c. sifted all-purpose flour
3 tsp. baking powder
1/2 tsp. salt
1/3 c. Florida orange juice
Orange Glaze

Cream margarine and sugar together in large bowl; stir in orange rind, cinnamon and nutmeg. Beat in egg substitute gradually; stir in carrots and walnuts. Sift flour, baking powder and salt together; blend into carrot mixture alternately with orange juice. Turn into greased 10-inch tube pan. Bake in 350-degree oven for 50 minutes to 1 hour or until cake tester inserted in cake comes out clean. Cool in pan for 15 minutes; turn out of pan and let cool completely. Cover top with Orange Glaze; sprinkle with additional chopped walnuts.

Orange Glaze

1 1/2 c. sifted confectioners' sugar
1 tbsp. pareve polyunsaturated margarine
1/2 tsp. grated orange rind
2 to 3 tbsp. Florida orange juice

Beat confectioners' sugar with margarine in small bowl. Add orange rind and enough juice to make a slightly runny glaze; mix well.
A pareve food is a food permissible in the kosher diet.

Photograph for this recipe on this page.

CHRISTMAS FRESH APPLE CAKE

2 c. sugar
1 1/3 c. Crisco oil
2 eggs
1 tsp. salt
1 tsp. soda
1 tsp. cinnamon
1 tsp. vanilla extract
3 c. flour
3 c. diced apples
1 c. chopped pecans

Beat sugar, oil and eggs together. Add salt, soda, cinnamon and vanilla; beat until well mixed. Add flour, 1 cup at a time, mixing well after each addition. Stir in apples and 1/2 of the pecans. Pour batter into greased 9 x 13-inch pan. Sprinkle remaining pecans over top of batter. Bake at 350 degrees for 45 minutes to 1 hour or until cake tests done.

G. G. Grimes, Pres.
Gamma Kappa No. 4595
Phoenix, Arizona

ISLES OF SPICE

1/4 c. shortening
3/4 c. (packed) brown sugar
1/4 tsp. salt
1 egg
1 c. sifted cake flour
1/2 tsp. cloves
1/4 tsp. cinnamon
3/4 tsp. soda
1/2 c. milk
8 tsp. cornstarch
6 tbsp. orange juice

2 tbsp. lemon juice
2 c. fruit cocktail syrup
2 c. fruit cocktail

Cream shortening with brown sugar. Add salt and egg; beat until fluffy. Sift cake flour, cloves, cinnamon and soda together; add to egg mixture alternately with milk, beginning and ending with flour mixture. Fill greased muffin tins 2/3 full. Bake at 375 degrees for about 20 minutes or until done. Dissolve cornstarch in orange juice and lemon juice. Heat fruit cocktail syrup to boiling point. Add cornstarch mixture; cook until thick, stirring constantly. Cook for 5 minutes longer. Add fruit cocktail; serve topping hot or cold. Serve topped with whipped cream, if desired. May top with sugar cubes soaked in lemon extract; ignite cubes and serve.

Lilah M. Floyd
MAL
Hays, Kansas

ITALIAN CREAM CAKE

1/2 c. butter
1/2 c. Crisco
2 c. sugar
5 eggs, separated
1 tsp. soda
2 c. flour
1 c. buttermilk
1 tsp. vanilla extract
1 c. chopped pecans
Creamy Pecan Icing

Cream butter and Crisco together. Add sugar; beat until smooth. Add egg yolks; beat well. Combine soda and flour; add to creamed mixture alternately with buttermilk, mixing well. Stir in vanilla; add pecans. Fold in stiffly beaten egg whites gently. Pour into 3 greased and floured 8-inch cake pans. Bake at 350 degrees for 25 minutes or until done. Fill layers and frost cake with Creamy Pecan Icing.

Creamy Pecan Icing

1   8-oz. package cream cheese,
softened
1/4 c. butter, softened

1 box confectioners' sugar
1 tsp. vanilla extract
1/2 c. chopped pecans

Beat cream cheese and butter together. Add sugar; mix well. Stir in vanilla and pecans.

Shirley Armbruster, V.P.
Sigma Chi No. 4689
Kenner, Louisiana

DOCTOR BIRD CAKE

3 c. sifted flour
1 tsp. soda
1 tsp. cinnamon
2 c. sugar
1 tsp. salt
2 c. diced bananas
1 1/2 c. cooking oil
1 1/2 tsp. vanilla extract
3 eggs, beaten
1   8-oz. can crushed pineapple and
juice
Easy Cheese Frosting

Sift dry ingredients together. Add bananas, oil, vanilla, eggs and pineapple; stir to mix well. Do not beat. Pour into greased tube pan. Bake at 350 degrees for 1 hour and 20 minutes or until done. Let cool before removing from pan. Frost with Easy Cheese Frosting.

Easy Cheese Frosting

1/2 c. margarine, softened
1   8-oz. package cream cheese,
softened
1 tsp. vanilla extract
1 box powdered sugar

Combine margarine and cream cheese; mix well. Add vanilla and powdered sugar; mix until smooth.

Louise Owen, Treas.
Alpha Mu No. 346
Muncie, Indiana
Anna Johnson, Pres.
Gamma Iota No. 3565
St. Louis, Missouri

NORWEGIAN BLOTKAKE

12 eggs
2 c. sugar
2 tsp. vanilla extract
3/4 c. all-purpose flour
2 tsp. baking powder
2 c. sweetened whipped cream
1 pkg. frozen berries

Grease two 9-inch round cake pans; line bottoms with waxed paper. Butter the waxed paper. Combine 8 whole eggs, 4 egg yolks, sugar and vanilla in a mixing bowl; beat until thick and lemon colored. Sift flour and baking powder together; fold into egg mixture. Whip egg whites until stiff; fold into batter. Pour batter into prepared pans. Bake in preheated 350-degree oven for 10 minutes. Reduce temperature to 325 degrees; bake for about 50 minutes longer or until cake tester comes out clean. Let cake cool. Serve with whipped cream and berries.

Marguerite Adams
Delta Upsilon No. 2842
Boca Raton, Florida

HOLIDAY MEXICAN FRUIT CAKE

1 c. sugar
2 c. flour
2 tsp. soda
1 19-oz. can crushed pineapple in heavy syrup
2 eggs, beaten
1 c. chopped walnuts
Fruit Cake Frosting

Combine all ingredients except Fruit Cake Frosting in bowl; mix well, using electric mixer. Pour into greased and floured 9 x 13-inch pan. Bake at 350 degrees for 35 to 40 minutes or until done. Frost hot or cooled cake with Fruit Cake Frosting.

Fruit Cake Frosting

1/4 c. margarine or butter
1 8-oz. package cream cheese, softened
1 1/2 to 2 c. powdered sugar

1 tsp. vanilla extract
Milk

Blend margarine and cream cheese together. Add powdered sugar and vanilla; mix in enough milk to make a thin frosting.

Alice L. Lubbers, Corr. Sec.
Beta Nu No. 510
Pueblo, Colorado

PINEAPPLE SHEET CAKE

2 eggs, beaten
2 c. sugar
2 c. flour
2 tsp. soda
1 20-oz. can crushed pineapple and juice
1 to 2 tsp. vanilla extract
1/2 c. chopped nuts (opt.)
Cream Cheese-Nut Topping

Combine all ingredients except Cream Cheese-Nut Topping; mix well. Pour into greased and floured sheet cake pan or jelly roll pan. Bake at 350 degrees for 20 to 25 minutes or until done. Spread Cream Cheese-Nut Topping over warm cake. Keep cake refrigerated.

Cream Cheese-Nut Topping

6 to 8 oz. cream cheese, softened
1/4 c. margarine, softened
1 3/4 c. powdered sugar
1/2 c. chopped nuts
1 tsp. vanilla extract

Combine all ingredients; mix well.

Carol Jensen
Alpha Sigma No. 4293
Conifer, Colorado
Arlene Karnes, Pres.
Eta Nu No. 2916
Wakeeney, Kansas

WARTIME CAKE

1 c. shortening
1 lb. raisins
2 c. sugar
1 tsp. allspice
1 tsp. cinnamon

1/2 tsp. nutmeg
4 c. flour
2 tsp. soda
4 tsp. baking powder
1 15-oz. can applesauce

Combine shortening, raisins, sugar, spices and 2 cups water in saucepan; boil for 15 minutes. Cool. Add flour, soda, baking powder and applesauce; mix well. Turn into greased angel food cake pan. Bake at 300 degrees for about 45 minutes.

Roberta L. Holmes
Alpha Kappa No. 3219
Green River, Wyoming

APRICOT YULE LOG

3/4 c. sifted cake flour
3/4 tsp. baking powder
1/4 tsp. salt
4 eggs
Sugar
1 tsp. vanilla extract
Confectioners' sugar
Apricot Filling
1 c. whipping cream

Sift flour, baking powder and salt together. Beat eggs in medium bowl until foamy. Add 3/4 cup sugar gradually; beat until thick and lemon colored. Fold in flour mixture and vanilla. Grease bottom and line 15 1/2 x 10 1/2 x 1-inch jelly roll pan with waxed paper. Spread batter evenly in pan. Bake in 400-degree oven for 13 minutes or until light brown. Dust dish towel lightly with confectioners' sugar. Invert cake onto towel; remove pan and peel off paper. Roll up cake in towel, starting at narrow end; let cool to room temperature on wire rack. Unroll; spread with Apricot Filling to within 1/2 inch of edges. Roll again without towel. Whip cream with 1 teaspoon sugar until stiff; spread over top of cake roll. Refrigerate until serving time. Decorate with dried apricots, orange slices and walnuts.

Apricot Filling

1 1/4 c. dried California apricots
1/2 c. orange juice

1/3 c. sugar
1 tbsp. cornstarch
2 tbsp. raisins
1/4 c. chopped walnuts

Reserve 5 apricots for garnish. Simmer remaining apricots in 1/2 cup water in covered saucepan for 10 minutes. Drain apricots; reserve juice. Add enough water to reserved juice to make 1/2 cup liquid. Chop drained apricots. Combine apricot liquid, orange juice, sugar and apricots in small saucepan. Combine cornstarch and 2 tablespoons water to make a smooth paste; add to apricot mixture. Cook over medium heat until mixture thickens and boils, stirring constantly. Stir in raisins and walnuts. Cool to room temperature before spreading on cake. Yield: 8-10 servings.

Photograph for this recipe on cover.

EGGNOG CAKE WITH HOT RUM GLAZE

1 pkg. yellow cake mix
1/8 tsp. nutmeg
2 eggs
1 1/2 c. eggnog
1/4 c. butter or margarine, melted
2 tbsp. rum or 1/4 tsp. rum flavoring

Combine all ingredients in large bowl; beat for about 4 minutes with electric mixer or until smooth. Pour batter into greased and floured bundt pan. Bake at 350 degrees for 45 to 55 minutes or until cake springs back when pressed lightly. Let cool in pan for 10 minutes. Invert on rack; cool completely.

Hot Rum Glaze

1/2 c. butter or margarine
1 c. sugar
1/4 c. light rum

Melt butter in saucepan; add sugar, rum and 1/4 cup water. Boil for 2 to 3 minutes. Drizzle over cooled cake.

Nancy Boland, Pres.
Epsilon Pi No. 2559
Pratt, Kansas

FAMILY REUNION CARROT-PUDDING CAKE

1 pkg. yellow cake mix
1 sm. package instant vanilla pudding
  mix
4 eggs
1/4 c. oil
3 c. grated carrots
1/2 c. raisins
1/2 c. chopped nuts
1/2 tsp. salt
2 tsp. cinnamon

Combine all ingredients in large mixing bowl; beat at medium speed for 4 minutes. Pour into greased and floured 13 x 9-inch baking dish. Bake at 350 degrees for about 45 minutes or until cake springs back when lightly touched and cake is beginning to pull away from sides of pan. Cool completely in baking dish.

Orange-Cream Cheese Frosting

1 tbsp. soft margarine
1 3-oz. package cream cheese,
  softened
1 tsp. grated orange rind
2 1/2 c. confectioners' sugar
1 tbsp. orange juice

Beat margarine, cream cheese and orange rind together until smooth. Add sugar and orange juice alternately, beating until smooth and creamy. Frost cake in baking dish.

Dianna L. Kelly
Delta Chi No. 3875
Shelbyville, Indiana

COCONUT-SOUR CREAM LAYER CAKE

1 18 1/2-oz. package butter-flavored
  cake mix
2 c. sugar
1 16-oz. carton sour cream
1 12-oz. package coconut, thawed
1 1/2 c. frozen whipped topping, thawed

Prepare cake mix according to package directions, making two 8-inch layers. Let cool completely. Split layers. Combine sugar, sour cream and coconut, blending well; chill. Reserve 1 cup coconut mixture for frosting; spread remaining mixture between layers. Combine reserved mixture with whipped topping; mix well. Frost cake. Seal cake in airtight container; refrigerate for 3 days before serving.

Lorene Johnstone, V.P.
Alpha Beta No. 165
Lincoln, Nebraska

VALENTINE STRAWBERRY CAKE

1/2 10-oz. box frozen strawberries
1 box yellow cake mix
1 3-oz. box strawberry gelatin
2 tbsp. flour
3/4 c. salad oil
4 eggs
1 tsp. vanilla extract

Combine all ingredients and 1/2 cup water; beat for at least 3 minutes. Pour into 3 layer cake pans. Bake at 350 degrees for about 30 minutes or until cake tests done. Cool. Remove from pans.

Strawberry Frosting

1 box powdered sugar
1/2 10-oz. box strawberries
1/2 c. butter or margarine

Combine all ingredients; mix until smooth. Spread between layers, over top and side of cake.

Linda Anderson, Sec.
Alpha Chi No. 4428
Carbondale, Kansas

HALLOWEEN GINGERBREAD UPSIDE-DOWN CAKE

3 tbsp. butter
1/4 c. (packed) brown sugar
1 1-lb. can pear or peach halves,
  well drained
1 pkg. gingerbread mix

Melt butter in 8-inch square pan. Sprinkle with brown sugar; arrange pears over brown sugar. Prepare gingerbread mix according to package directions. Pour batter over pears. Bake according to package directions, adding about 10 minutes to baking time. Serve warm with whipped cream or ice cream. Garnish children's servings with orange and brown M and M candies.

Blanche M. Druker, Ed. Dir.
Alpha Lambda No. 3592
Alexandria, Virginia

BITE-SIZED CHEESECAKES

2 8-oz. packages cream cheese, softened
3 eggs
2/3 c. sugar
1 tsp. almond extract
Cheesecake Topping

Combine first 4 ingredients; pour into miniature paper cupcake liners to 3/4 full. Bake at 350 degrees for 20 minutes. Let cool. Spread topping over cheesecakes; bake for 5 to 8 minutes longer.

Cheesecake Topping

1 c. sour cream
1 tsp. vanilla extract
3 tbsp. sugar

Combine ingredients; mix well.

Sueanne Field, Scrapbook Chm.
Alpha Lambda No. 3952
Springfield, Virginia

BLUEBERRY CHEESECAKE

11 graham crackers, crushed
1/4 c. melted butter
1 1/2 c. sugar
2 eggs
2 8-oz. packages cream cheese, softened
1 tsp. vanilla extract
1 can blueberry pie filling

Combine crumbs, butter and 1/2 cup sugar; mix well. Pat into 8 x 10-inch pan. Beat eggs

well; add cream cheese. Beat until smooth and light. Add remaining 1 cup sugar and vanilla; blend well. Spread mixture into crust. Bake in 375-degree oven for 12 to 15 minutes. Cool. Spread pie filling on top; chill for 8 hours. Cut into squares to serve. Yield: 16 servings.

Peggy Healy
Zeta Tau No. 2064
Colorado Springs, Colorado

SPECIAL PARTY CHERRY CHEESECAKE

1 c. graham cracker crumbs
1/2 c. finely chopped walnuts
1/3 c. butter or margarine
1 3/4 c. sugar
3 8-oz. packages cream cheese, softened
6 eggs
1 16-oz. carton sour cream
2 tbsp. cornstarch
Lemon juice
2 tsp. vanilla extract
1 21-oz. can cherry pie filling
1 tbsp. grated lemon peel

Combine crumbs, walnuts, butter and 1/4 cup sugar in medium bowl; mix well. Press firmly on bottom and side of deep 9-inch springform pan to within 1 1/2 inches of top; set aside. Beat cream cheese in large bowl of electric mixer at medium speed until smooth; beat in 1 1/2 cups sugar. Beat in eggs with mixer at low speed; add sour cream, cornstarch, 1 tablespoon lemon juice and vanilla. Beat for 3 minutes, scraping bowl. Pour mixture into crumb crust. Bake in preheated 350-degree oven for 1 hour or until lightly browned. Turn off oven; let cheesecake stand in oven for 30 minutes. Remove cheesecake; let cool in pan. Cover; refrigerate until ready to serve. Remove side of pan; slide cheesecake onto serving platter. Combine pie filling, lemon peel and 1/2 teaspoon lemon juice; mix carefully. Spoon cherry topping evenly over top of cheesecake.

Sandie Blount, V.P.
Gamma Nu No. 4508
Orlando, Florida

CHRISTMAS CHEER CHEESECAKE

1 3-oz. package lemon gelatin
1 8-oz. package cream cheese, softened
1 c. sugar
1 c. evaporated milk, well chilled
24 sq. graham crackers, crushed
1/2 c. margarine, softened

Dissolve gelatin in 1 cup hot water; cool. Beat cream cheese and sugar together until creamy; add gelatin. Whip milk until fluffy; fold into cheese mixture. Combine crumbs and margarine; press into springform pan. Pour cheese mixture into crust. Refrigerate until firm. Yield: 10 servings.

Jane Highfield, Treas.
Gamma Kappa Chap.
Panama City, Florida

EASY MOCK LEMON CHEESECAKE

1 pkg. graham crackers, crushed
3 tbsp. sugar
1/2 c. melted margarine
1 lg. carton Cool Whip
1 6-oz. can frozen lemonade concentrate
1 can sweetened condensed milk

Combine cracker crumbs, sugar and margarine; press into 9-inch square pan. Thaw Cool Whip and lemonade; add milk. Mix until well blended. Pour into crust. Refrigerate for several hours before serving. Very simple and very refreshing.

Alvita Cates
Sigma Kappa No. 4684
Claflin, Kansas

GEORGIA PRIZE PEANUT CHEESECAKE

1/3 c. butter or margarine
1 c. graham cracker crumbs
3/4 c. finely chopped dry roasted peanuts
12 oz. cream cheese, softened

2/3 c. creamy peanut butter
1 14-oz. can sweetened condensed milk
1/3 c. fresh or reconstituted lemon juice
1 tsp. vanilla extract
1 4 1/2-oz. carton frozen nondairy whipped topping, thawed

Melt butter in small saucepan; stir in cracker crumbs and peanuts. Reserve 2 tablespoons peanut mixture for garnish; press remaining mixture on bottom of 9-inch springform pan. Chill thoroughly. Beat cream cheese and peanut butter in large mixer bowl until fluffy. Add milk; beat until smooth. Stir in lemon juice and vanilla; fold in whipped topping. Turn into prepared pan; garnish with reserved crumbs. Chill for 2 to 3 hours. Keep cheesecake refrigerated.

Martha R. Lansky, Rec. Sec.
Epsilon Delta No. 2618
Urbana, Illinois

MEMORIAL DAY QUICK CHEESECAKE

1 recipe graham cracker crust
2 c. milk
1 8-oz. package cream cheese, softened
1 3-oz. package instant lemon pudding mix

Pat graham cracker crust mixture into 8-inch square pan. Combine 1/2 cup milk and cream cheese; mix until smooth. Add remaining milk, then quickly mix in pudding mix. Pour into graham cracker crust. Chill until firm.

Sharon Kindler
Beta Eta No. 2970
Goldendale, Washington

GERMAN CHOCOLATE BROWNIE CHEESECAKE

1 pkg. German chocolate cake mix
1/2 c. shredded coconut
1/3 c. margarine, softened
3 eggs
2 8-oz. packages cream cheese, softened

1 c. sugar
3 tsp. vanilla extract
2 c. sour cream

Beat cake mix, coconut, margarine and 1 egg together at low speed of electric mixer until mixture is crumbly. Press very lightly in ungreased 13 x 8 x 2-inch baking pan. Beat cream cheese, remaining 2 eggs, 3/4 cup sugar and 2 teaspoons vanilla together until smooth and fluffy. Spread over cake mixture. Bake in preheated 350-degree oven for 20 to 25 minutes. Combine sour cream, remaining 1/4 cup sugar and remaining 1 teaspoon vanilla; mix well. Spread over cheesecake. Let cool; refrigerate for at least 8 hours. Yield: 20 servings.

Barbara Culpepper
MAL
Lafayette, Indiana

MINIATURE CHEESECAKES

Vanilla wafers
2 8-oz. packages cream cheese,
   softened
2 eggs, beaten
3/4 c. sugar
1 tsp. vanilla extract
1 tsp. ReaLemon juice
1 can cherry pie filling

Place vanilla wafer in each cupcake liner in muffin tin. Combine all ingredients except pie filling; beat until smooth. Fill each cup 3/4 full with cream mixture. Bake at 350 degrees for 15 minutes. Top with pie filling. Chill thoroughly in muffin tin.

Clyda Bernasconi, Pres.
Zeta Upsilon No. 2229
Temple City, California

BANANA SPLIT DESSERT

1 box vanilla wafers
1/2 c. melted margarine
1 8-oz. package cream cheese
1/2 c. margarine, softened
2 c. powdered sugar
1 tsp. vanilla extract
6 bananas, sliced
1 qt. strawberries or crushed
   pineapple

1 lg. carton Cool Whip
Nuts (opt.)

Crush vanilla wafers; mix with melted margarine. Pat into 9 x 13-inch pan. Let stand for 1 hour. Combine cream cheese, 1/2 cup softened margarine, powdered sugar and vanilla; beat for 10 minutes. Spread into wafer crust. Place bananas over cream cheese mixture; place strawberries over bananas. Spread Cool Whip over top; sprinkle with nuts. Chill until ready to serve.

Carol Cragen, Rec. Sec.
Alpha Chi No. 463
Whiteland, Indiana

EASY CAKE ROLLS

1 lg. box vanilla wafers, crushed
2 pkg. pitted dates, ground
1 lb. walnuts, ground
1 pkg. colored marshmallows
1 can sweetened condensed milk

Combine all ingredients in large mixing bowl; mix well by hand. Divide into 5 parts; shape each part into long roll. Wrap rolls in plastic wrap; chill until ready to serve. Cut into slices to serve. Can be frozen.

Lola L. Bridge, Sec.
Alpha Delta No. 1711
Milford, Utah

CHERRY ANGEL DESSERT

2 env. whipped topping mix
1 c. milk
1 8-oz. package cream cheese at
   room temperature
1 c. powdered sugar
1 sm. angel food cake, torn into
   pieces
1 can cherry pie filling

Prepare topping mix according to package directions, using milk. Combine cream cheese and sugar in small bowl; beat until smooth. Add to whipped topping. Place cake in bowl; add cheese mixture. Mix well. Place in 8 x 13-inch dish; cover with pie filling. Chill for several hours.

Jane Mathiasmeier, Pres.
Beta Kappa No. 3124
Arkansas City, Kansas

CHOCOLATE EASTER EGG DESSERT

> 2 env. unflavored gelatin
> 1 c. sugar
> 1/4 c. salt
> 2 1/2 c. milk
> 2 6-oz. packages semisweet
>   chocolate pieces
> 2 tsp. vanilla extract
> 2 c. heavy cream, whipped

Combine gelatin, sugar and salt in medium saucepan; stir in milk and chocolate pieces. Place over low heat; cook, stirring constantly, for about 10 minutes or until gelatin dissolves and chocolate is melted. Remove from heat; beat with rotary beater until chocolate is blended. Stir in vanilla. Chill, stirring occasionally, until mixture mounds slightly when dropped from spoon. Fold in whipped cream. Turn into 10-cup melon mold or round mixing bowl. Chill until firm. Unmold onto serving platter. Yield: 12 servings.

Velda Adolf, Sec.
Kappa Tau No. 4527
Burlington, Colorado

FRESH STRAWBERRY ICEBOX CAKE

> 1 lb. vanilla wafers
> 1/4 c. melted butter
> 1/2 c. butter
> 1 1/2 c. sugar
> 2 eggs
> 1 qt. strawberries, cut in half
> 1 pt. whipping cream, whipped

Crush wafers very fine; mix with melted butter. Spread 2/3 of the crumbs firmly in bottom of 9 x 13-inch pan. Cream butter with sugar until light and fluffy. Add eggs, one at a time, beating well after each addition. Spread evenly over crumbs. Add strawberries. Spread whipped cream over strawberries. Sprinkle with remaining crumbs. Refrigerate overnight. Yield: 12-16 servings.

Linda Malone, Jonquil Girl
Gamma Alpha No. 3455
Poseyville, Indiana

COCONUT-RASPBERRY BAVARIAN

> 1 3-oz. package Royal raspberry
>   gelatin
> 1/4 tsp. almond extract
> 1 4-oz. can flaked coconut
> 1 c. heavy cream, whipped
> 1 10-oz. package frozen raspberries,
>   thawed
> 2 tsp. cornstarch

Dissolve gelatin in 1 cup boiling water; stir in 1 cup cold water and almond extract. Chill until slightly thickened. Set aside 1 tablespoon coconut; fold remaining coconut and whipped cream into slightly thickened gelatin. Pour into 4-cup mold. Chill until firm. Drain raspberries, reserving syrup. Blend reserved syrup into cornstarch in saucepan; cook, stirring, until thickened. Remove from heat; add raspberries. Chill. Unmold gelatin. Serve with raspberry sauce and additional whipped cream; sprinkle with reserved coconut. Yield: 6 servings.

Photograph for this recipe above.

STRAWBERRY MARSHMALLOW WHIP

> 1 3-oz. package Royal strawberry
>   gelatin
> 2 c. prepared whipped topping

1 1/2 c. miniature marshmallows
1 13 1/2-oz. can crushed pineapple,
   drained

Dissolve gelatin in 1 cup boiling water; add 1 cup cold water. Chill until partially congealed. Place bowl of gelatin firmly in bowl of ice; whip until light and fluffy. Blend into whipped topping; fold in marshmallows and pineapple. Pour into 8-cup mold; chill until firm. Unmold; garnish with fresh strawberries, if desired. Yield: 8-10 servings.

Photograph for this recipe on opposite page.

PUDDING TORTE

1/2 c. butter
1 c. flour
1/2 c. ground pecans
1 8-oz. package cream cheese
1 c. powdered sugar
1 carton Cool Whip
2 sm. boxes instant lemon pudding mix
3 c. milk

Melt butter; add flour and pecans. Spread in 9 x 13-inch pan. Bake at 350 degrees for 15 minutes. Cool. Combine cream cheese, sugar and half the Cool Whip. Spread over crust. Refrigerate for 1 hour. Combine pudding mix and milk; spread over cream cheese layer. Chill until set. Spread remaining Cool Whip over top. Chill for several hours. Any flavor of pudding mix may be used, if desired.

Sondra McNamara
Beta Delta No. 658
Mount Vernon, Indiana

CHOCO-MINT MOUSSE

1 6-oz. package semisweet mint
   chocolate pieces
3 eggs
1 tsp. vanilla extract
1 10-oz. container Pet Whip, thawed

Melt chocolate pieces in double boiler over hot water. Remove from heat; cool slightly. Add 1 whole egg and 2 egg yolks, one at a time, beating well after each addition. Stir in vanilla. Beat egg whites until soft peaks form; fold egg whites and Pet Whip into

chocolate mixture. Pour into dessert dishes; garnish with slivered almonds. Chill until firm.

Photograph for this recipe on page 128.

STRAWBERRY-PECAN ICEBOX DESSERT

1 10-oz. package vanilla wafers,
   crushed
5 c. powdered sugar
1 1/2 c. margarine
4 eggs
3 pkg. frozen strawberries, thawed
   and drained
1 c. chopped pecans
2 pt. heavy whipping cream, whipped

Spread crumbs over bottom of 9 x 13-inch pan, reserving small amount for topping. Combine sugar, margarine and eggs; beat until fluffy. Arrange alternate layers of egg mixture and strawberries on crust. Sprinkle with pecans. Spread with whipped cream. Top with reserved crumbs. Refrigerate for at least 3 to 4 hours before serving. May be frozen. May substitute 6 cups fresh strawberries, when available, for frozen strawberries, if desired.

Linda Brodersen, Pres.
Gamma Omicron No. 8850
Manhattan, Kansas

TIPSY CAKE

2 pkg. vanilla pudding mix
1 2-lb. pound cake
1/2 c. Bourbon
2 1/2 pt. whipping cream, whipped
1 10-oz. package chopped pecans

Prepare pudding mix according to package directions. Let cool. Break up pound cake into bite-sized pieces; sprinkle with Bourbon. Combine cake and pudding. Reserve 1 cup whipped cream; fold remaining cream into cake mixture. Stir in pecans; place in serving bowl. Top with reserved whipped cream. Chill until ready to serve. Yield: About 20 servings.

Fran Lanning, Pres.
Beta Gamma No. 4267
Hampton, Virginia

WHIPPED LIME DESSERT

2 c. chocolate wafer crumbs
1/3 c. melted butter
1 3-oz. package lime gelatin
1/4 c. lime juice
2 tbsp. lemon juice
1 13-oz. can evaporated milk, well
 chilled
1 c. sugar

Combine chocolate wafer crumbs and butter; press into 13 x 9 x 2-inch pan. Dissolve gelatin in 1 3/4 cups hot water; stir in lime juice and lemon juice. Chill until partially congealed. Whip gelatin. Whip chilled evaporated milk until fluffy; beat in sugar. Fold into whipped gelatin; pour over crumb crust. Chill until firm. Top with grated semisweet chocolate and English walnut halves.

Delberta Roberts, Educational Dir.
Kappa Omicron No. 4041
Wakeeney, Kansas

DANISH RUM PUDDING

1 env. unflavored gelatin
2 c. eggnog
1/3 c. sugar
1 tbsp. cornstarch
1 tsp. rum extract
1 c. whipping cream
Raspberry Sauce

Soften gelatin in 1/4 cup water. Heat eggnog. Combine sugar and cornstarch; stir into eggnog. Cook until thickened, stirring constantly. Remove from heat; stir in gelatin until dissolved. Cool. Blend in rum extract. Beat whipping cream until stiff; fold in eggnog mixture. Pour into 6 custard cups; chill for several hours or overnight. Unmold custards in shallow dishes; top with Raspberry Sauce.

Raspberry Sauce

1 10-oz. package frozen raspberries,
 thawed
1/2 c. currant jelly
1 tbsp. cornstarch
1 tbsp. butter
1/4 c. orange juice

Heat 3/4 cup raspberries and currant jelly together until simmering. Combine cornstarch with remaining 1/4 cup raspberries; add to hot fruit mixture. Cook until thickened, stirring constantly. Remove from heat; stir in butter until melted. Cool. Stir in orange juice; chill thoroughly.

Photograph for this recipe on this page.

HOMEMADE CHUNKY FRESH APRICOT ICE CREAM

2 lb. fresh California apricots
1 1/4 c. sugar
1/8 tsp. salt
1 c. milk
3 egg yolks, slightly beaten
1 tsp. vanilla extract
2 c. heavy cream

Dip apricots into boiling water for about 30 seconds or until skins will slip off easily. Plunge into cold water; remove skins. Cut apricots in half; remove pits. Chop 12 apricot halves into small chunks; add 1/4 cup sugar. Puree remaining apricot halves in electric blender; add 1/4 cup sugar to puree. Stir remaining 3/4 cup sugar, salt, milk and egg yolks together in medium saucepan. Stir over medium heat until small bubbles appear around edge of liquid. Remove from heat; stir in vanilla. Cool. Stir in unwhipped cream, chopped apricots and apricot puree. Fit dasher into ice cream freezer canister. Pour apricot mixture into canister. Freeze according to freezer instructions. Remove dasher; cover with foil and replace lid. Empty water from bucket. Repack bucket with salt and ice so canister is completely covered with ice. Let ripen for at least 1 hour before serving. Yield: 2 1/4 quarts.

Photograph for this recipe on page 102.

QUICKY CHUNKY FRESH APRICOT ICE CREAM

1 qt. vanilla ice cream, softened
8 fresh California apricots, peeled and diced

Stir ice cream and apricots together quickly in large bowl to combine; spoon into freezer container. Freeze for 1 hour; stir to distribute apricots evenly. Return to freezer; freeze for 3 hours or until firm. Place ice cream in refrigerator for 15 minutes before serving time to soften lightly for easier serving.

Photograph for this recipe on page 102.

RED AND WHITE PARFAITS

3 or 4 fresh apricots
1 c. sugar
Dash of salt
1/4 tsp. vanilla extract
Melba Sauce
Chunky Fresh Apricot Ice Cream

Dip apricots in boiling water for about 30 seconds or until skins slip off easily. Cut apricots in half; remove pits. Combine sugar, 1/2 cup water, salt and vanilla in saucepan. Bring to a boil over medium heat, stirring constantly. Boil for 2 minutes. Add apricot halves; simmer for 3 minutes. Chill apricots and syrup. Cut each apricot half into 4 slices. Spoon about 2 teaspoons Melba Sauce into each of 6 parfait glasses. Add 2 pieces apricots to each glass, then add scoop of apricot ice cream. Repeat layers until glasses are full. Garnish with whipped cream, fresh apricot slices and fresh raspberries.

Melba Sauce

1 c. fresh raspberries
1/4 c. sugar
1/4 c. currant jelly
3/4 tsp. cornstarch

Mash raspberries; stir in sugar. Combine raspberries and jelly in saucepan; bring to a boil. Combine cornstarch and 1 tablespoon water; stir into raspberry mixture. Cook over low heat, stirring constantly, until thickened and translucent. Strain sauce; cool.
Recipe for Chunky Fresh Apricot Ice Cream can be found in Ice Cream Desserts.

Photograph for this recipe on page 102.

COT AND CAKE ROLL-UP

3/4 c. sifted cake flour
3/4 tsp. baking powder
1/4 tsp. salt
4 eggs at room temperature
3/4 c. sugar
1/2 tsp. almond extract
Confectioners' sugar
1 qt. Chunky Fresh Apricot Ice Cream

Grease bottom of 15 x 10 x 1-inch jelly roll pan; line with waxed paper. Grease paper. Do not grease or line sides of pan. Sift flour, baking powder and salt together. Beat eggs in electric mixer bowl; add sugar gradually, beating for about 10 minutes or until thick and lemon colored. Add almond extract. Fold in dry ingredients gradually. Pour batter into prepared pan. Bake in 400-degree oven for 13 minutes or until cake tests done. Turn out immediately onto cloth sprinkled with confectioners' sugar. Remove paper carefully; trim off crisp edges of cake. Roll up cake and cloth in jelly roll fashion, beginning at narrow end. Place on rack to cool. Soften apricot ice cream at room temperature until spreadable. Unroll cake carefully; spread ice cream evenly over cake. Roll cake and ice cream; place on serving plate with edge of cake on underside. Cover with waxed paper; freeze. Garnish cake with apricot slices and mint leaves; sprinkle with confectioners' sugar, if desired.
Recipe for Chunky Fresh Apricot Ice Cream can be found in Ice Cream Desserts.

Photograph for this recipe on page 102.

SEVEN SWANS A SWIMMING

6 tbsp. Nucoa or Mazola margarine
1/4 tsp. salt
3/4 c. sifted flour
3 eggs
1 qt. (about) vanilla ice cream
1 recipe Chocolate Sauce

Bring 1/2 cup water, margarine and salt to a full boil in small saucepan. Add flour, all at once; beat rapidly over low heat until mixture leaves side of pan and forms smooth compact ball. Remove from heat. Add eggs, one at a time, beating well after each addition. Mixture should be thick when last egg has been added. Divide mixture into fourths. Press through 1/4 inch pastry tube or paper cone onto ungreased cookie sheet, as follows. Use 1/4 of the mixture for necks; make 7 curved strips resembling printed numeral 2, each 2 1/2 inches tall. Use 1/4 of the mixture for right wings; make 7 continuous curved ribbons resembling script letter N, about 2 inches tall with first loop higher than second. Follow directions for right wings to make left wings, making second loop higher. Use remaining mixture for tails. Pipe 7 dots the size of a marble onto cookie sheet. Bake in preheated 400-degree oven for about 15 minutes or until golden brown. Cool on wire rack. Make ice cream ball by packing slightly softened ice cream into 1/2 cup measure. Place in dessert dish. Working quickly so ice cream will not melt, press a swan neck, two wings and tail into ball. Repeat, making 7 swans. Swans may be placed in freezer until serving time, if desired. Pour Chocolate Sauce into dish around swan just before serving.

Chocolate Sauce

3/4 c. cocoa
2/3 c. sugar
3/4 c. red or blue label Karo syrup
1/4 tsp. salt
2 tbsp. Nucoa or Mazola margarine
1 tsp. vanilla extract

Combine cocoa and sugar in saucepan. Add syrup, salt and 1 cup water. Cook over medium heat, stirring constantly, until mixture comes to boil. Boil for 5 minutes. Remove from heat. Stir in margarine and vanilla. Cool. Serve warm or cold.

Photograph for this recipe on opposite page.

FROZEN YULE LOG

1   1-lb. 4-oz. can sliced pineapple
1 c. salad dressing
1/4 c. honey
1 c. quartered red and green
    maraschino cherries
2/3 c. slivered toasted almonds
2 c. whipping cream, whipped

Drain pineapple, reserving 1/4 cup syrup. Combine salad dressing, honey, reserved syrup, cherries and almonds; fold in whipped cream. Arrange alternate layers of salad dressing mixture and pineapple slices in 2-pound coffee can. Cover with plastic wrap; freeze until ready to use. Slide spatula around inside of can. Cut bottom from can; do not remove bottom. Wrap can in warm towel; push on bottom to slide out log. Sprinkle with additional almonds; garnish with mint, if desired. Yield: 12-14 servings.

Bonnie Spell, Soc. Chm.
Gamma Chi No. 3194
Escondido, California

HOT FUDGE SAUCE FOR ICE CREAM

2 tbsp. (heaping) cocoa
1/2 c. milk
3/4 c. sugar
1/4 c. margarine
Dash of salt
1 tsp. vanilla extract

Combine cocoa, milk and sugar in saucepan. Cook over low heat until mixture is smooth and blended, stirring constantly. Add margarine and salt; cook for 3 to 5 minutes longer or until slightly thickened. Remove from heat; stir in vanilla. Yield: 1 1/2 cups sauce.

Helen Roe Skaggs
Alpha Lambda No. 2785
Columbus, Indiana

GERMAN CHOCOLATE ICE CREAM

1 c. sugar
1/4 c. all-purpose flour
1/4 tsp. salt
1/4 tsp. cinnamon
1 qt. milk
2   4-oz. bars sweet cooking
    chocolate, melted
3 eggs, beaten
1 c. shredded coconut
1 qt. light cream or half and half
1 c. chopped pecans

Combine sugar, flour, salt and cinnamon in a heavy 3-quart saucepan. Add milk gradually. Cook over medium heat, stirring constantly, until thickened. Cook for 2 minutes longer. Remove from heat. Blend in melted chocolate. Blend small amount of hot mixture into eggs; return to pan. Cook for 1 minutes. Do not boil. Remove from heat; add coconut. Cool. Blend in cream. Chill thoroughly. Stir in pecans. Place in freezer container. Freeze according to freezer directions. Yield: About 1 gallon.

Ione Trapp, V.P.
Gamma Omega No. 2910
North Vernon, Indiana

MAPLE NUT ICE CREAM

2 1/4 c. sugar
5 eggs, beaten
1 can evaporated milk
1 1/2 qt. milk
1 qt. half and half
4 1/2 tsp. maple flavoring
1/2 tsp. salt
1 c. chopped walnuts

Add sugar gradually to eggs, beating until mixture is stiff. Add remaining ingredients; mix thorougly. Pour into ice cream freezer container. Freeze according to freezer instructions.

Ruthanne Rocha
Gamma Tau No. 3523
Miranda, California

BROWNIE SANDWICHES

1   15-oz. package brownie mix
1 c. chopped pecans
3 pt. vanilla ice cream

Prepare brownie mix according to package directions for cake-type brownies. Divide batter into 2 greased 15 1/2 x 10 1/2-inch pans. Sprinkle each pan with 1/2 cup chopped pecans. Bake in a 350-degree oven for 20 minutes. Cut each pan of hot brownies into eighteen 3 1/4 x 2 1/2-inch cookies. Remove from pan; cool on rack. Cut each pint of ice cream into 6 slices. Place slice of ice cream between 2 cookies. Wrap in Saran Wrap or waxed paper; keep frozen until serving time. Yield: 18 sandwiches.

Photograph for this recipe above.

PEACH ICE CREAM

2 qt. canned peaches
6 eggs
Sugar to taste
1 lg. can evaporated milk
1   3-oz. box instant vanilla pudding
    mix
1 tsp. vanilla extract
Milk

Reserve 2 cups peaches; combine remaining peaches with next 5 ingredients. Process in

blender until peaches are pureed. Pour into ice cream freezer. Cut up reserved peaches; add to freezer. Add milk to fill to line of freezer. Stir to mix all ingredients. Freeze according to freezer directions.

Lois Bradley, Pres.
Alpha Phi No. 2051
Churchville, Virginia

QUICK AND GOOD HOMEMADE ICE CREAM

2 pt. half and half
2 c. milk
2 cans sweetened condensed milk
2 tsp. vanilla extract
Chopped fruit (opt.)

Combine all ingredients; mix well. Pour into freezer container; freeze according to freezer directions.

Janie Allmendinger, Pres.
Beta Omicron No. 3701
Rogers, Arkansas

EASTER LEMON FRUIT FREEZE

2/3 c. butter
1/3 c. sugar
3 c. crushed Rice or Corn Chex
1   14-oz. can sweetened condensed milk
1/2 c. lemon juice
1   21-oz. can lemon pie filling
1   17-oz. can fruit cocktail, well
    drained
2 c. whipped topping.

Melt butter in medium saucepan; stir in sugar, then crumbs. Reserve 1/3 cup crumb mixture for garnish. Pat remaining crumb mixture firmly on bottom of 13 x 9-inch baking pan. Bake at 300 degrees for 12 minutes. Cool. Combine milk and lemon juice in large bowl; stir in pie filling and fruit cocktail. Pour over crust. Top with whipped topping and reserved crumbs. Freeze for 4 hours. Remove from freezer 20 minutes before cutting.

Cheryl Wahlenmaier, Reporter
Beta Kappa No. 3124
Arkansas City, Kansas

ICY LEMON SURPRISES

6 lg. lemons
Lemon sherbet
1/2 c. heavy cream
2 tbsp. confectioners' sugar
1/2 tsp. vanilla extract
Chocolate curls or chocolate sprinkles

Wash lemons and dry well. Cut each lemon lenthwise to remove 1/3 of the lemon. Scoop out all pulp to make shell. Fill with sherbet. Place in freezer; freeze until firm. Whip cream with sugar and vanilla until stiff. Press through pastry tube to form rosettes or dollops on each lemon. Decorate with chocolate curls. Yield: 6 servings.

Vivienne Ozuna
Las Coronas Reg. Coun. Pres.
Sigma Psi No. 4605
Canyon Country, California

MINCEMEAT ICE CREAM BALLS

1 qt. vanilla ice cream, softened
1/2 jar mincemeat
1 c. flaked coconut
Maraschino cherries, halved

Combine ice cream and mincemeat in medium bowl; mix well. Freeze until firm. Scoop into balls; dredge with coconut. Place on flat pan; return to freezer. Serve in sherbet dishes; garnish with cherry halves.

Melinda Fadely, Rec. Sec.
Alpha Omega No. 4709
Anderson, Indiana

POPSICLES

1 pkg. unsweetened Kool-Aid
1 c. sugar
1 sm. package fruit-flavored gelatin

Dissolve Kool-Aid and sugar in 1 1/2 cups cold water. Dissolve gelatin in 1 cup hot water; stir into Kool-Aid mixture. Pour into molds; freeze until firm.

Sue Been, Pres.
Gamma Alpha No. 2909
Springdale, Arkansas

HALLOWEEN PUMPKIN SQUARES

1 1-lb. can pumpkin
1 c. sugar
1 tsp. salt
1 tsp. ground ginger
1 tsp. ground cinnamon
1 tsp. ground nutmeg
1 c. chopped toasted pecans
1/2 gal. vanilla ice cream, softened
36 gingersnaps

Combine pumpkin, sugar, salt, ginger, cinnamon and nutmeg; mix well. Stir in pecans. Fold pumpkin mixture into ice cream in chilled bowl. Line bottom of 13 x 9 x 2-inch pan with half the gingersnaps; spread half the ice cream mixture over gingersnaps. Repeat layers; place in freezer. Freeze for about 5 hours or until firm. Cut into squares to serve. Garnish with whipped cream and pecan halves. Yield: 12-16 servings.

Martha Montgomery, Pres.
Alpha Omega No. 886
Columbus, Ohio

PUMPKIN STACKUPS

1 c. canned pumpkin
1/2 c. sugar
1/2 tsp. salt
1/2 tsp. ginger
1/2 tsp. cinnamon
1/4 tsp. nutmeg
1/2 c. chopped pecans (opt.)
1 qt. vanilla ice cream, softened
16 (about) gingersnaps, crushed

Combine pumpkin, sugar, salt and spices; add pecans. Stir ice cream; fold in pumpkin mixture. Line bottom of shallow pan or refrigerator tray with half the gingersnap crumbs; top with half the ice cream mixture. Cover with remaining gingersnaps; top with remaining ice cream mixture. Freeze until firm. Cut in wedges; garnish with pecan halves. Yield: 6-8 servings.

Irene Fife
Lamplighter, Past State Pres.
Theta Lambda No. 2920
Colorado Springs, Colorado

CHEESE-STRAWBERRY CREME

2 env. unflavored gelatin
3/4 c. milk
3 c. cottage cheese
1/3 c. sour cream
3/4 c. sugar
1/4 tsp. salt
1 1/2 tsp. vanilla extract
2 egg yolks
1 tbsp. grated lemon peel
1 tsp. lemon juice
1/2 c. raisins
1/3 c. finely chopped almonds

Sprinkle gelatin over 1/2 cup cold water in small saucepan. Heat over low heat, stirring until dissolved. Add milk. Beat cottage cheese and sour cream together on high speed of mixer for 5 minutes, scraping bowl occasionally. Beat in sugar, salt, vanilla, egg yolks, lemon peel, lemon juice and gelatin mixture. Chill for 10 minutes or just until mixture begins to thicken. Stir in raisins and almonds. Pour into a cold water rinsed 6-cup mold. Chill until set or overnight. Unmold; garnish with pink-tinted whipped cream and strawberries, if desired. Yield: 8-10 servings.

Photograph for this recipe on page 88.

APRICOT LINZER TORTE

1 c. diced dried California apricots
1 8-oz. can crushed pineapple in
    unsweetened juice
Sugar
1/2 c. butter or margarine, softened
1 egg
1/2 tsp. grated lemon peel
1/4 tsp. ground cinnamon
3/4 c. all-purpose flour
3/4 c. ground toasted blanched
    almonds
Confectioners' sugar

Place apricots, undrained pineapple, 1/2 cup water and 2/3 cup sugar in saucepan. Cover; simmer for 15 minutes or until mixture is very thick, stirring occasionally. Cool. Cream butter and 1/4 cup sugar together in large bowl until light and fluffy. Beat in egg; mix in lemon peel, cinnamon, flour and almonds.

Chill pastry for about 1 hour. Chill 1/5 of the pastry for later use. Press remaining 4/5 of the pastry onto bottom and 1 inch up side of 9-inch round cake pan with removable bottom. Spoon in cooled apricot filling. Bake in 350-degree oven for 35 to 40 minutes or until pastry is browned. Remove outer rim of cake pan; let torte cool thoroughly. Roll out remaining 1/5 of the pastry on lightly floured board. Cut out 9 small pastry stars, using 1-inch star-shaped cookie cutter. Place on baking sheet. Bake at 350 degrees for 3 minutes or until lightly browned. Let cool. Place on waxed paper. Cover torte filling with circle of aluminum foil. Sprinkle torte pastry edge and pastry stars with confectioners' sugar. Remove foil from torte; place stars on torte filling. Garnish torte with red glace cherry quarters.

Photograph for this recipe on page 101.

CHRISTMAS COMPOTE

1 box pitted prunes
1 can pineapple tidbits and juice
1 can cherry pie filling
1 pkg. dried apricots
1 c. Sherry or water

Combine all ingredients; pour into baking dish. Bake in 350-degree oven for 1 hour. Serve warm or cool.

Faye Knackstedt
Delta Tau No. 3684
Ellisville, Missouri

CHRISTMAS CRANBERRY CRUNCH

1 c. sugar
1 tbsp. cornstarch
1 tsp. vanilla extract
Pinch of salt
2 c. fresh cranberries
1/2 c. seedless raisins
1 c. oatmeal
1 c. (firmly packed) brown sugar
1/2 c. flour
1/3 c. butter

Combine sugar, cornstarch, 1/2 cup water, vanilla and salt in saucepan; stir in cranberries and raisins. Bring to a boil over medium heat. Simmer for 5 minutes; let cool slightly. Combine oatmeal, brown sugar and flour in bowl; cut in butter until mixture is crumbly. Sprinkle 1/2 of the oatmeal mixture in greased 8 x 8-inch pan. Spread cooled cranberry mixture over oatmeal mixture; top with remaining oatmeal mixture. Bake at 350 degrees for 45 minutes. Serve warm or cold. Top with vanilla ice cream, if desired. Yield: 6-9 servings.

Joyce Zimmer
Alpha Lambda No. 618
Vermillion, South Dakota

GLAZED HOLIDAY APPLES

9 Roman Beauty apples, cored
3/4 c. sugar
1/4 c. white syrup
Grated lemon rind to taste
1 tbsp. lemon juice
4 tbsp. red hot cinnamon candies

Peel apples about 1/3 of the way down from stem ends. Combine remaining ingredients and 1/4 cup water; pour mixture into electric skillet. Place apples, stem ends down, in skillet; cover. Cook at 225 degrees for 20 minutes. Turn apples over; reduce skillet temperature to simmer. Cook for 15 minutes longer. Remove apples. Spoon pan juices over apples to serve.

Wannell McBride, Rec. Sec.
Gamma Eta No. 3416
Farmington, New Mexico

STUFFED CINNAMON APPLES

6 tart med. apples
3/4 c. red cinnamon candies
1 3-oz. package cream cheese, softened
2 tbsp. milk
1 tsp. lemon juice
1/3 c. chopped pitted dates

1 9-oz. can pineapple tidbits, drained
2 tbsp. chopped walnuts

Pare and core apples. Cook candies in 2 cups water until dissolved. Add apples; cook slowly, uncovered, for about 15 to 20 minutes or until just tender, turning once during cooking. Chill apples in syrup for several hours, turning once while chilling. Combine cream cheese, milk and lemon juice. Add dates, pineapple and walnuts; mix well. Drain apples; place in serving dishes. Stuff centers with cream cheese mixture.

Marguerite W. Widdop, Past State Pres.
Alpha Pi No. 2042
Colonial Heights, Virginia

MERINGUE EASTER EGG NESTS

Green food coloring
Coconut
6 egg whites
1/2 tsp. salt
1/2 tsp. cream of tartar
1 1/2 c. sugar
1 tsp. vanilla extract
Strawberry ice cream
Colored jelly beans or small Easter egg candies

Mix a drop of food coloring with a small amount of water; mix into coconut to color evenly. Set aside. Beat egg whites until frothy. Add salt and cream of tartar; beat until stiff but not dry. Beat in sugar and vanilla gradually. Cover a baking sheet with unglazed paper or brown paper. Shape meringue mixture into 8 nests on the paper, using spoon or pastry bag. Build up sides to height of about 1 1/2 inches and make slight hollows in centers. Sprinkle with coconut. Bake in 275-degree oven for about 50 minutes or until delicately browned. Remove from paper; cool on cake rack. Place a dip of ice cream in center of the nests; top with candies.

Ellary Simms
MAL
Corrales, New Mexico

SAVOY PEARS

Sugar
1 2-in. piece of lemon peel
1 tbsp. lemon juice
4 pears, peeled, halved and cored
1/4 c. cornstarch
1/2 c. white wine
1 egg, slightly beaten
1/2 c. heavy cream

Combine 3 cups water, 1/2 cup sugar, lemon peel and lemon juice in 3-quart saucepan; bring to a boil over medium heat. Add pear halves. Cover; cook gently until tender but firm. Reserve 1 cup pear syrup. Remove pears from pan; place in bowl. Cover; chill in refrigerator. Combine cornstarch, 2 tablespoons sugar, reserved pear syrup, wine and egg in 1-quart saucepan. Bring to a boil over medium heat, stirring constantly; boil for 1 minute. Remove from heat; cool to room temperature, stirring occasionally. Whip cream until soft peaks form; fold in wine mixture. Chill until ready to use. Arrange pears in serving bowl; spoon whipped cream mixture around pears. Garnish with strips of lemon peel. Yield: 6-8 servings.

Photograph for this recipe on page 136.

CREAM PUFFS WITH CREAMY COT FILLING

1 16-oz. can apricot halves, drained
2/3 c. sugar
1/4 tsp. ground cinnamon
1 c. sour cream
1/2 c. butter or margarine
1 c. all-purpose flour
4 eggs
1 c. confectioners' sugar
2 to 3 tbsp. milk or cream

Puree apricots in electric blender or press through sieve. Combine apricots and sugar in medium saucepan. Bring to a boil; simmer, uncovered, for about 15 minutes or until very thick. Let mixture cool; stir in cinnamon and sour cream. Chill until ready to use. Bring 1 cup water and butter to a full boil in large saucepan. Stir in flour; stir vigorously over low heat for about 30 seconds or until mixture forms a ball. Remove from heat. Beat in eggs, all at one time; beat until smooth. Drop 1/4 cup dough for each cream puff 3 inches apart onto ungreased baking sheet. Bake in 400-degree oven for 35 to 40 minutes or until puffed and golden brown. Let cool. Cut off top third of each cream puff; pull out excess soft dough. Place about 1 1/2 tablespoons chilled apricot filling in each cream puff; replace tops. Blend confectioners' sugar and enough milk to make a glaze; spoon glaze over each cream puff. Garnish with a slice of canned apricot, a sliver of red maraschino cherry and a sprig of fresh mint leaves, if desired. Yield: 12 cream puffs.

Photograph for this recipe on page 101.

APRICOT CREAM TARTS

1 16-oz. can apricot halves, drained
1 3 1/4-oz. package vanilla pudding
   and pie filling mix
1 c. light cream
3/4 tsp. grated lemon peel
1/2 c. sugar
10 baked tart shells 3 1/2 in. in
   diameter
Apricot halves, drained and chilled
1/2 c. strained apricot preserves, warmed
1/2 c. heavy cream, whipped and
   sweetened

Puree apricots in electric blender or press through sieve. Combine apricots, pie filling mix, cream, lemon peel and sugar in medium saucepan; bring to a boil, stirring constantly. Remove from heat. Spoon into prepared tart shells. Let cool, then chill tarts until ready to use. Arrange apricot halves in desired patterns on top of tarts, allowing space for whipped cream garnish. Brush preserves over apricots. Pipe rosettes or place spoonfuls of whipped cream on tarts. Maraschino cherry halves, fresh strawberry halves, grape halves or fresh blueberries may be used as fruit topping, if desired.

Photograph for this recipe on page 101.

OBSTTORTE

1/4 c. margarine
Sugar

2 egg yolks
1 tsp. grated lemon rind
1 c. flour
2 tbsp. cornstarch
Dash of salt
1 c. milk
2 tbsp. lemon juice
1/4 tsp. vanilla extract
4 drops of yellow food coloring
Apple slices, pear slices, seedless
   grapes, mandarin orange segments
   or halved strawberries
Fruit Tart Glaze

Beat margarine in small bowl of electric mixer at low speed. Add 1/4 cup sugar, 1 egg yolk and lemon rind; beat well. Mix in flour gradually until thoroughly blended. Press into 9-inch pie pan with fingers. Bake in 400-degree oven for 12 to 15 minutes or until edge is lightly browned. Cool. Combine cornstarch, 2 tablespoons sugar and salt in 1-quart saucepan. Add milk gradually; stir until smooth. Cook over low heat until mixture comes to a boil, stirring constantly; boil for 1 minute. Remove from heat. Combine lemon juice, remaining egg yolk, vanilla and food coloring; stir into cornstarch mixture. Let cool. Spread in tart shell. Arrange apple slices over filling; cover with Fruit Tart Glaze. Chill until serving time. Serve with whipped cream, if desired.

Fruit Tart Glaze

   1 1/2 tsp. unflavored gelatin
   1/4 c. light corn syrup
   1 tbsp. lemon juice

Pour 6 tablespoons water into saucepan; sprinkle gelatin over water to soften. Place over low heat until gelatin dissolves, stirring constantly. Remove from heat. Stir in syrup and lemon juice; mix well. Chill until partially congealed.

Photograph for this recipe on page 136.

APPLE-WHISKEY-MINCEMEAT PIE

   1/4 c. whiskey or Bourbon
   1 1-lb. 6-oz. jar prepared mincemeat

1/2 c. (packed) brown sugar
3 tbsp. flour
3 c. peeled sliced apples
1 unbaked 10-inch pie shell
6 peeled cored apple rings
2 tbsp. butter or margarine

Mix whiskey with mincemeat; set aside. Combine sugar and flour. Arrange sliced apples in layers in pie shell, sprinkling each layer with sugar mixture. Spread 1 1/2 cups spirited mincemeat over apples. Arrange apple rings on top, filling centers with remaining 1/2 cup mincemeat. Dot with butter. Bake in 425-degree oven for 40 minutes or until crust is well browned. May cover pie shell edge with aluminum foil to keep edge from getting too brown, if desired.

Jo Ross, Treas.
Delta Xi No. 3038
Clearwater, Florida

GRASSHOPPER PIE

   2 3-oz. packages lime gelatin
   4 tbsp. sugar
   1/8 tsp. salt
   1/3 c. Creme de Menthe
   1/3 c. Creme de Cacao
   1 tsp. vanilla extract
   1 egg white
   1 env. whipped topping mix
   1 unbaked 9-in. chocolate crumb crust

Dissolve gelatin, 2 tablespoons sugar and salt in 2 cups boiling water; add 3/4 cup cold water, liqueurs and vanilla. Chill until partially congealed. Beat egg white until foamy. Add remaining 2 tablespoons sugar gradually; beat until stiff peaks form. Prepare topping mix according to package directions. Reserve 1/2 cup gelatin mixture. Blend egg white and prepared topping into remaining gelatin mixture; chill until thick. Pile into pie crust; drizzle reserved gelatin mixture over top. Swirl spoon through filling to marbelize.

Peggy Diehl, Treas.
Alpha Iota No. 3365
Waynesboro, Virginia

NEW YEAR'S EVE PIE

   2 tbsp. butter or margarine
   1 1/2 c. coconut
   1 1-lb. 1-oz. can fruit cocktail
   1 env. unflavored gelatin
   1 6-oz. can frozen limeade concentrate
   1/4 c. sugar
   Green food coloring (opt.)
   1 1/2 c. whipping cream, whipped

Spread butter evenly on bottom and side of 9-inch pie plate. Press coconut evenly into butter to form crust. Bake in 300-degree oven for 15 minutes or until golden brown. Drain fruit cocktail; reserve 1/2 cup syrup. Soften gelatin in syrup; dissolve over heat. Combine limeade, sugar and green food coloring; stir in gelatin. Cool until partially congealed. Set aside 1/4 cup fruit cocktail; add remaining to limeade mixture. Reserve 1/4 cup whipped cream; fold in remaining whipped cream. Pour into prepared crust. Chill until firm. Make balloons of whipped cream; decorate with reserved fruit cocktail. Yield: 8 servings.

Photograph for this recipe above.

PECAN FUDGE PIE

   1 12-oz. package semisweet
      chocolate chips
   4 eggs
   1/2 tsp. salt
   2 tbsp. butter, melted
   2 tsp. vanilla extract
   1 c. light Karo syrup
   1 1/2 c. pecan halves
   1 unbaked deep 9 or 10-in. pie shell

Melt chocolate chips over low heat. Beat eggs, salt, butter, vanilla and syrup together. Add melted chocolate slowly, stirring rapidly. Fold in pecans; pour into pie shell. Bake in preheated 350-degree oven for 50 minutes to 1 hour or until center is set. Cool before cutting.

Dee Ann Archer, Pres.
Gamma Xi No. 4615
Oklahoma City, Oklahoma

FRENCH MINT PIE

   2 sq. chocolate
   1 c. powdered sugar

1/2 c. butter
2 eggs
1/4 tsp. mint flavoring
1   9-in. graham cracker crust

Melt chocolate over hot water; let cool. Beat sugar and butter together until smooth. Add eggs, one at a time, beating well after each addition. Add chocolate and mint flavoring; mix well. Spread into graham cracker crust; place in refrigerator. Chill for several hours.

Eula Koelling
MAL
Denver, Colorado

CHOCOLATE EGGNOG PIE

1 1/3 c. chocolate wafer crumbs
Sugar
1/4 c. butter, melted
1 env. unflavored gelatin
2 tbsp. cornstarch
1/4 tsp. salt
2 c. eggnog
1 tsp. vanilla extract
1/2 tsp. rum extract
2 c. whipping cream
1/4 c. confectioners' sugar

Combine crumbs and 2 tablespoons sugar; stir in butter. Press mixture firmly and evenly against bottom and side of 9-inch pie plate. Bake in preheated 350-degree oven for 5 minutes. Let cool. Sprinkle gelatin over 1/4 cup cold water to soften. Combine 1/3 cup sugar, cornstarch and salt in heavy saucepan; stir in eggnog gradually. Cook over medium heat until thickened, stirring constantly. Cook for 2 minutes longer. Remove from heat; stir in softened gelatin until dissolved. Add vanilla extract and rum extract. Chill until slightly thickened. Beat 1 cup cream until stiff; fold into eggnog mixture. Pour into cooled crust. Chill until set. Beat remaining 1 cup whipping cream in chilled bowl until foamy. Add confectioners' sugar gradually; beat until soft peaks form. Spread over pie; garnish with chocolate curls and stemmed maraschino cherries. Yield: 8 servings.

Photograph for this recipe on page 67.

COCONUT AND PINEAPPLE CHESS PIE

1/2 c. melted butter
2 c. sugar
2 tsp. flour
2 tsp. cornmeal
4 eggs, beaten
1 c. crushed pineapple, well drained
1/2 c. coconut
2 tsp. vanilla flavoring
1 unbaked lg. or 2 sm. pie shells

Combine first 8 ingredients; mix well. Pour into large pie shell. Bake at 375 degrees for about 30 minutes or until center of pie is firm.

Peggy Shelton, Sec.
Theta Phi No. 1620
Lake Dallas, Texas

FATHER'S FROSTED APPLE PIE

7 c. thinly sliced apples
2 tbsp. lemon juice
1 c. sugar
2 tbsp. flour
1 tsp. cinnamon
1/8 tsp. nutmeg
1/4 tsp. salt
1 recipe 2-crust pie pastry
2 tbsp. butter or margarine
1 egg yolk, slightly beaten
Apple Pie Frosting
Chopped walnuts

Combine apples and lemon juice; toss to coat well. Combine next 5 ingredients; mix with apples. Pour into pastry-lined pie plate; pile high in center. Dot with butter. Add top crust. Mix egg yolk with 1 tablespoon water; brush over top crust. Bake at 425 degrees for 45 to 50 minutes or until done. Spread Apple Pie Frosting over hot pie; sprinkle with walnuts.

Apple Pie Frosting

1 c. confectioners' sugar
1 tbsp. light corn syrup
1/2 tsp. vanilla extract

Combine ingredients; mix well.

June Lamb, Ed. Chm.
Epsilon Pi No. 2104
Bedford, Indiana

DOROTHY'S PECAN PIE

1/4 c. butter, softened
2/3 c. (packed) brown sugar
3 eggs, beaten
3/4 c. dark Karo syrup
1/4 tsp. salt
1 tsp. vanilla extract
1 recipe 1-crust pie pastry
1 c. pecan halves

Cream butter and sugar together until fluffy. Add next 4 ingredients; mix well. Line pie pan with pastry; sprinkle in pecans. Pour egg mixture over pecans. Bake in 450-degree oven for 10 minutes. Reduce temperature to 350 degrees; bake for 35 minutes longer or until knife inserted in center comes out clean.

Dorothy W. Wilkinson
Delta Chap.
Hotchkiss, Colorado

PECAN CRUST-PUMPKIN PIE

1 1/2 c. graham cracker crumbs
1/2 c. chopped pecans
1 1/4 c. sugar
1/4 c. margarine, melted
1 env. unflavored gelatin
1/2 tsp. cinnamon
1/2 tsp. ginger
1/8 tsp. cloves
1/4 tsp. allspice
1/2 tsp. salt
4 eggs, separated
1   1-lb. can pumpkin
3/4 c. milk
1/2 c. whipping cream, whipped

Combine crumbs, pecans, 1/4 cup sugar and margarine; blend well. Press evenly into 9-inch pie pan. Bake in 300-degree oven for 10 minutes. Let cool. Combine 3/4 cup sugar, gelatin, spices and salt in top of double boiler; stir in slightly beaten egg yolks, pumpkin and milk. Cook for 15 minutes or until mixture coats a spoon, stirring constantly. Pour into bowl; let chill. Beat egg whites in large bowl until foamy. Add remaining 1/4 cup sugar gradually; beat until stiff but not dry. Place bowl of pumpkin

mixture in pan of ice; beat until mixture is fluffy. Fold in meringue; spoon into pie shell. Chill until ready to serve. Garnish with dollops of whipped cream; sprinkle with nutmeg.

Photograph for this recipe on page 33.

FLUFFY PUMPKIN PIE

1/2 c. sugar
1 env. unflavored gelatin
1 tsp. pumpkin pie spice
1/2 tsp. salt
1 c. milk
1 egg, slightly beaten
1   16-oz. can pumpkin
1 c. Cool Whip or Dream Whip
1 baked pie shell

Combine sugar, gelatin, spice and salt in saucepan; blend in milk. Cook, stirring, over medium heat until gelatin is dissolved. Stir small amount of gelatin mixture into egg, then stir slowly into saucepan. Blend in pumpkin. Chill until very thick. Fold in Cool Whip. Spoon into pie shell. Chill for about 4 hours or until firm. Top with Cool Whip, if desired.

Zada Terzenbach, V.P.
Alpha Upsilon No. 3295
Federal Way, Washington

LEMON ANGEL PIE

4 eggs, separated
1 1/2 c. sugar
1/4 tsp. cream of tartar
1 tsp. vanilla extract
1 tsp. vinegar
3 tbsp. lemon or orange juice
Whipped cream or Cool Whip

Beat egg whites until soft peaks form; add 1 cup sugar and cream of tartar gradually, beating until stiff peaks form. Beat in vanilla and vinegar. Line pie pan with meringue mixture. Bake in 350-degree oven for 1 hour. Cool. Combine beaten egg yolks with remaining 1/2 cup sugar and lemon juice in saucepan; cook, stirring constantly, until thick. Cool. Pour over cooled meringue shell.

Cover generously with whipped cream. Chill for 4 hours.

Reggie Souder, Rec. Sec.
Delta Iota No. 3525
Huntington, Indiana

DEEP-DISH MINCE APPLE PIE

1 28-oz. jar mincemeat or mincemeat
   with Brandy and rum
2 21-oz. cans apple pie filling
2 tsp. vanilla extract
2 tbsp. margarine
1 recipe 2-crust pie pastry
2 tbsp. milk, cream or evaporated milk
2 tbsp. sugar

Combine mincemeat, apple pie filling and vanilla; place in 13 x 9 x 2-inch baking pan. Dot with margarine. Roll out pastry to fit pan; place on top of filling, pressing and fluting edges to sides of pan. Cut several vents in crust. Brush pastry crust with milk; sprinkle with sugar. Bake in preheated 425-degree oven for 45 minutes or until crust is golden brown and filling is bubbly.

Barbara Mooney, Educational Dir.
Theta Beta No. 3670
Pleasant Hill, Oregon

OHIO LEMON SLICE PIE

Pastry for 8-in. 2-crust pie
2 lemons
1 3/4 c. sugar
4 eggs

Line 8-inch pie plate with pastry; set aside. Grate rind from lemons to measure 2 tablespoons; set aside. Peel lemons, removing all white membrane. Cut lemons into very thin slices; remove seeds. Combine lemon slices, rind and sugar in bowl. Let stand for 20 minutes, stirring occasionally. Beat eggs well. Stir into lemon mixture; pour into pastry-lined plate. Adjust top crust; cut slits for steam to escape. Seal and flute edges. Bake at 400 degrees for 35 to 40 minutes or until

done. Cover pastry edges with foil to prevent overbrowning, if necessary.

Kay Baker, Historian
Beta Eta No. 3696
Fairfield, Illinois

EASY COCONUT PIE

2 eggs
1 c. sugar
1 tbsp. flour
1/4 c. butter, melted
1 c. frozen coconut, thawed
Pinch of salt
1/4 tsp. vanilla extract
1/2 c. milk
1 unbaked pie shell

Beat eggs well. Add next 7 ingredients in order listed; mix well. Pour into pie shell. Bake in 400-degree oven for 30 minutes or until done.

Peggy F. Thompson, Philanthropic Chm.
Delta Rho No. 4512
Front Royal, Virginia

SOUR CREAM-RAISIN PIE

1 c. (packed) light brown sugar
1 c. sour cream
3 tbsp. cornstarch
1/2 c. milk
3 eggs, separated
1 c. seedless raisins
Pinch of salt
1 baked 9-in. pie shell

Combine brown sugar and sour cream in saucepan; bring to boiling point, stirring constantly. Dissolve cornstarch in milk. Beat egg yolks; stir into milk. Stir slowly into hot mixture; cook until thick, stirring constantly. Add raisins and salt. Cook slowly for 5 minutes longer. Let cool. Pour into pie shell. Make meringue using egg whites; spread over pie, sealing to edge. Brown meringue in 350-degree oven.

Belle Flinn, W. and M. Com.
Alpha Phi No. 1148
Thermopolis, Wyoming

MACADAMIA NUT PIE

8 eggs
2 c. corn syrup
1 c. sugar
1/2 c. butter, melted
1/4 c. flour
2 tsp. vanilla extract
Dash of salt
1 unbaked 9-in. pastry shell
1 c. chopped macadamia nuts

Combine eggs, corn syrup, sugar, butter, flour, vanilla and salt; beat with rotary beater until smooth. Pour into pastry shell; sprinkle with macadamia nuts. Bake at 350 degrees for 1 hour or until knife inserted in center comes out clean. Cool before serving.

Jacquie Randlett
Alpha Iota No. 2992
Anchorage, Alaska

MILE-HIGH STRAWBERRY PIE

2 egg whites
Sugar
1   10-oz. box frozen strawberries,
  thawed
1 tbsp. lemon juice
1 c. whipping cream
1 baked 10-in. deep-dish pie shell

Beat egg whites until frothy, adding 1 cup sugar gradually. Add strawberries and lemon juice. Beat at high speed for 15 minutes, scraping bowl frequently. Beat cream with 3 tablespoons sugar until stiff peaks form; fold into strawberry mixture. Pile high in pie shell; freeze until firm. Remove from freezer about 5 minutes before serving. May substitute 2 cups fresh strawberries for frozen strawberries, adding 1/2 cup sugar.

Joan Adolfson, Ed. Dir.
Delta Omega No. 4662
Moses Lake, Washington

STRAWBERRY-CREAM CHEESE PIE

1   6-oz. package cream cheese,
  softened

3 tbsp. sour cream
1   9-in. graham cracker crust
1 to 1 1/2 qt. fresh strawberries
1 c. sugar
3 tbsp. cornstarch
Red food coloring (opt.)

Beat cream cheese until fluffy. Add sour cream; beat until smooth. Spread over bottom of graham cracker crust; refrigerate. Mash enough uneven strawberries to measure 1 cup. Force through sieve; add enough water to measure 1 cup. Combine sugar and cornstarch in saucepan. Add 1 cup water and sieved strawberries; cook over medium heat until mixture is clear and thickened, stirring constantly. Boil for about 1 minute. Stir to cool slightly; add a small amount of red food coloring. Fill crust with remaining strawberries, tip end up; pour glaze over top. Chill for 1 hour.

Elaine C. Thomas
Alpha Epsilon No. 3548
Newport News, Virginia

CARAMEL TREATS

1 pkg. Kraft caramels
3 tbsp. milk
1 c. Rice Krispies
1 c. Frosted Flakes
1 c. coconut
1 c. chopped nuts

Melt caramels and milk in double boiler or in saucepan over low heat. Add all remaining ingredients at once; stir rapidly. Roll about 1 teaspoon of cereal mixture at a time into very small balls with buttered hands. Let stand for about 30 minutes or until balls are firm.

Ann Graham, Past Pres.
Beta Upsilon No. 748
Lebanon, Indiana

CHOCOLATE-COATED COCONUT CANDY

1/2 c. butter or margarine
1 can sweetened condensed milk
2 boxes confectioners' sugar
Pinch of salt

1 can flaked coconut
1/4 c. chopped pecans
2 pkg. chocolate chips
1/3 cake paraffin

Melt butter; add milk slowly. Stir in sugar and salt; mix well. Add coconut and pecans; stir well. Chill until mixture can be easily handled. Roll into small balls; insert a toothpick into each ball. Place in refrigerator; chill until firm. Melt chocolate chips and paraffin in top of double boiler. Dip balls into chocolate; remove quickly and place on waxed paper. Stir chocolate often to keep well mixed. Remove toothpick using another toothpick. Smooth any holes with spoon and a small amount of melted chocolate mixture. Store in refrigerator in covered container.

Nancy Headley
Gamma Kappa No. 4595
Mesa, Arizona

CHRISTMAS PEANUT BUTTER BALLS

1 c. margarine
1 c. peanut butter
1 1-lb. box powdered sugar
1 12-oz. package choclate chips
1 6-oz. Hershey bar
1/3 bar paraffin

Melt margarine and peanut butter together; add enough powdered sugar to make a very stiff mixture. Shape into balls; place on cookie sheet. Refrigerate for 10 minutes. Melt chocolate chips, Hershey bar, and paraffin in top of double boiler. Dip balls into chocolate mixture; place on foil. Refrigerate until hard. Yield: 4 dozen balls.

Joyce Davis
Alpha Psi No. 2841
Kokomo, Indiana

DATE AND FIG BALLS

1 8-oz. package dates, coarsely ground
1 12-oz. package dried figs, coarsely ground

1/2 c. lemon juice
1/2 c. candied cherries, diced
Flaked coconut

Combine all ingredients except coconut; mix thoroughly. Shape into small balls; roll in coconut.

Eleanor Hardy, Ed. Dir.
Beta Eta No. 3696
Fairfield, Illinois

PEANUT BUTTER CANDY BALLS

1/2 c. margarine
2 c. chunky peanut butter
1 box powdered sugar
3 c. Cocoa Rice Krispies
1 bar paraffin
1 12-oz. package chocolate chips

Melt margarine and peanut butter together; fold in powdered sugar and Rice Krispies. Mix well. Shape into balls; place on waxed paper to dry. Melt paraffin and chocolate chips in double boiler. Dip balls into mixture with fork; place on waxed paper to harden. Stir chocolate mixture occasionally. Yield: 6 1/2 dozen.

Dorothy Ross
Alpha Xi No. 1861
West Des Moines, Iowa

RUM BALLS

2 c. fine vanilla wafer crumbs
1 c. confectioners' sugar
1 c. finely chopped pecans
2 tbsp. dark corn syrup
1/4 c. light rum

Combine crumbs, sugar, pecans, corn syrup and rum; mix well. Form into 1-inch balls; roll in additional confectioners' sugar. Store in glass or plastic container; refrigerate until ready to serve. Flavor improves with age.

Linda Young, Treas.
Delta Alpha No. 2664
Saint Cloud, Florida

SAINT PATRICK'S PING-PONG BALLS

1 6-oz. package chocolate bits
1/2 c. sugar
1/4 c. light corn syrup
2 1/2 c. crushed vanilla wafer crumbs
1 c. finely chopped nuts
1 tsp. vanilla extract or rum
Green sugar

Melt chocolate bits over hot water; remove pan from water. Stir in sugar and corn syrup. Blend in 1/4 cup water, crumbs, nuts and vanilla. Mix well. Form in 1-inch balls; roll in green sugar. Place in airtight container for at least overnight. Keeps for 3 to 4 weeks and improves in flavor with age.

Lora Lee Davis, Pres.
Sigma Chi No. 4689
Metairie, Louisiana

CANDIED STRAWBERRIES

1 c. coconut
1 c. ground nuts (opt.)
2 3-oz. packages strawberry
*   gelatin*
3/4 c. sweetened condensed milk
1/2 tsp. vanilla extract
Red sugar
Green food coloring
Slivered almonds

Combine first 5 ingredients; mix thoroughly. Chill for 1 hour. Form into strawberry shapes. Roll in red sugar. Place several drops of food coloring in jar; add almonds. Shake to tint almonds. Insert tinted sliver of almond for stem. These strawberries freeze well and are very decorative for dessert trays.

Janet Pattison, Awards Chm.
Gamma Delta No. 2208
Peru, Indiana

CHERRY CANDY

1 can sweetened condensed milk
2 lb. powdered sugar
1 sm. can coconut

1 c. chopped pecans
1 jar candied cherries, chopped
1/4 tsp. salt
1 tsp. vanilla extract

Combine all ingredients; mix well. Divide into 4 parts. Shape into rolls; wrap in foil. Refrigerate until ready to serve; slice.

Charlene Walters
Theta No. 598
North Manchester, Indiana

CHOCOLATE-COVERED PRETZELS

1 6-oz. package semisweet
*   chocolate morsels*
2 tbsp. corn syrup
2 tbsp. shortening
30 (about) 3-in. twisted pretzels

Combine chocolate morsels, corn syrup, shortening and 1 1/2 teaspoons water in top of double boiler; place over hot but not boiling water. Stir until chocolate is melted. Remove pan from heat but keep chocolate mixture over hot water. Dip each pretzel into chocolate mixture to coat thoroughly; place on wire rack over waxed paper. Chill in refrigerator for about 10 minutes or until coating sets. Remove from refrigerator; let stand at room temperature for about 1 hour or until surface dries.

Barbara Doherty, Pres.
Alpha Omega No. 4576
West Chester, Pennsylvania

CHRISTMAS BUTTER FUDGE

4 c. sugar
2 c. milk
1/2 c. butter
1/4 tsp. salt
1 tsp. vanilla extract
1/4 finely chopped candied cherries
1/4 c. blanched pistachios

Combine sugar, milk, butter and salt in large saucepan. Bring to a boil, stirring constantly until sugar is dissolved. Cook over moderate heat, stirring occasionally, to 236 degrees on candy thermometer or until candy forms a

soft ball when dropped into cold water. Remove from heat immediately; place pan in cold water. Do not stir or beat until cooled to lukewarm. Add vanilla; beat until candy becomes thick and creamy and loses shine. Fold in cherries and pistachios quickly just before fudge is to the setting stage. Pour candy into buttered 8-inch square pan; let stand at room temperature until firm. Cut into squares and decorate with candied fruit, if desired.

Photograph for this recipe above.

CHOCOLATE FUDGE

1 1/4 c. milk
4   1-oz. squares unsweetened
*   chocolate*
3 c. sugar
2 tbsp. corn syrup
1/4 c. butter
1 tsp. vanilla extract
1 1/2 c. coarsely chopped nuts

Heat milk and chocolate together in heavy pan over low heat until chocolate melts. Add sugar and corn syrup; stir until sugar dissolves. Wash sugar crystals from sides of pan with damp cloth wrapped around a fork. Cook to 234 degrees on candy thermometer or to soft-ball stage, stirring occasionally. Remove from heat; add butter. Cool to 110 degrees or lukewarm, without stirring. Add vanilla and nuts; beat until candy holds shape and begins to lose gloss. Pour onto buttered platter or pan. Cut into squares and decorate with pecan halves when set, if desired. Yield: About 3 pounds fudge.

Photograph for this recipe on this page.

MICROWAVE FUDGE

1 lb. powdered sugar
1/2 c. cocoa
1/4 c. milk
1/4 lb. margarine
1 tbsp. vanilla extract
1/2 c. chopped nuts

Place sugar and cocoa in mixing bowl; add milk and margarine. Do not stir. Microwave for 3 minutes. Remove from oven; stir just enough to mix. Add vanilla and nuts; stir until blended. Pour into greased pan; place in refrigerator to harden for 1 hour.

Louise T. McCullough, Pres.
Alpha Kappa No. 1172
Fort Myers, Florida

WHITE CHRISTMAS FUDGE

2 1/4 c. sugar
1/2 c. sour cream
1/4 c. milk
2 tbsp. butter
1 tbsp. Karo syrup
1/4 tsp. salt
2 tsp. vanilla extract
1 c. pecans, chopped

Combine sugar, sour cream, milk, butter, syrup and salt in heavy saucepan. Cook over medium heat until sugar is dissolved and mixture comes to a boil, stirring constantly. Cook to 238 degrees on candy thermometer. Remove from heat; let stand until lukewarm. Add vanilla; beat until mixture begins to lose gloss and hold shape. Stir in pecans quickly; turn into buttered 8 x 8-inch pan. Let stand until firm before cutting. Yield: 1 1/2 pounds.

Olivia Harrington
Theta Pi No. 3408
Duncanville, Texas

NO-FAIL DIVINITY

Butter
3 c. sugar
3/4 c. light corn syrup
1/4 tsp. salt
2 egg whites
3 tbsp. flavored gelatin
Vanilla extract to taste
1 c. chopped nuts

Butter sides of heavy 2-quart saucepan; add sugar, corn syrup, 3/4 cup hot water and salt. Cook, stirring constantly, until sugar dissolves and mixture reaches boiling point. Cook, without stirring, to 250 degrees on candy thermometer or to hard-ball stage. Remove from heat. Beat egg whites until soft peaks form, adding gelatin gradually and beating until stiff peaks form. Stir in vanilla. Pour hot syrup slowly over egg white mixture; beat constantly at high speed of mixer until soft peaks form and mixture begins to lose gloss. Stir in nuts. Drop from teaspoon onto waxed paper. Cool. Yield: 4 1/2 dozen pieces.

Clela Chapman, Corr. Sec.
Alpha Omicron No. 577
Enid, Oklahoma

ORANGE-GLAZED PECANS

1 orange
1 1/2 c. sugar
4 c. pecans

Grate enough rind from orange to measure 1 teaspoon. Squeeze orange; reserve juice. Cook sugar, 1/2 cup water and reserved orange juice to soft-ball stage. Add orange rind and pecans; cook until pecans are coated and turn white. Pour onto waxed paper; separate pecans. Let cool.

Wilma Endsley, 2nd V.P.
Gamma Iota No. 4063
Laurel, Mississippi

PEANUT BRITTLE

3 c. sugar
1 c. white Karo syrup
3 c. fresh peanuts

3 tsp. butter
1 tsp. salt
2 tsp. soda

Combine sugar, syrup and 1/2 cup water in heavy Dutch oven. Boil to 234 degrees on candy thermometer or until mixture spins a thread. Add peanuts, stirring constantly. Cook to 305 degrees or until mixture turns golden brown. Remove from heat; add butter, salt and soda. Mixture will bubble. Pour quickly and carefully into 2 buttered cookie sheets, spreading evenly with wooden spatula or spoon. Cool. Break into pieces.

Helen Grabiec, Past State Pres.
Delta Gamma No. 2478
Brecksville, Ohio

POPCORN EASTER BUNNIES

7 c. popped popcorn, Kix or Cheerios
1 c. sugar
1/3 c. light corn syrup
1 tsp. salt
1/4 c. butter
1 tsp. vanilla extract
Marshmallows
Pipe cleaners

Place popcorn in large bowl. Combine sugar, 1/3 cup water, syrup, salt and butter in saucepan; cook to 250 degrees on candy thermometer or to hard-ball stage. Remove from heat; stir in vanilla. Pour in thin stream over popcorn, stirring constantly to mix well. Shape into bunny shapes with buttered hands. Attach marshmallow slices for ears and marshmallow halves for tails. Attach pipe cleaners for whiskers.

Carrie Hahnenberg, Ed. Dir.
Alpha Omega No. 886
Westerville, Ohio

SO-EASY CARAMEL CORN

2 c. (packed) brown sugar
1/2 c. light corn syrup
1 c. margarine
Dash of salt

Pinch of cream of tartar
1/2 tsp. soda
6 to 7 qt. warm popped popcorn

Combine first 4 ingredients in saucepan; bring to a full boil. Stir and boil for 3 minutes. Remove from heat; add cream of tartar and soda. Stir until foamy. Pour over popcorn. Stir until popcorn is well coated with syrup. Spread on 2 cookie sheets. Bake at 200 degrees for 45 minutes. Remove immediately to cool. Store in airtight containers.

Ruth Hennon, Treas.
Eta Beta No. 2286
Arvada, Colorado

CHRISTMAS CARAMELS

2 c. sugar
1 c. (packed) brown sugar
1 c. light corn syrup
1 c. heavy cream
1 c. milk
1 c. butter
1 1/2 tbsp. vanilla extract
1 c. chopped nuts

Combine all ingredients except vanilla and nuts in heavy saucepan. Cook slowly to 260 degrees on candy thermometer or to firm-ball stage, stirring occasionally. Remove from heat. Add vanilla and nuts. Pour into buttered 8 x 8 x 2-inch pan. Cool until firm. Turn out on cutting board. Cut into 1-inch pieces. Wrap in waxed paper or Saran Wrap.

Georgia Stephen
Beta Tau No. 472
Grand Junction, Colorado

CHRISTMAS GOODIES

1/2 c. white Karo syrup
1/2 c. sugar
3/4 c. peanut butter
3 c. Special K cereal
1 pkg. chocolate bits
1 pkg. butterscotch bits

Bring syrup and sugar to boiling point; add peanut butter. Stir in Special K; mix well. Pat into buttered pan; smooth with fingers. Melt chocolate bits and butterscotch bits; pour over Special K mixture. Cut into squares while still hot. Refrigerate; cut again.

Carla Krueger
Kappa Chi No. 4457
Brush, Colorado

MOUND BARS

2 c. crushed graham crackers
1/2 c. butter, melted
1/4 c. sugar
1 sm. package flaked coconut
1 sm. can sweetened condensed milk
1 pkg. chocolate chips
1 tbsp. peanut butter

Combine graham cracker crumbs, butter and sugar; spread in 12 x 9 x 2-inch pan. Bake at 350 degrees for 10 minutes. Combine coconut and milk; spread over graham cracker mixture. Bake at 350 degrees for 15 minutes. Let cool. Melt chocolate chips and peanut butter together; spread on top of coconut mixture. Chill until firm. Cut into bars.

Mrs. Leo Frieden, Philanthropic Com.
Theta No. 598
North Manchester, Indiana

PEANUT BUTTER CUPS

1 2/3 c. graham cracker crumbs
1 c. margarine, melted
1 lb. powdered sugar
1 c. peanut butter
2 c. chocolate chips

Combine first 4 ingredients; spread in 13 x 9-inch pan. Melt chocolate chips in double boiler; spread over peanut butter mixture. Chill for 1 hour or until ready to use. Cut into squares.

Chris Flinn, Treas.
Eta Psi No. 2693
Colorado Springs, Colorado

CINNAMON-SPANGLED STARS

6 c. puffed rice
3 c. miniature marshmallows
1/3 c. butter or margarine
1/2 tsp. vanilla extract
Thick white confectioners' sugar
frosting
Red cinnamon candies
12 birthday candles

Heat puffed rice in shallow baking pan in preheated 350-degree oven for about 10 minutes. Pour into large greased bowl. Melt marshmallows and butter over low heat, stirring occasionally; stir in vanilla. Pour over puffed rice; stir until all kernels are evenly coated. Press into 12 greased individual star-shaped molds, using greased hands. Let stand for about 30 minutes; remove from molds. Pipe frosting to form a circle about 1 1/2 inches in diameter in center of each star. Press red cinnamon candies into frosting; attach a cinnamon candy with frosting to each star point. Make a small hole in center of each star. Insert candle and light. Make a star pattern as a guide and shape stars free form, if star molds are not available.

Photograph for this recipe above.

BANANA-OATMEAL COOKIES

3/4 c. shortening
3/4 c. sugar
2 sm. bananas, mashed
1 egg, well beaten
1 1/2 c. sifted flour
1/2 tsp. soda
1/4 tsp. salt
1 tsp. cinnamon
1 tsp. nutmeg
1/2 c. chopped nuts
3/4 c. oatmeal

Cream shortening and sugar together; add bananas and egg. Sift flour, soda, salt and spices together; add to creamed mixture. Add nuts and oatmeal mixture. Drop by rounded teaspoonfuls onto greased cookie sheet. Bake at 400 degrees until done.

Billie Anderson, V.P.
Beta Eta No. 3696
Fairfield, Illinois

ANGEL BITS

1/2 tsp. salt
3 egg whites, stiffly beaten
1 c. sugar
1/2 tsp. vanilla extract
1 c. chopped pecans
1   6-oz. package chocolate chips

Add salt to stiffly beaten egg whites. Add sugar gradually, beating constantly until sugar is dissolved. Fold in vanilla, pecans and chocolate chips. Drop from teaspoon onto greased and floured cookie sheet. Bake at 300 degrees for 30 minutes. Yield: 65 cookies.

Gloria Davis, Pres.
Beta Nu No. 4719
Cadiz, Kentucky

CHERRY BROWNIES

1/2 c. butter
2 oz. unsweetened chocolate
1 c. sugar
1/2 tsp. baking powder
2 eggs

1/2 c. flour
1/2 c. chopped nuts
1/3 c. finely chopped maraschino
cherries, drained
1 tsp. vanilla extract

Melt butter and chocolate in saucepan. Blend in sugar and baking powder. Add eggs, one at a time, beating well after each addition. Stir in remaining ingredients; mix well. Spread in greased 8-inch square pan. Bake at 350 degrees for 30 to 35 minutes.

Brownie Cherry Frosting

1 tbsp. butter, melted
1 c. sifted confectioners' sugar
1 oz. chocolate, melted
Vanilla extract to taste
1 to 2 tbsp. maraschino cherry juice
2 tbsp. finely chopped maraschino
cherries

Combine butter, sugar, chocolate and vanilla. Stir in enough cherry juice to make of spreading consistency. Blend in cherries. Frost brownies; cut into bars.

Hilda Franz, Pres.
Alpha Rho No. 3735
Biloxi, Mississippi

SNOWFLAKES

2 egg whites
1 tsp. vanilla extract
Pinch of salt
2/3 c. sugar
1 c. chopped pecans
1 c. chocolate chips

Beat egg whites until soft peaks form; add vanilla and salt. Beat until firm peaks form. Add sugar gradually, beating until stiff peaks form. Stir in pecans and chocolate chips. Drop from spoon onto a cookie sheet covered with greased foil. Place in preheated 375-degree oven; turn off heat immediately. Leave in oven until oven cools thoroughly. Yield: 2 dozen cookies.

Dorotha Trouslot, W. and M. Chm.
Kappa Nu No. 4415
Newton, Kansas

CHRISTMAS MOCHA BALLS

1 c. butter
1/2 c. sugar
1 tsp. vanilla extract
2 c. sifted flour
1/4 c. cocoa
1 tsp. instant coffee powder
1 c. finely chopped nuts
1/2 c. chopped maraschino cherries
Confectioners' sugar

Cream butter and sugar together; stir in vanilla. Sift dry ingredients together. Add to creamed mixture gradually; mix well. Stir in nuts and cherries. Form dough into rolls 1 inch in diameter; wrap in waxed paper. Refrigerate overnight. Cut rolls into 1/2-inch slices; roll in palms of hands to form balls. Bake at 325 degrees for 20 minutes. Sift confectioners' sugar over warm cookies; let cool on rack. Yield: 6 dozen.

Judy Patterson, V.P.
Beta Iota No. 2748
Madison, Wisconsin

CHRISTMAS COOKIES

1 c. butter
1 c. (packed) brown sugar
1 c. sugar
2 eggs
1 tsp. vanilla extract
2 1/2 c. flour
1 tsp. soda
1 tsp. baking powder
1 c. oatmeal
1 c. salted peanuts

Cream butter and sugars together; add eggs and vanilla. Beat until well blended. Sift flour, soda and baking powder together. Add to butter mixture; mix well. Stir in oatmeal and peanuts. Chill dough for several hours or overnight. Shape balls of 1 teaspoon of dough; place on baking sheet. Bake at 350 degrees for about 15 to 18 minutes or until browned.

Judith Eberle, V.P.
Eta Epsilon No. 4501
Wakeeney, Kansas

DATE STRIPS

2 c. rolled oats
1 1/2 c. flour
1 c. (packed) brown sugar
1 tsp. soda
1/4 tsp. salt
3/4 c. butter, melted
Date Filling

Combine first 5 ingredients; mix well. Stir in butter. Press half the mixture into baking pan. Spread filling over oats mixture; spread remaining oats mixture over top. Bake in 350-degree oven for 40 minutes. Cut into strips or squares to serve.

Date Filling

1/2 c. chopped nuts
1 lb. chopped dates
1 c. sugar
1 tbsp. flour
1 tsp. vanilla extract

Combine first 4 ingredients with 1 cup water in saucepan; mix well. Bring to a boil, stirring constantly; boil until thick. Stir in vanilla. Let cool.

Jean DeGooyer, Past State Pres.
Beta Chi No. 2443
Kirkland, Washington

FRUITED LAYER BARS

1 1/2 c. sifted all-purpose flour
Sugar
1/2 tsp. salt
6 tbsp. butter
2 eggs, separated
1 c. sour cream
1/2 tsp. vanilla extract
1 c. finely snipped dates
1/3 c. apricot preserves
2 tsp. grated orange peel
1/2 tsp. cinnamon
1/3 c. chopped walnuts

Sift flour, 1 tablespoon sugar and salt together; cut in butter until mixture resembles coarse crumbs. Combine egg yolks, 1/4 cup sour cream and vanilla; stir into flour mixture. Pat mixture into greased 13 x 9 x 2-inch pan. Bake in preheated 350-degree oven for 20 minutes. Combine dates, remaining 3/4 cup sour cream, apricot preserves and orange peel; spread over baked layer. Beat 2 egg whites until soft peaks form; add 7 tablespoons sugar and cinnamon gradually. Beat until stiff peaks form. Spread meringue carefully over date mixture; sprinkle with walnuts. Bake at 350 degrees for 30 minutes; cool.

Mardi Albright
Delta Nu No. 517
Kalama, Washington

HEDGEHOGS

1 c. (packed) brown sugar
2 eggs
2 c. chopped nuts
1 1/2 c. coconut
1 c. chopped dates

Combine brown sugar and eggs; beat until light and fluffy. Add nuts, coconut and dates; mix well. Form into small balls; place on greased cookie sheet. Bake at 350 degrees for 15 minutes.

Myrtle Weber, Pres.
Alpha Zeta No. 226
Tacoma, Washington

FLAKY PINEAPPLE SQUARES

1 lb. butter or margarine
4 c. flour
1 c. sour cream
1 tsp. vanilla extract
3 c. drained crushed pineapple
1 c. sugar
3 tbsp. cornstarch
Confectioners' sugar

Cut butter into flour with pastry blender or 2 knives. Add sour cream and vanilla; mix well. Refrigerate for 2 hours. Combine pineapple, sugar and cornstarch in saucepan; cook over medium heat, stirring constantly, until thick and clear. Cool. Roll out half the dough; place in ungreased jelly roll pan. Add pineapple filling; spread over dough. Roll out remaining dough; cover pineapple filling.

Bake in preheated 325-degree oven for 55 minutes or until golden brown. Sprinkle with confectioners' sugar; cut into squares.

Sue Ann Van Cleave, V.P.
Alpha Chi No. 463
Franklin, Indiana

ICED WALNUT SQUARES

1 c. butter or margarine
1/2 c. sugar
2 c. flour
1/2 c. cornstarch
Vanilla extract
4 eggs, beaten
1 lb. brown sugar
1/2 tsp. baking powder
1 c. shredded coconut
1 1/2 c. chopped walnuts
1/2 c. soft margarine
1 lb. powdered sugar
1 lg. package cream cheese, softened

Cream butter and sugar until light; blend in flour and cornstarch. Pat into 11 x 17-inch pan. Bake at 300 degrees for 15 minutes. Combine 2 teaspoons vanilla and next 5 ingredients, mixing well. Remove pan from oven; spread walnut mixture over top. Bake at 300 degrees for 15 minutes. Increase temperature to 350 degrees. Bake for 5 minutes longer. Cool. Combine margarine, powdered sugar, cream cheese and vanilla to taste; beat until smooth. Spread over cooled layer. Cut into squares.

Mary Balkowitsch
Alpha Epsilon No. 414
Vancouver, Washington

THREE-WAY ORANGE SPICE COOKIES

4 c. sifted flour
1 c. sugar
1 tsp. soda
1 c. Karo light or dark corn syrup
1 c. Nucoa or Mazola margarine
4 tsp. grated orange rind
1/2 tsp. ginger
1/2 tsp. ground cloves

2 eggs
Orange Butter Icing

Sift flour, sugar and soda together. Combine corn syrup, margarine, orange rind and spices in saucepan; bring to a boil over medium heat. Beat eggs in large bowl; stir in hot mixture slowly. Stir in flour mixture, all at once; blend well. This batter may be used for drop cookies, refrigerator cookies or squares. Drop batter onto greased cookie sheet by teaspoonfuls 1 inch apart. Shape well-chilled batter into 1/2-inch balls or roll out and cut with cookie cutter. Squares may be made by spreading batter in 2 greased jelly roll pans. Bake in preheated 350-degree oven until done. Frost as desired with Orange Butter Icing.

Orange Butter Icing

2 tbsp. margarine
1 c. confectioners' sugar
1 tbsp. orange juice
1 tbsp. Karo light or dark corn syrup
1 tsp. grated orange rind
Few grains of salt

Melt margarine in small saucepan; remove from heat. Add remaining ingredients; beat until smooth.

Photograph for this recipe below.

Beverages

Too often, the imaginative choice of a beverage is overlooked by a hostess when she is planning a special occasion meal. And, much of the time, all of the bustle and activity that marks any holiday season just makes "what to drink" seem unimportant. But, for a truly balanced and pleasing meal, the choice of a beverage is an important key. Think of it: a group of friends gather for a festive Fourth of July picnic on the beach. During the day, they boil seafood and grill chicken and spareribs over a roasting pit dug into the sand. They play volleyball, jog, swim and just get generally hot, tired, sun-burned, and *thirsty*.

There are better ways to quench your thirst than just unadorned iced tea or sugary, tasteless colas. Why settle for iced tea when an iced, spiced tea com-bined with favorite fruit juices revives a sun-drenched soul so much better? Why bother with the expense of empty-calorie colas for a crowd when the same amount of ginger ale combined with pineapple, pear, cranberry and lemon juices can satisfy the same number of people with far more sparkle and nutrition? Moreover, these fruit juice punches can be prepared in advance and served from thermal jugs, eliminating the sure mess and possible danger of pop-top cans and glass bottles.

There are many summertime holidays, as well as birthdays and other cele-brations where ice cream is an expected item on the menu. Let ice creams and sherbets make an unexpected appearance on the menu in a frosty bever-age. Scoops of ice cream add personality to milk and are delightful and refreshing with various flavors of carbonated drinks, while rich chocolate ice cream mellows a steaming cup of hot coffee. Scoops of icy sherbet are also tantalizing in cold tumblers of lemonade, limeade and other fruit juices. Hot beverages are almost a necessity on nippy holiday evenings. But, happily, these can go far beyond delicious, yet overdone, favorites such as coffee and hot chocolate. The electric excitement of a holiday atmosphere calls for hot cider stirred with a cinnamon stick, or a hot and pungent cranberry tea.

Special occasions, such as wedding receptions, showers, and bridge luncheons are often large enough to include more than one beverage on the menu, spiced hot tea, Irish coffee, wine punch or champagne punch to name a few. Extra touches for party beverages can be decorative ideas. Also, a punch bowl ice-ring filled with cherries, strawberries or other fresh fruits or thin-sliced oranges and lemons, a mint leaf garnish, a dollop of whipped cream, tinted and sprinkled with cinnamon, nutmeg or ginger served in attractive mugs, tumblers, or a pretty punch bowl set can add interest and color to the holiday theme.

Imaginative beverages have their place in menus all the year through. Chilled coffee is often a most refreshing finish for a light lunch on a hot summer day. When the children come home from school ready for their peanut but-ter and crackers, surprise them with an icy fruit slush to accompany their snack. Most teen-agers are known for their endless appetites, but should avoid sugary junk foods. For a filling and nourishing drink for them, run orange juice, ice and dry whipped topping mix in a blender until fluffy and frothy, then serve in a tall tumbler garnished with slices of fresh fruit.

No party beverage needs ever be plain or repetitive in the way it tastes or looks because there are just too many ingredients and preparation methods perfectly suited to beverage making. A beverage can be designed to fit the meal or the occasion, and will always be a delightful surprise to the guests. As for serving imaginative beverage recipes with everyday family meals, they can be a nutritious and exciting alternative that will complement your meals rather than just wash them down.

Members of ESA believe that special beverages are just one more way for talented homemakers to show off their artistic skills and round out holiday, party, and family meals with a distinctive and refreshing touch. Choose from the tongue-tickling array of beverages that follow and you are sure to find all the right beverages to delight your family and friends.

BRANDY SLUSH

2 c. sugar
4 bags green tea or 4 tbsp. instant
 tea
1 12-oz. can frozen orange juice,
 thawed
1 12-oz. can frozen lemonade, thawed
2 c. Brandy
7-Up

Boil 7 cups of water and sugar together until sugar is dissolved; set aside to cool. Steep tea in 2 cups boiling water for 20 minutes or until dark in color. Combine with sugar mixture; cool. Add orange juice, lemonade and Brandy. Mix well. Freeze in plastic container. Place 2 scoops slush in glass; pour in desired amount of 7-Up.

Bonnie Revers, Pres.
Delta Beta No. 3935
Naperville, Illinois

DAIQUIRIS IN A PUNCH BOWL

2 cans frozen daiquiri mix
 concentrate
2 lg. cans frozen lemonade
 concentrate
1 qt. sparkling water
Rum (opt.)

Combine all ingredients and 1 1/2 quarts water in punch bowl. Float ice ring in punch.

Joyce Ahlstrom, Past Pres.
Gamma Zeta No. 4534
Boise, Idaho

STRAWBERRY DAIQUIRIS

2 c. fresh or frozen strawberries
1 c. lime juice
3/4 c. powdered sugar
1 c. white rum
1 qt. club soda

Combine first 4 ingredients in blender container; process, adding ice cubes or crushed ice to make a very thick mixture. Pour into cocktail glasses; stir in a small amount of club soda and additional lime juice to thin to desired consistency.

Janie Weiler, Pres.
Beta Eta No. 3696
Fairfield, Illinois

FROZEN DAIQUIRIS

1 6-oz. can frozen lemonade
 concentrate
1 6-oz. can frozen limeade
 concentrate
1 10-oz. bottle 7-Up
1 1/2 juice cans light rum
2 drops of green food coloring
2 to 4 tbsp. sugar

Combine all ingredients and 1 1/2 juice cans water; mix well. Freeze. Yield: 8-10 servings.

Linda Santman, Jonquil Girl
Theta Chi No. 39380
Coos Bay, Oregon

SNOWY CHRISTMAS EGGNOG

5 eggs, separated
10 tbsp. sugar
4 c. half and half
3/4 c. Brandy
1/2 c. rum
1/2 c. Bourbon
3 c. milk
Grated nutmeg

Beat egg yolks with 5 tablespoons sugar in blender container until thick and lemon-colored. Add 2 cups half and half. Add Brandy, rum, and Bourbon slowly with blender at low speed. Pour into 1-gallon container; add remaining half and half and milk. Blend well; chill for several hours. Beat egg whites until soft peaks form; add remaining 5 tablespoons sugar gradually, beating until stiff peaks form. Pour egg yolk mixture into chilled punch bowl; fold in 2/3 of the egg white mixture. Spoon remaining egg white mixture in large mounds on top. Sprinkle generously with freshly grated nutmeg. Yield: 25 servings.

Shirley Dreyer, Past State Pres.
Alpha Psi No. 3549
High Point, North Carolina

EGGNOG PUNCH

    3   13-oz. cans Pet evaporated milk
    4 eggs, slightly beaten
    1/2 c. sugar
    1   1-in. piece of fresh orange rind
    4 tsp. rum flavoring or 1 c. rum

Combine milk, 2 cups water, eggs, sugar and orange rind in large saucepan; stir over medium heat until steaming hot. Stir in rum flavoring. Serve warm topped with whipped cream and nutmeg. Yield: About 12 servings.

Photograph for this recipe above.

COFFEE EGGNOG

    2 eggs, separated
    1/3 c. cinnamon-flavored instant
        coffee
    1/4 c. honey
    1/2 to 3/4 c. Brandy
    1 qt. milk

    Whipping cream
    3 tbsp. sugar

Beat egg yolks, instant coffee, honey and Brandy together until blended. Beat in milk gradually; chill. Beat egg whites until stiff; fold into coffee mixture. Whip 1 cup cream with sugar until soft peaks form; fold into eggnog. Chill thoroughly. Serve in punch cups. Top with whipped cream; garnish with sprinkling of Cafe Cinnamon.

Tincy Perry, V.P.
Alpha Chi No. 877
Big Spring, Texas

FOURTH OF JULY MOLLY HOGANS

    1   12-oz. can frozen orange juice,
        thawed
    6 tbsp. lemon juice
    1/2 c. sugar
    1 pt. gin
    3 eggs
    1 tsp. vanilla extract
    2 or 3 bottles 7-Up or lemon-lime soda

Place all ingredients except 7-Up in a large mixing bowl; add 1 1/2 orange juice cans water. Mix with mixer or egg beater until foamy. Place 1 1/2 jiggers egg mixture in 12-ounce glass with ice. Fill glass with 7-Up.

Madith Johnson, Pres.
Beta Eta No. 3431
Saint Charles, Missouri

HALLOWEEN COCOA

1   1-lb. box instant cocoa mix
1   8-qt. box powdered milk
1   6-oz. jar powdered cream
1/2 c. (heaping) powdered sugar

Combine all ingredients. Store in airtight container. Place 1/3 cup mix in cup; fill with hot water to serve.

Kathy Gill, Pres.
Alpha Epsilon No. 3907
Coeur d'Alene, Idaho

BATTER FOR HOT BUTTERED RUM

1 qt. vanilla ice cream, softened
2 1/4 c. (packed) brown sugar
1 lb. butter, softened
Rum

Process small amounts of first 3 ingredients in blender at a time until smooth. Store in freezer. Thaw partially before using. Place 4 tablespoons batter in cup; add 3 tablespoons rum. Fill cup with hot water.

Margaret Weil, Pres.
Epsilon Epsilon No. 3475
Gresham, Oregon

HOLIDAY HOT BUTTERED RUM

1 lb. butter, softened
1 lb. brown sugar
1 qt. vanilla ice cream, softened
Rum

Combine butter, brown sugar and ice cream; mix well. Freeze until ready to use. Place 1 heaping tablespoon ice cream mixture in cup; fill with hot water and 1 jigger of rum.

Marsha Beery
Delta Tau No. 4264
Yakima, Washington

HONEYED HOT BUTTERED RUM

1 c. butter
1 1/3 c. (packed) brown sugar
6 tbsp. honey
Rum
2 tsp. nutmeg
2 tsp. cinnamon
2 tsp. vanilla extract

Cream butter; beat in brown sugar. Add honey, 3/4 cup rum, spices and vanilla. Refrigerate until ready to use. Butter mixture will keep indefinitely in refrigerator. Add heaping tablespoon butter mixture and 1 jigger rum to each cup of boiling water or hot apple cider. Jigger of rum may be omitted, if desired.

Catherine Harre
Gamma Iota No. 3936
Carbondale, Illinois

SPICY HOT BUTTERED RUM

3 eggs
1 lb. butter, melted
2 lb. brown sugar
1 tsp. ground cloves
1 tsp. ground cinnamon
1 tsp. ground nutmeg
1 tsp. ground allspice
Rum

Beat eggs thoroughly in blender. Mix eggs, butter, brown sugar and spices in large pan. Cook over low heat, stirring constantly until mixture is smooth. Keep warm. Add 2 heaping tablespoons egg mixture and 1 1/2 jiggers rum to 1 cup boiling water. Mix well in cup and serve.

Alice Robinson
Kappa Tau No. 4527
Burlington, Colorado

HOT CHOCOLATE MIX

1   16-oz. box Nestles Quik
1   8-oz. jar Coffee-Mate
1 lb. powdered sugar

Combine all ingredients, mixing well. Store in airtight container. Place about 1/4 cup chocolate mixture in mug; add hot water and stir.

Marguerite Frey, Pres.
Beta Omicron No. 2997
Middleton, Wisconsin

MILK MOCHA

2 qt. milk
6 tbsp. powdered chocolate drink
6 tbsp. instant coffee
1/4 c. (firmly packed) light brown
    sugar
1 tsp. vanilla extract

Combine milk, chocolate mix, instant coffee and sugar in a 3-quart saucepan. Heat to serving temperature, stirring occasionally. Add vanilla extract. Beat with rotary beater until foamy just before serving.

Photograph for this recipe on page 112.

CAFE AU LAIT

4 c. milk
4 c. hot coffee

Heat milk in heavy saucepan over low heat, beating constantly until hot and foamy. Pour milk into a warmed 1-quart serving pitcher. Pour coffee into a second warmed 1-quart serving pitcher. Pour both simultaneously into cups so that milk and coffee blend as poured.

Photograph for this recipe on page 88.

WITCHES' BREW

4 c. milk
3 tbsp. sugar
3 tbsp. instant coffee

1/3 c. quick chocolate-flavored
    drink mix
1/2 tsp. cinnamon

Heat milk. Combine sugar, coffee, chocolate-flavored drink mix and cinnamon; stir in hot milk. Heat. Pour into serving cups or mugs. Garnish with a dollop of whipped cream and cinnamon stick, if desired. Yield: 4 servings.

Photograph for this recipe above.

HOT MOCHA

2 c. Swiss Miss
2 c. nondairy creamer or 2 c. powdered
    milk
1 c. instant coffee
1 1/2 c. sugar or 1 1/2 c. Sugar Twin
1 tsp. cinnamon
1/2 tsp. nutmeg

Combine all ingredients; store in airtight container. Powdered milk and Sugar Twin keep calories low while creamer and sugar give a richer flavor. Add 2 heaping teaspoons or more to coffee cup of boiling water for a delicious beverage at any time.

Barbara Kendall, Treas.
Gamma Beta No. 4577
Mount Vernon, Washington

HOT MULLED APPLE CIDER

1/2 c. (packed) brown sugar
1 tsp. whole allspice
1 tsp. whole cloves
1/4 tsp. salt
Dash of nutmeg
1   3-in. stick cinnamon
2 qt. apple cider

Combine all ingredients in a large pan; bring slowly to a boil. Cover; simmer for 20 minutes. Strain. Pour hot cider over clove-studded orange wedges in warmed glass pitcher.

Pat Bolin, Parliamentarian
Alpha Omicron No. 577
Enid, Oklahoma

HOT RUM SWIZZLES

6 c. grapefruit juice
3 c. orange juice
1 qt. cider
12 whole cloves
2   2-in. pieces of cinnamon stick
2 c. grenadine
1 to 2 c. amber rum
3 or 4 drops of angostura bitters
8 drops of red food coloring

Combine grapefruit juice, orange juice, cider, cloves and cinnamon sticks in 6-quart saucepan; bring to a boil. Reduce heat; simmer, covered, for 30 minutes. Strain to remove spices. Return liquid to large saucepan. Stir in grenadine, rum, bitters and food coloring; mix well. Cover; bring to a boil. Serve hot; garnish each serving with a cinnamon stick and orange slice, if desired. May serve cold in chilled punch bowl over ice cubes. Float orange slices studded with cloves on top. Yield: About 4 quarts.

Betty Sanders
Intl. State Presidents Chm.
Gamma Rho No. 2537
Fort Myers, Florida

HOT SPICED LEMONADE

1/2 c. sugar
1/2 tsp. whole cloves

1   2-in. stick cinnamon
1/2 tsp. allspice
Juice of 4 lemons
Lemon slices

Combine 4 cups water, sugar and spices; bring to a boil. Simmer for 5 minutes; strain. Add 4 cups boiling water and lemon juice when ready to serve. Serve hot with slice of lemon. Yield: 2 quarts.

Mrs. Jeanne Williamson, Rec. Sec.
Alpha Upsilon No. 3337
Milwaukee, Wisconsin

CRANBERRY TEA

2 1/2 c. sugar
3/4 c. red hot cinnamon candies
12 whole cloves
1/2 can frozen lemon juice
1/2 can frozen orange juice
    concentrate
1 qt. cranberry juice

Combine sugar, candies, cloves and 1 quart water in kettle; bring to a boil. Remove from heat; let cool slightly. Add lemon juice concentrate, orange juice concentrate, 3 quarts water and cranberry juice; serve hot.

Pat Schuler, Sec.
Alpha Gamma No. 3089
Chillicothe, Missouri

GYPSY HOT APPLE WINE

3 c. apple cider
1/4 c. sugar
1   3-in. stick cinnamon
6 whole cloves
Peel of 1/4 lemon, cut in strips
1 fifth dry white wine
2 tbsp. lemon juice

Combine apple cider, sugar, cinnamon, cloves and lemon peel in saucepan; bring to a boil. Stir until sugar dissolves. Simmer, uncovered, for 15 minutes. Strain to remove spices and peel. Add wine and lemon juice. Heat but do not boil. Serve in preheated mugs. Yield: 6-8 servings.

Dorothy Howard, Rec. Sec.
Zeta Chi No. 3878
Fort Collins, Colorado

RUSSIAN TEA

> 1 1/2 c. Tang
> 1/2 c. instant tea
> 1/2 tsp. ground cloves
> 1 c. sugar
> 1 tsp. cinnamon

Combine all ingredients; mix well. Store in covered jar. Dissolve about 2 teaspoons tea mixture in cup of hot water.

Alice E. Genta, Treas.
Alpha Zeta No. 206
Tacoma, Washington

SPICY HOT WINE

> 1/2 gal. Mogan David wine
> 1 c. sugar
> Grated rind and juice of 1 lemon
> Grated rind and juice of 1 orange
> 3 or 4 sticks cinnamon
> 10 to 12 whole allspice

Combine all ingredients in saucepan; simmer for 1 hour. Serve hot.

Virginia Bigbee, Pres.
Delta Omega No. 1628
Manhattan, Kansas

NEW YEAR'S EVE BANANA PUNCH

> 4 c. sugar
> 1 lg. can pineapple juice
> 1 med. can frozen lemonade
>   concentrate
> 1 med. can frozen orange juice
>   concentrate
> 5 bananas, quartered

Boil 6 quarts water and sugar to make a syrup; let cool. Stir in next 3 ingredients. Scrape seeds from bananas; place bananas in blender container. Process to puree; stir into juice mixture. Freeze until needed. Remove from freezer 2 to 3 hours before serving. Punch should be slushy when served.

Elaine Couch, Ed. Dir.
Alpha Theta No. 4623
Owensville, Indiana

TANGERINE NEW YEAR'S PUNCH

> 1 qt. Florida grapefruit juice,
>   chilled
> 1 c. Florida tangerine juice or
>   orange juice, chilled
> 1 16-oz. bottle low-calorie
>   raspberry soda, chilled
> Florida tangerine or orange sections

Combine all ingredients except tangerine sections in punch bowl. Add sections; serve over ice. Yield: 14 servings.

Photograph for this recipe on page 172.

APRICOT FIZZ

> 2 1/2 c. apricot nectar, chilled
> 1 1/2 c. unsweetened pineapple juice,
>   chilled
> Chunky Fresh Apricot Ice Cream
> 2 c. carbonated soda
> Fresh apricot slices, pineapple
>   chunks and maraschino cherries

Combine apricot nectar and pineapple juice; set aside. Place 1 or 2 scoops of apricot ice cream in bottom of each of six 12-ounce soda glasses. Pour about 2 tablespoons of juice mixture into each glass; stir slightly to combine ice cream and juice. Divide remaining juice among sodas, using about 1/2 cup per glass. Add large scoop of apricot ice cream to each soda; fill to top with carbonated soda. Thread 1 apricot slice, 1 pineapple chunk and 1 maraschino cherry on straw; place in soda for garnish.
Recipe for Chunky Fresh Apricot Ice Cream can be found in Ice Cream Desserts.

Photograph for this recipe on page 102.

SPARKLING BANANA PUNCH

> 6 bananas, blended
> 1 lg. can frozen orange juice, thawed
> 1 sm. can frozen lemonade, thawed
> 1 46-oz. can pineapple juice
> 2 c. sugar
> 4 qt. 7-Up

Combine all ingredients except 7-Up; add 3 cups water. Freeze in large plastic bowl. Remove from freezer 1 hour before serving. Unmold punch into punch bowl. Pour 7-Up over top; mash as much as possible. Let stand for 30 minutes before serving.

Diane Newman, V.P.
Gamma Kappa No. 4595
Phoenix, Arizona

CHRISTMAS CRANBERRY PUNCH

1 pt. bottle cranberry juice
1 6-oz. can frozen lemonade
*   concentrate*
1 lg. bottle ginger ale
2 pt. lime sherbet

Combine cranberry juice, lemonade concentrate and 2 1/4 cups water in punch bowl. Add ginger ale slowly; float scoops of sherbet on top.

Ernestine Babcock, Philanthropic Chm.
Alpha Omicron No. 1827
Burlington, Iowa

CHRISTMAS WASSAIL

2 sm. juicy oranges
Whole cloves
5 cinnamon sticks
2 qt. apple cider or apple juice
1 sm. can frozen lemonade concentrate
1 sm. can frozen orange juice
*   concentrate*
1 c. rum

Stud oranges generously with cloves; place in shallow pan. Bake at 325 degrees for 30 minutes. Tie several cloves and cinnamon sticks in cheesecloth bag. Combine apple cider, lemonade and orange juice in large pan; add cheesecloth bag. Bring to a boil. Pierce baked oranges with a fork; place oranges in juice mixture. Simmer for about 15 minutes. Remove cheesecloth bag and oranges. Pour mixture into silver punch bowl; add rum. Clove-studded oranges can be reused.

Harriett L. Hahn
Epsilon Lambda No. 1029
Indianapolis, Indiana

CITRUS RUM PUNCH

1 12-oz. can frozen orange juice
*   concentrate*
1 6-oz. can frozen limeade
*   concentrate*
1 6-oz. can frozen lemonade
*   concentrate*
1 46-oz. can pineapple juice,
*   chilled*
2 bottles ginger ale, chilled
1 1/2 c. rum

Thaw concentrates until slushy; pour into punch bowl. Stir in remaining ingredients. Add ice ring, if desired.

Dot Harcum, State Pres.
Alpha Epsilon No. 3548
Newport News, Virginia

FIESTA PUNCH

2 fifths Sauterne
1 46-oz. can pineapple juice
1 6-oz. can frozen lemonade
1 qt. sparkling water

Combine first 3 ingredients in punch bowl. Add sparkling water just before serving. Add ice ring to cool and for decoration.

Carolyn M. Hayes
Beta Omicron No. 2997
Waunakee, Wisconsin

HOLIDAY JOY JUICE

1 6-oz. can frozen pink lemonade
1 13-oz. can crushed pineapple
1 10-oz. package frozen strawberries
1 fifth vodka or gin (opt.)
3 lg. bottles 7-Up

Combine first 3 ingredients in blender container; blend until smooth. Pour into punch bowl. Add vodka and 7-Up when ready to serve. Add ice or ice ring. Garnish with whole strawberries and mint sprigs.

Tedde Holcomb, Pres.
Epsilon Alpha No. 2951
Pilot Rock, Oregon

GRADUATION PUNCH COOLER

3 6-oz. cans frozen limeade
  concentrate
3 6-oz. cans frozen lemonade
  concentrate
1 qt. grapefruit juice, chilled
2 qt. ginger ale, chilled
Sugar
Green food coloring

Pour limeade and lemonade into punch bowl. Stir in 4 quarts water. Add grapefruit juice and ginger ale. Add sugar to taste. Add several drops of green food coloring to tint until a light shade of green. Add ice cubes. Garnish with lime slices and strawberries. Serve with petit fours and various party accompaniments.

Photograph for this recipe above.

POINSETTIA PUNCH

2 cans cherry juice or 2 bottles
  cranberry juice
1 can Hawaiian punch

2 cans frozen pineapple-orange juice,
  thawed
2 tbsp. lemon juice
1/4 c. sugar
2 qt. ginger ale

Combine all ingredients except ginger ale; stir until sugar is dissolved. Add ginger ale just before serving. Serve with ice cubes and garnish with orange and lemon slices.

Shirley Haugen, Corr. Sec.
Alpha Theta No. 1616
Moorhead, Minnesota

SNOWBALL PUNCH

1 46-oz. can pineapple juice,
  chilled
1 6-oz. can frozen lemonade
  concentrate
1/2 gal. vanilla ice cream, softened

Combine pineapple juice and lemonade concentrate; pour into punch bowl. Float scoops of ice cream in punch. Serve immediately. Appropriate coloring for special occasions can be added. Substitute sherbet or fruit-flavored ice cream to match color scheme.

Rolaine H. Little, VIA State Dir.
Beta Lambda No. 3199
Gainesville, Florida

SPARKLING HOLIDAY PUNCH

2 c. sugar
1/2 c. lemon juice
1/2 c. lime juice
2 c. grapefruit juice
2 1/2 c. orange juice
2 c. Rhine wine
1 qt. extra dry Champagne
2 tbsp. grenadine (opt.)

Combine 2 cups water, sugar and lemon juice. Boil for 1 minute. Add 2 cups cold water; let cool. Stir in lime juice, grapefruit juice and orange juice. Pour into punch bowl; add ice cubes. Add Rhine wine, Champagne and grenadine. Stir and serve.

Donna Schumaker
Beta Beta No. 4142
Winter Springs, Florida

STRAWBERRY-TEA PUNCH

3 family-size tea bags
1/2 c. sugar
1 6-oz. can frozen lemonade
1 10-oz. package frozen
strawberries, thawed

Pour 6 cups boiling water over tea bags; steep for 4 minutes. Remove tea bags. Stir in sugar, lemonade and strawberries. Serve over ice. Yield: 8-10 servings.

Darlene Solberg, Treas.
Gamma Pi No. 1200
Longmont, Colorado

VALENTINE SPARKLING STRAWBERRY PUNCH

2 10-oz. packages frozen sweetened
strawberries, slightly thawed
1 6-oz. can frozen lemonade
concentrate, slightly thawed

1 4/5 qt. bottle Rose wine, chilled
2 28-oz. bottles ginger ale,
chilled
1 28-oz. bottle club soda, chilled
2 trays ice cubes
1/4 c. sugar

Blend strawberries and lemonade concentrate in blender container at high speed until well blended. Pour into large punch bowl. Add wine and stir. Add remaining ingredients; stir until sugar is dissolved. Garnish punch with orange slices and strawberries. Yield: 26 servings.

Shirley Campbell, Sec.
Beta Beta No. 4096
Leadville, Colorado

HOLIDAY PARTY PUNCH

1 bottle apricot or black raspberry
brandy
1 bottle white wine
1 bottle club soda
1 bottle Champagne

Pour brandy and white wine into punch bowl. Add club soda and Champagne; stir gently. Serve immediately.

Marian Wood, Treas.
Beta Gamma No. 4647
Homosassa, Florida

VODKA PUNCH

1 lg. can frozen orange juice
concentrate
2 cans orange Hi-C
2 lg. cans unsweetened pineapple
juice
1 sm. can apricot nectar
1 sm. can frozen lemonade concentrate
2 qt. ginger ale
1 qt. vodka

Combine all ingredients in large punch bowl. Float orange ice ring on top.

Joan Dickman, Pres.
Alpha Rho No. 4184
Nebraska City, Nebraska

Wine Chart

RED WINES (Serve at Room Temperature, in 6 to 9-oz. glass) 	**CALIFORNIA** — (Light and very fruity): Gamay, Grignolino, Pinot St. George, Ruby Cabernet, Zinfandel; (Robust flavor): Barbera, Cabernet Sauvignon, Petite Sirah, Pinot Noir.
	EUROPEAN — (France) Bordeaux: Pomerol, Medoc, St. Emilion, Graves; Burgundy: Chambertin, Musigny, Clos Vougeot, Beaujolais, la Tache, Volnay: Rhone: Hermitage, Chateauneuf du Pape. (Italy): Barolo, Chianti, Barbera, Alcatico. (Spain): Marques de Riscal, Rioja. (Greece): Castel Danielis, Robola, St. Helena.
WHITE WINES (Serve Slightly Chilled, in 6 to 9-oz. glass) 	**CALIFORNIA** — (Light, full flavor): Emerald Riesling, Gewurztraminer, Green Hungarian, Grey Riesling, Johannisburg or White Riesling, Sylvaner; (Full-Bodied, Robust): Semillon, Chardonnay or Pinot Chardonnay, Sauvignon Blanc, Chenin Blanc.
	EUROPEAN — (France) Bordeaux: Sauternes, Chateau d' Yquem, Bursac; Burgundy: Montrachet, Chablis, Pouilly-Fuisse, Pouilly-Fume, Meursault. (Italy) Soave, White Chianti, Lachrymu Christi, Est Est Est, Frascati. (Germany) Rhine: Rheingau, Rheinhessen; Moselle: Wehlener, Sounenuhr, Liebfraumilch, Piesport. (Spain): Sherry, Vinho Verdes. (Greece) Aphrodite, Retsina. (Switzerland): Dezaley, Neuchatel.
VIN ROSE (Serve Slightly Chilled, in 6 to 9-oz. glass) 	**CALIFORNIA** — Grenache
	EUROPEAN — (France) Loire Valley: Sweet Roses, Rose Cabernet d'Anjou; Rhone: Dry Roses, Tavel. (Italy): Vermintino. (Greek): Roditys, Kokineli.
DESSERT WINES (Serve at Room Temperature in 2½ to 4-oz. glass) 	Rare Tawny and Tinta Port, Muscatel, Tokay, Sweet Champagne, Cream Sherry, Sweet Sherry, Sauternes, Marsala, Malaga, Mavrodaphne, Muscot-Samos.

Charcoaling - By The Rules

HOW TO LIGHT THE FIRE — THE RIGHT WAY

Every successful cookout begins with a good fire.

1. Line the grill with heavy duty aluminum foil — for faster cooking and easier clean-up later.

2. Stack the briquets in a pyramid; they'll light faster since air can circulate around them.

3. Use a good starter. Try the electric or chimney type, or choose a liquid, jelly or solid fibrous cubes.

4. Be patient! Let the briquets burn to just the right stage before adding food. Generally they'll require 20 to 40 minutes.

HOW TO JUDGE THE TEMPERATURE OF A CHARCOAL BRIQUET FIRE

- *To tell when it's cooking time:* Different brands of charcoal give off varying degrees of heat in a given time ... thus some are ready for cooking sooner than others. In daylight, the coals are ready for cooking when they are covered by a layer of gray ash; at night they'll have a bright red glow. At this stage, spread the briquets into a single layer with tongs and place food on the grill.

- *Quick temperature test:* Hold your hand at the cooking height, palm side down. If you can keep it in position for 2 seconds, the temperature is high or hot; 3 seconds, medium-high or hot; 4 seconds, medium; 5 seconds, low.

- *To lower the temperature:* Raise the grid, or spread out the coals.

- *To raise the temperature:* Tap ash from coals, or push them closer.

- *When more coals are needed:* Add to the outer edge of hot coals.

- *If spattering fat causes flare-ups:* Put flames out by raising grid, spreading out coals, or removing a few coals. If all else fails, have a water bottle handy (remove food before sprinkling). For rotisserie cooking, place foil drip pan in front of the coals in the fire box to catch the drippings, thus eliminating flare ups before they start.

HOW TO MAKE CLEAN-UP EASY

- *Prevention:* Line the grill with heavy duty aluminum foil ... spray the grill rack with a non-stick coating.

- *Cure:* To remove grease and grilled-on food particles, sprinkle dry baking soda on a damp sponge and scour; rinse with water/soda solution.

- *Store:* Clean after each use; then cover the grill and store in a clean, dry place.

NUTRITION LABELING

Modern Americans have become very diet and nutrition conscious, and in response, commercial food producers have begun to include nutrition information on the labels of their products. Nutrition Labeling is an invaluable service in many ways. There are many persons on special diets (diabetic, low-sodium, low-cholesterol) who must know the specifics of the foods they eat. However, whether the homemaker cooks for a special diet or not, Nutrition Labeling on the foods she buys helps her to know the part they play to her overall nutrition and menu planning.

The United States Food and Drug Administration has determined how much of every important nutrient is needed by the average healthy person in the United States, well known as the Recommended Daily Dietary Allowance (RDA). The United States RDA reflects the highest amounts of nutritives for all ages and sexes. Pregnant and nursing women, as well as persons with special dietary needs, should consult their doctors for any recommended increases or decreases in their daily diet.

UNITED STATES RECOMMENDED DAILY ALLOWANCE CHART

Protein	45-65 Grams
Carbohydrates	125 Grams
Vitamin A	5,000 International Units
Thiamine (Vitamin B_1)	1.5 Milligrams
Riboflavin (Vitamin B_2)	1.7 Milligrams
Vitamin B_6	2 Milligrams
Vitamin B_{12}	6 Micrograms
Folic Acid (B Vitamin)	0.4 Milligrams
Pantothenic Acid (B Vitamin)	10 Milligrams
Vitamin C (Ascorbic Acid)	55-60 Milligrams
Vitamin D	400 International Units
Vitamin E	30 International Units
Iron	18 Milligrams
Calcium	1 Gram
Niacin (Nicotinic Acid)	13-20 Milligrams
Magnesium	400 Milligrams
Zinc	15 Milligrams
Copper	2 Milligrams
Phosphorus	1 Gram
Iodine	150 Micrograms
Biotin (Vitamin H)	0.3 Milligrams

IMPORTANT NUTRIENTS YOUR DIET REQUIRES

PROTEIN

Why? Absolutely essential in building, repairing and renewing of all body tissue. Helps body resist infection. Builds enzymes and hormones, helps form and maintain body fluids.

Where? Milk, eggs, lean meats, poultry, fish, soybeans, peanuts, dried peas and beans, grains and cereals.

CARBOHYDRATES

Why? Provide needed energy for bodily functions, provide warmth, as well as fuel for brain and nerve tissue. Lack of carbohydrates will cause body to use protein for energy rather than for repair and building.

Where? Sugars: sugar, table syrups and jellies, jams, etc., as well as dried and fresh fruits. Starches: cereals, pasta, rice, corn, dired beans and peas, potatoes, stem and leafy vegetables, and milk.

FATS

Why? Essential in the use of fat soluble vitamins (A, D, E, K), and fatty acids. Has more than twice the concentrated energy than equal amount of carbohydrate for body energy and warmth.

Where? Margarine, butter, cooking oil, mayonnaise, vegetable shortening, milk, cream, ice cream, cheese, meat, fish, eggs, poultry, chocolate, coconut, nuts.

VITAMIN A

Why? Needed for healthy skin and hair, as well as for healthy, infection-resistant mucous membranes.

Where? Dark green, leafy and yellow vegetables, liver. Deep yellow fruits, such as apricots and cantaloupe. Milk, cheese, eggs, as well as fortified margarine and butter.

THIAMINE (VITAMIN B$_1$)

Why? Aids in the release of energy of foods, as well as in normal appetite and digestion. Promotes healthy nervous system.

Where? Pork, liver, kidney. Dried peas and beans. Whole grain and enriched breads and cereals.

RIBOFLAVIN (VITAMIN B$_2$)

Why? Helps to oxidize foods. Promotes healthy eyes and skin, especially around mouth and eyes. Prevents pellagra.

Where? Meats, especially liver and kidney, as well as milk, cheese, eggs. Dark green leafy vegetables. Enriched bread and cereal products. Almonds, dried peas and beans.

VITAMIN B$_6$

Why? Helps protein in building body tissues. Needed for healthy nerves, skin and digestion. Also helps body to use fats and carbohydrates for energy.

Where? Milk, wheat germ, whole grain and fortified cereals. Liver, kidney, pork and beef.

VITAMIN B$_{12}$

Why? Aids body in formation of red blood cells, as well as in regular work of all body cells.

Where? Lean meats, milk, eggs, fish, cheese, as well as liver and kidney.

VITAMIN C (ASCORBIC ACID)

Why? Promotes proper bone and tooth formation. Helps body utilize iron and resist infection. Strengthens blood vessels; lack of it causes bones to heal slowly,

failure of wounds to heal, and fragile vessels to bleed easily.

Where? Citrus fruits, cantaloupe and strawberries. Broccoli, kale, green peppers, raw cabbage, sweet potatoes, cauliflower, tomatoes.

VITAMIN D

Why? Builds strong bones and teeth by aiding utilization of calcium and phosphorus.

Where? Fortified milk, fish liver oils, as well as salmon, tuna and sardines. Also eggs.

VITAMIN E

Why? Needed in maintaining red blood cells.

Where? Whole grain cereals, wheat germ, beans and peas, lettuce and eggs.

IRON

Why? Used with protein for hemoglobin production. Forms nucleus of each cell, and helps them to use oxygen.

Where? Kidney and liver, as well as shellfish, lean meats, and eggs. Deep yellow and dark green leafy vegetables. Dried peas, beans, fruits. Potatoes, whole grain cereals and bread. Enriched flour and bread. Dark molasses.

CALCIUM

Why? Builds and renews bones, teeth, other tissues, as well as aids in the proper function of muscles, nerves and heart. Controls normal blood clotting. With protein, aids in oxidation of foods.

Where? Milk and milk products, excluding butter. Dark green vegetables, oysters, clams and sardines.

NIACIN

Why? Helps body to oxidize food. Aids in digestion, and helps to keep nervous system and skin healthy.

Where? Peanuts, liver, tuna, as well as fish, poultry and lean meats. Enriched breads, cereals and peas.

MAGNESIUM

Why? Aids nervous system and sleep.

Where? Almonds, peanuts, raisins and prunes. Vegetables, fruits, milk, fish and meat.

ZINC

Why? Needed for cell formation.

Where? Nuts and leafy green vegetables. Shellfish.

COPPER

Why? Helps body to utilize iron.

Where? Vegetables and meats.

PHOSPHORUS

Why? Maintains normal blood clotting function, as well as builds bones, teeth, and nerve tissue. Aids in utilization of sugar and fats.

Where? Oatmeal and whole wheat products. Eggs and cheese, dried beans and peas. Nuts, lean meat, and fish and poultry.

IODINE

Why? Enables thyroid gland to maintain proper body metabolism.

Where? Iodized salt. Saltwater fish and seafood. Milk and vegetables.

BIOTIN (VITAMIN H)

Why? Helps to maintain body cells.

Where? Eggs and liver. Any foods rich in Vitamin B.

CAN SIZE CHART

8 oz. can or jar . . . . .1 c.	1 lb. 13 oz. can or jar
10 1/2 oz. can (picnic can) . . . . .1 1/4 c.	or No. 2 1/2 can or jar . . . . .3 1/2 c.
12 oz. can (vacuum) . . . . .1 1/2 c.	1 qt. 14 fl. oz. or 3 lb. 3 oz.
14-16 oz. or No. 300 can . . . . .1 1/4 c.	or 46 oz. can . . . . .5 3/4 c.
16-17 oz. can or jar	6 1/2 to 7 1/2 lb.
or No. 303 can or jar . . . . .2 c.	or No. 10 can . . . . 12-13 c.
1 lb. 4 oz. or 1 pt. 2 fl. oz.	
or No. 2 can or jar . . . . .2 1/2 c.	

EQUIVALENT CHART

3 tsp. . . . . 1 tbsp.	2 pt. . . . . .1 qt.
2 tbsp. . . . . .1/8 c.	1 qt. . . . . .4 c.
4 tbsp. . . . . .1/4 c.	5/8 c. . . . . .1/2 c. + 2 tbsp.
8 tbsp. . . . . .1/2 c.	7/8 c. . . . . .3/4 c. + 2 tbsp.
16 tbsp. . . . . .1 c.	1 jigger . . . . .1 1/2 fl. oz.(3 tbsp.)
5 tbsp. + 1 tsp. . . . . .1/3 c.	2 c. fat .1 lb.
12 tbsp. . . . . .3/4 c.	1 lb. butter . . . . 2 c. or 4 sticks
4 oz. . . . . .1/2 c.	2 c. sugar . . . . .1 lb.
8 oz. . . . . .1 c.	2 2/3 c. powdered sugar . . . . .1 lb.
16 oz. . . . . .1 lb.	2 2/3 c. brown sugar . . . . .1 lb.
1 oz. . . . . 2 tbsp. fat or liquid	4 c. sifted flour . . . . .1 lb.
2 c. . . . . .1 pt.	4 1/2 c. cake flour . . . . .1 lb.

3 1/2 c. unsifted whole wheat flour	. . . . .1 lb.
8 to 10 egg whites	. . . . .1 c.
12 to 14 egg yolks	. . . . .1 c.
1 c. unwhipped cream	. . . . .2 c. whipped
1 lb. shredded American cheese	. . . . .4 c.
1/4 lb. crumbled blue cheese	. . . . .1 c.
1 chopped med. onion	. . . . .1/2 c. pieces
1 lemon	. . . . 3 tbsp. juice
1 lemon	. . . . 1 tsp. grated peel
1 orange	. . . . .1/3 c. juice
1 orange	. . . . about 2 tsp. grated peel
1 lb. unshelled walnuts	. . . . .1 1/2 to 1 3/4 c. shelled
1 lb. unshelled almonds	. . . . .3/4 to 1 c. shelled
4 oz. (1 to 1 1/4 c.) uncooked macaroni	. . . . 2 1/4 c. cooked
7 oz. spaghetti	. . . . .4 c. cooked
4 oz. (1 1/2 to 2 c.) uncooked noodles	. . . . .2 c. cooked
28 saltine crackers	. . . . .1 c. crumbs
4 slices bread	. . . . .1 c. crumbs
14 square graham crackers	. . . . .1 c. crumbs
22 vanilla wafers	. . . . .1 c. crumbs

SUBSTITUTIONS FOR A MISSING INGREDIENT

1 square *chocolate* (1 ounce) = 3 or 4 tablespoons cocoa plus 1/2 tablespoon fat.

1 tablespoon *cornstarch* (for thickening) = 2 tablespoons flour.

1 cup sifted *all-purpose flour* = 1 cup plus 2 tablespoons sifted cake flour.

1 cup sifted *cake flour* = 1 cup minus 2 tablespoons sifted all-purpose flour.

1 teaspoon *baking powder* = 1/4 teaspoon baking soda plus 1/2 teaspoon cream of tartar.

1 cup *sour milk* — 1 cup sweet milk into which 1 tablespoon vinegar or lemon juice has been stirred; or
       1 cup buttermilk (let stand for 5 minutes).

SUBSTITUTIONS FOR A MISSING INGREDIENT

1 cup *sweet milk* = 1 cup sour milk or buttermilk plus 1/2 teaspoon baking soda.

1 cup *canned tomatoes* = about 1 1/3 cups cut-up fresh tomatoes, simmered 10 minutes.

3/4 cup *cracker crumbs* = 1 cup bread crumbs.

1 cup *cream, sour, heavy* = 1/3 cup butter and 2/3 cups milk in any sour milk recipe.

1 cup *cream, sour, thin* = 3 tablespoons butter and 3/4 cup milk in sour milk recipe.

1 cup *molasses* = 1 cup honey.

1 teaspoon *dried herbs* = 1 tablespoon fresh herbs.

1 *whole egg* = 2 egg yolks for custards.

1/2 cup *evaporated milk* and 1/2 cup *water* or 1 cup *reconstituted nonfat dry milk* and 1 tablespoon
      butter = 1 cup whole milk.

1 package *active dry yeast* = 1 cake compressed yeast.

1 tablespoon *instant minced onion, rehydrated* = 1 cake compressed yeast.

1 tablespoon *instant minced onion, rehydrated* = 1 small fresh onion.

1 tablespoon *prepared mustard* = 1 teaspoon dry mustard.

1/8 teaspoon *garlic powder* = 1 small pressed clove of garlic

METRIC CONVERSION CHARTS FOR THE KITCHEN

VOLUME

1 tsp.	4.9 cc	2 c.	473.4 cc
1 tbsp.	14.7 cc	1 fl. oz.	29.5 cc
1/3 c.	28.9 cc	4 oz.	118.3 cc
1/8 c.	29.5 cc	8 oz.	236.7 cc
1/4 c.	59.1 cc	1 pt.	473.4 cc
1/2 c.	118.3 cc	1 qt.	.946 liters
3/4 c.	177.5 cc	1 gal.	3.7 liters
1 c.	236.7 cc		

CONVERSION FACTORS:

Liters	X	1.056	=	Liquid Quarts
Quarts	X	0.946	=	Liters
Liters	X	0.264	=	Gallons
Gallons	X	3.785	=	Liters
Fluid Ounces	X	29.563	=	Cubic Centimeters
Cubic Centimeters	X	0.034	=	Fluid Ounces
Cups	X	236.575	=	Cubic Centimeters
Tablespoons	X	14.797	=	Cubic Centimeters
Teaspoons	X	4.932	=	Cubic Centimeters
Bushels	X	0.352	=	Hectoliters
Hectoliters	X	2.837	=	Bushels
Ounces (Avoir.)	X	28.349	=	Grams
Grams	X	0.035	=	Ounces
Pounds	X	0.454	=	Kilograms
Kilograms	X	2.205	=	Pounds

WEIGHT

1 dry oz.	28.3 Grams
1 lb.	.454 Kilograms

LIQUID MEASURE AND METRIC EQUIVALENT

(NEAREST CONVENIENT EQUIVALENTS)

CUPS SPOONS	QUARTS OUNCES	METRIC EQUIVALENTS
1 teaspoon	1/6 ounce	.5 milliliters 5 grams
2 teaspoons	1/3 ounce	10 milliliters 10 grams
1 tablespoon	1/2 ounce	15 milliliters 15 grams
3 1/3 tablespoons	1 3/4 ounces	50 milliliters
1/4 cup (4 tablespoons)	2 ounces	60 milliliters
1/3 cup (5 1/3 tablespoons)	2 2/3 ounces	79 milliliters
1/3 cup plus 1 tablespoon	3 1/2 ounces	100 milliliters
1/2 cup (8 tablespoons)	4 ounces	118 milliliters
1 cup (16 tablespoons)	8 ounces	1/4 liter 236 milliliters
2 cups	1 pint 16 ounces	1/2 liter less 1 1/2 tablespoons 473 milliliters
2 cups plus 2 1/2 tablespoons	17 ounces	1/2 liter
4 cups	1 quart 32 ounces	946 milliliters
4 1/3 cups	1 quart, 2 ounces	1 liter 1000 milliliters

CONVERSION FORMULAS:

To convert Centigrade to Fahrenheit: multiply by 9, divide by 5, add 32.

To convert Fahrenheit to Centigrade: subtract 32, multiply by 5, divide by 9.

DRY MEASURE AND METRIC EQUIVALENT

(MOST CONVENIENT APPROXIMATION)

POUNDS AND OUNCES	METRIC	POUNDS AND OUNCES	METRIC
1/6 ounce	5 grams	1/4 pound (4 ounces)	114 grams
1/3 ounce	10 grams	4 1/8 ounces	125 grams
1/2 ounce	15 grams	1/2 pound (8 ounces)	227 grams
1 ounce	30 grams (28.35)	3/4 pound (12 ounces)	250 grams
		1 pound (16 ounces)	454 grams
1 3/4 ounces	50 grams	1.1 pounds	500 grams
2 2/3 ounces	75 grams	2.2 pounds	1 kilogram
3 1/2 ounces	100 grams		1000 grams

Index

COLOR PHOTOGRAPH RECIPES

PHOTOGRAPHY CREDITS

California Apricot Advisory Board; Spanish Green Olive Commission; United Dairy Industry Association; National Live Stock and Meat Board; Best Foods: A Division of CPC International, Inc.; R. T. French Company; McIlhenny Company; Pet, Inc.; Schieffelin & Company; California Avocado Advisory Board; Olive Administrative Committee; Pineapple Growers Association; Campbell Soup Company; Calvo Growers of California; Green Giant Company; California Beef Council; Brussels Sprout Marketing Program; Louisiana Yam Commission; Fleischmann's Yeast; Fleischmann's Margarine; Florida Citrus Commission; Royal Puddings and Gelatins; National Pecan Shellers and Processors Association; Cling Peach Advisory Board; Quaker Oats Company and Pickle Packers International, Inc.